falling off the bone

Jean Anderson
PHOTOGRAPHY BY JASON WYCHE

WILEY

JOHN WILEY & SONS, INC

Copyright © 2010 by Jean Anderson. All rights reserved
Photography Copyright © 2010 by Jason Wyche. All rights reserved
Line Drawings © 2010 by Ben Downard. All rights reserved

Published by John Wiley & Sons, Inc., Hoboken, New Jersey
Published simultaneously in Canada

For general information on our other products and services or for technical support, please contact our Customer Care Department within the United States at (800) 762-2974, outside the United States at (317) 572-3993 or fax (317) 572-4002.

Wiley also publishes its books in a variety of electronic formats. Some content that appears in print may not be available in electronic books. For more information about Wiley products, visit our web site at www.wiley.com.

Library of Congress Cataloging-in-Publication Data:

Anderson, Jean, 1929–
  Falling off the bone / Jean Anderson.
    p. cm.
  Includes index.
  ISBN 978-0-470-46713-8 (cloth)
1. Cookery (Meat) 2. Stews. 3. Low budget cookery. I. Title.
  TX749.A687 2010
  641.6'6—dc22

                                              2009043720

JAN 1 8 2011

Printed in China

10 9 8 7 6 5 4 3 2 1

ALSO BY JEAN ANDERSON

*The Doubleday Cookbook** (with Elaine Hanna)
The Family Circle Cookbook (with the Food Editors of Family Circle)
*Half a Can of Tomato Paste & Other Culinary Dilemmas*** (with Ruth Buchan)
The New Doubleday Cookbook (with Elaine Hanna)
*The Food of Portugal****
The New German Cookbook (with Hedy Würz)
The American Century Cookbook
The Good Morning America Cut the Calories Cookbook (co-edited with Sara Moulton)
Dinners in a Dish or a Dash
*Process This! *****
Quick Loaves
*A Love Affair with Southern Cooking: Recipes and Recollections ******

*Winner, R.T. French Tastemaker Award, Best Basic Cookbook (1975) and Best Cookbook of the Year (1975)
**Winner, Seagram/International Association of Culinary Professionals Award, Best Specialty Cookbook of the Year (1980)
***Winner, Seagram/International Association of Culinary Professionals Award, Best Foreign Cookbook of the Year (1986)
****Winner, James Beard Cookbook Awards, Best Cookbook, Tools & Techniques Category (2003)
*****Winner, James Beard Cookbook Awards, Best Cookbook, Americana Category (2008)

CONTENTS

BEEF 1

Brisket, Chuck (Shoulder), Flank, Oxtail, Rump, Shanks, and such

----

- THE BEST WAYS TO COOK EACH
- NUTRITIONAL PROFILE
- GRADES
- SHOPPING, STORAGE, AND FREEZING TIPS

RECIPES
- My Illinois Grandmother's Hearty Beef and Vegetable Soup
- Root Soup
- Joe Booker
- Oxtail Soup
- Best-Ever Borsch
- Swiss Steak with Tomato Gravy
- Onion-Smothered Chicken-Fried Steak
- Biscuit, Beef, and Vegetable Pie
- Slow 'n' Easy Austrian Goulash
- Deviled Short Ribs
- Yankee Boiled Dinner
- AND MORE

VEAL 83

Breast, Riblets, Round, Rump, Shanks, and Shoulder

- THE BEST WAYS TO COOK EACH
- NUTRITIONAL PROFILE
- GRADES
- SHOPPING, STORAGE, AND FREEZING TIPS

RECIPES
- Tuscan Veal Pot Roast in Lemon Sauce
- Sauerkraut-Stuffed Rolled Veal Shoulder
- Hassle-Free Braised Rump of Veal
- Slow Cooker Blanquette de Veau
- Vitello Tonnato (Cold Sliced Veal with Tuna Mayonnaise)
- Ossobuco
- Russian Crumb-Crusted Veal and Beef Loaf with Sour Cream Gravy
- AND MORE

LAMB 121

Breast, Neck, Riblets, Shanks, and Shoulder

- THE BEST WAYS TO COOK EACH
- NUTRITIONAL PROFILE
- GRADES
- SHOPPING, STORAGE, AND FREEZING TIPS

RECIPES
- Umbrian Mushroom, Lamb, and Cannellini Soup
- Anglesey Cottage Caul
- Old-Fashioned Irish Stew
- Andalusian Shepherd's Stew
- Flavors-of-the-East Sicilian Lamb Bake
- Slow Cooker Lamb with Raisins and Toasted Almonds
- Braised Blade Chops of Lamb with Coffee and Cream Gravy
- Curried Lamb Shanks with Almond Pilaf
- AND MORE

PORK 183

Fresh Ham, Pig's Feet, Spareribs

- THE BEST WAYS TO COOK EACH
- NUTRITIONAL PROFILE
- GRADES
- SHOPPING, STORAGE, AND FREEZING TIPS

RECIPES
- Gingery Lacquered Spareribs
- Jade Soup with Pork-and-Veal-Dumpling-Balls
- Gypsy Goulash
- Milwaukee "Brew" Stew
- Pueblo Posole with Pork and Green Chiles
- Slow Cooker Pork Ossobuco
- Alsatian Fresh Ham Braised with Sauerkraut and Vermouth
- Spicy Braised Pork Belly with Glazed Carrots
- Crispy Fried Trotters with Milk and Cornmeal Gravy
- AND MORE

ACKNOWLEDGMENTS

I should like to thank, first and foremost, good friends and colleagues Georgia Chan Downard and Joanne Lamb Hayes for lending a hand with the recipe testing and development. Few food people are more professional, more imaginative, or more dedicated.

In addition, I'd like to thank Lynne Whiteley Novy, John Soltys, Kathy Ketterman, and Barbara von Wahlde, willing "guinea pigs" who came running when there were recipe tests to taste and critique. And Frank Stasio of NC Public Radio's *The State of Things* for sharing the good news that the more unusual cuts of lamb could be found at the Farmer's Market in Durham—all home-grown. I'd complained that local supermarkets, even the high-end groceries, carried little more than tender chops and legs—most of them imported from New Zealand. And I'd be remiss without a word of thanks to long-time colleagues, sounding boards, and best buds Sara Moulton and Jim Villas.

Thanks, too, to David Black, my agent and rock, who found a home for this book; and my easy-to-work-with Wiley editor, Justin Schwartz, for his wisdom, guidance, support, and not least for overseeing the want-to-dive-right-in food photographs. Finally, I'm indebted to gifted young artist Ben Downard for such informative and appealing line drawings of beef, veal, lamb, and pork, which show exactly where the tough cuts are.

INTRODUCTION

PEOPLE LAUGH WHEN I TELL THEM I TOOK A MEAT-CUTTING COURSE IN COLLEGE AND IN TRUTH, I THOUGHT IT A LARK UNTIL I SHOWED UP FOR CLASS. NO CRIP COURSE THIS BUT AN INTENSIVE, HANDS-ON, SEMESTER-LONG SERIES OF LESSONS THAT TAUGHT ME MORE THAN I EVER EXPECTED TO KNOW ABOUT BEEF, VEAL, LAMB, AND PORK.

People laugh when I tell them I took a meat-cutting course in college and in truth, I thought it a lark until I showed up for class. No crip course this but an intensive, hands-on, semester-long series of lessons that taught me more than I ever expected to know about beef, veal, lamb, and pork.

The practical exam at the end of the course was a doozy, in fact my good buddy, former *Gourmet* executive chef Sara Moulton, was so impressed when I described it to her she still talks about it.

There, on butcher-paper-covered tables laid end-to-end in a room the size of a small gymnasium were more than a hundred anonymous cuts of meat. My challenge: ID them one by one noting type of meat (beef, veal, lamb, pork), animal part (shoulder, rib, loin, and so forth), retail cut (not only name—flank, butt, boned and rolled rump—but also whether Chicago cut, Kansas City, or New York), grade (Prime, Choice, Good, etc.), and finally, best ways to cook (broil, braise, stew, etc.) plus the reasons why.

I no longer make fun of that meat-cutting class, indeed it was one of the most valuable courses I took in my years at Cornell. Soon after settling in New York, I told my West Village butcher that I could bone and roll a rump roast. He laughed, then put me to the test. Once again I passed.

I'd never go boning-knife-to-boning-knife with a butcher today, but the basics of those long-ago meat-cutting lessons have served me well. I can recognize a pork arm roast at twenty paces, spot baby beef passed off as veal, and know at a glance whether lamb shoulder chops are freshly sliced.

More important, I know that tough cuts of meat come from well exercised parts of the animal (neck, shoulder, shank, tail, etc.), that cooking can tenderize them, and that they're endlessly versatile. Not so pricey steaks, chops, and roasts cut from the gold-plated rib and loin. "Such cuts," I remember my professor saying, "will never be more tender than they are raw."

So why is the reverse true of the bony, sinewy, cheaper cuts of meat? What sort of magic takes place in the stew pot and Dutch oven? The muscles in these economical cuts are shot through or sheathed with connective tissue (ligaments, tendons, gristle)—shoe-leather-tough when raw. But when slowly cooked in liquid—even the smallest amount of it—that sinew, or to be more precise, the collagen it contains, turns to gelatin. And all the more so if that liquid contains something acidic like tomatoes, vinegar, wine, or lemon juice.

Struggling to make ends meet on a meager college professor's salary, my mother was forever turning tough budget cuts into pot roasts and stews while my wealthier school chums dined on pork chops and prime ribs. To be honest, I preferred stew then and do to this day.

Without shanks, shoulders, spareribs, and such there'd be no beef bourguignon or ossobuco, no barbecued ribs or oxtail soup. Every country, every culture, has counted on the "lesser cuts" in lean times and as a result, created some of the world's most cherished meat recipes. How many great classics begin with steaks, chops, or prime ribs? Precious few.

My focus here: the tough cuts (or "less tender," as the meat industry prefers to classify them) widely available across America—external cuts, not offal (innards and organs rarely seen beyond big metropolitan areas). Supermarkets carry many of these sinewy budget cuts. Elsewhere, high-end groceries and good butchers will either have them or be willing to order them for you (also see Sources, page 243).

In our rush to put dinner on the table in thirty minutes or less, we've forsaken the soups, stews, and pot roasts that laze away, largely unattended, gaining tenderness and flavor every step of the way. And we're losing the comfort foods that fill the house with tantalizing aromas no jiffy recipe can match. Ever. Isn't it time to rediscover the versatility, the value of the so-called lesser cuts of meat not to mention the pure pleasure of anticipation?

In the pages that follow you will find exactly that—scores of recipes for bony and/or sinewy cuts of beef, veal, lamb, and pork—old favorites that recapture the joy of hours spent in our grandmothers' kitchens plus plenty of unknowns and a few exotics. It's a round-the-world collection of the recipes I've enjoyed at home and abroad, recipes that concentrate on the most widely available tough cuts of beef, veal, lamb, and pork.

Try substituting them for pricey steaks and chops. They'll not only add welcome variety to your meals, they'll also stretch your food dollar. Easily. Impressively. Deliciously.

—*Jean Anderson, Chapel Hill, NC*

HOW TO USE THIS BOOK

PLEASE READ THIS SECTION CAREFULLY. THE INFORMATION GIVEN HERE NOT ONLY INCLUDES BASICS TO GUIDE YOU AS YOU COOK, BUT ALSO SUGGESTS SHORTCUTS AND— I HOPE—ANTICIPATES AND ANSWERS QUESTIONS THAT MAY ARISE.

GENERAL INFORMATION

Before beginning any recipe in this book, read it— twice, if necessary—so that you know exactly what you are to do. Also:

- Check to see that you have all necessary ingredients and equipment at hand.
- Measure all recipe ingredients before you begin cooking.
- Do as much advance prep as possible (peeling, slicing, chunking, etc.) so that you don't have to pause mid-recipe.
- Preheat the oven to the desired temperature for 20 minutes before anything goes into it. Preheat the broiler 15 minutes.
- Do not substitute one ingredient for another unless a recipe suggests alternatives

HOW TO TENDERIZE MEAT

Early on, cooks learned that there were two basic ways of tenderizing tough cuts of meat, chemical and mechanical. One or both may be used in a single recipe.

First, the Chemical:

- **Marinating:** A preliminary soak in a marinade made tart with vinegar, wine, citrus juice, or tomatoes can jump-start the tenderization, particularly if that marinade is also used as a cooking liquid or basting sauce. Tests have shown that raw meats marinated in vinegar or wine as long as 48 hours cook to far greater tenderness than those never marinated.
- **Using Commercial Tenderizers:** Less popular than they were ten or 20 years ago, these powdered, protein-digesting plant enzymes (papain from papayas and bromelin from pineapples) are effective when rubbed or pounded into raw meat. Use sparingly. Too

much and the meat turns mushy. I haven't seen commercial tenderizers in my supermarket lately, but they can be ordered online.

• **Cooking via Moist Heat:** This means stewing (cooking meat in a large amount of liquid) or braising (browning meat, then cooking with a small amount of liquid in a covered pot). Soups and stews often contain tomatoes, wine, or beer as well as water or broth and not just for flavor. Being acidic, these three help soften connective tissue as do two less frequently used ingredients—vinegar and lemon juice. For the same reason, Swiss steaks and pot roasts are often braised in tomato or wine sauces. The key to successful stewing and braising? Keep the liquid at a gentle simmer. If it actively boils for any length of time, the meat will be tough.

The Mechanical:

• **Cubing:** Surfing the web recently, I was surprised to see a variety of hand-cranked gadgets that will "cube" meat (imprint slim, boneless cuts with waffle-like patterns), severing much of the tough connective tissue. There are also cutlet bats and meat pounders—for the most part cheaper but equally effective tenderizers. Any good kitchen shop sells them.

• **Grinding:** The single most effective way to tenderize meat. In the old days, women did the job themselves using grinders clamped to kitchen counters. My mother had one of those meat grinders and I remember feeding chunks of beef into the hopper and cranking, cranking, cranking. Not easy! Today, of course, packages of ground beef (with varying degrees of fat) are as near as the closest supermarket. So, too, meatloaf mixes—usually a blend of beef and pork, or beef, pork, and veal (these, by the way, are equally good for meatballs). Butchers at high-end groceries will grind meat to order though probably not pork unless they have a pork-only grinder. Methods of raising pork are markedly improved, it's true, still some pork may contain a microscopic parasite that causes trichinosis, a sometimes fatal illness. *NOTE: Though cooking kills the parasite at an internal temperature of 140°F and though some chefs cook pork only to internal temperatures of 145°F, the US Department of Agriculture recommends that all pork—the tough cuts as well as the tender—be cooked to internal temperatures of 160°F—minimum.*

• **Pounding:** Boneless slices of round (beef or veal) are usually the target and there's no doubt that energetic pounding with a cutlet bat flattens them nicely and ruptures much of the tough connective tissue. Country-fried steaks are routinely pounded before they're dredged and braised.

• **Scoring and Slicing:** Scoring (making crisscross cuts over the surface of meat, most often a thick, boneless shoulder steak) is usually done before meat is cooked. Slicing, on the other hand, occurs after cooking. Take flank steak (a.k.a. London broil): It's a long, flat, fibrous steak cut from the belly of the beast that's sliced across the grain—tissue-thin—as soon as it emerges from the broiler. "Across the grain" is the operative phrase here, for without those fiber-splitting cross-cuts at sixteenth-of-an-inch intervals, broiled flank steak is too tough to chew.

INDIVIDUAL INGREDIENTS

Bacon, Bacon Drippings: Several of my recipes call for slab bacon—smoked or cured bacon sold by the chunk instead of pre-sliced. Most good butchers carry it and a few high-end groceries, too. If unavailable, choose the thickest sliced bacon you can find—hickory-smoked—then stack and cut or snip as recipes direct. Avoid bacons that have been injected with water—"water added" on the label is your clue. Frugal cooks have always saved bacon drippings for frying and for seasoning. My mother kept a little jar of them in the fridge, topping it off each time we had bacon for breakfast. I do the same and frequently sauté onions, carrots, even meats in them because of the flavor they impart.

Bay Leaves: Once you discover the lemony/spicy evergreen flavor of fresh bay leaves, you'll abandon the dried, which not only have little flavor but also tend to break into brittle shards that can cut the tongue or stick in the throat. Fortunately, supermarkets now sell slim plastic packets of fresh bay leaves (crinkle them as you add to soups and stews to release their flavor). Even better, buy a little potted plant and stand it on a sunny windowsill. Just make sure what you buy is *edible*—sweet bay is what you want or *Laurus nobilis*, to give its botanical name (some varieties of bay are poisonous). *NOTE: Always remove bay leaves from a dish before serving lest someone choke. Bay leaves are there to impart flavor, not to be eaten.*

Black Pepper: My recipes call occasionally for peppercorns (no need to remove them before serving) but more often for freshly ground black pepper. For the record: 10 energetic grinds of the peppermill = about ¼ teaspoon freshly ground black pepper, 20 grinds = ½ teaspoon.

Breadcrumbs: Certain recipes call for breadcrumbs—meatloaves and meatballs, stuffings, and crisp coatings. In each case, the bread to use is firm-textured or home-style white bread (Arnold and Pepperidge Farm are two familiar brands). To make breadcrumbs:
> Tear the slices—crusts and all—directly into a food processor fitted with the chopping blade and alternately pulse and churn until the crumbs are as coarse or fine as you like.

For the record: one slice bread = ½ cup crumbs. *TIP: If you often use breadcrumbs, reduce an entire loaf to moderately fine crumbs (a good all-purpose size), pop into a large plastic zipper bag, label, date, and stash in the freezer. What a time-saver it is just to open the bag and scoop out the amount of crumbs you need. Maximum storage time: three months.*

Butter: Unsalted stick butter is the one to use. Make no substitutions unless recipes suggest them. Ghee is clarified butter. Its advantage, apart from its 24-karat flavor, is that it doesn't burn. I like to keep a little jar of ghee on hand to use for sautéing and seasoning meats, fish, and vegetables; it keeps well for about two weeks if tightly capped and stored in the refrigerator. To make ghee:
> Melt unsalted butter, let stand a few minutes, then skim off all milk solids. I usually make ghee by microwave, "nuking" 1½ sticks unsalted but-

ter in an uncovered 1-quart oven-proof glass measuring cup 10 minutes on Warm. Oven wattages vary, however, so if you have a powerful new model (1,000 watts or more), try five minutes at the lowest setting. Yield: 1½ sticks unsalted butter = about 1 cup ghee.

Cayenne Pepper: The preferred term today is ground hot red pepper because the fiery powder in that little glass jar may be a blend of hot red peppers, among them cayenne. *NOTE: When a recipe calls for hot pepper (either ground or flakes), I usually give a range—¼ to ½ teaspoon, for example, then add "depending upon how 'hot' you like things." The smaller amount will give you a fairly tepid dish, the second a tolerably hot one. If you like things truly hot, taste as you go, upping the amount to suit you..*

Chili Flakes: What we used to call crushed dried hot red chili peppers. The formula hasn't changed, only the name. See Cayenne Pepper, above, for seasoning tips.

Citrus Juice: Lemon, orange, and lime juices are called for in more than a few recipes—*fresh* juices. When it comes to cooking meat, citrus juices play two major roles: they add flavor and being acidic, they help tenderize tough cuts whether used in marinades or cooking liquids. *TIP: To save time, juice the fruit directly into a spouted glass measuring cup and stop when you have the amount you need.*

Citrus Zest: Lemon, lime, and orange zest (the colored part of the rind) are powerful flavor boosters and particularly compatible with beef, veal, lamb, and pork. *TIP: If a recipe calls for both juice and zest, remove the zest first. Use a Microplane to grate the zest, a swivel-bladed vegetable peeler to remove long strips of it. Once the zest is removed, halve and juice the fruit.*

Cippolini: Some stews call for whole small white onions (silverskins, see below) and because they're not as available as they once were, I often substitute these popular newcomers. Small and sweet, these

Italian onions are only slightly larger than silver-skins, flattish rather than round, and superb in any meaty stew. My supermarket usually carries little mesh bags of them and my high-end grocery always has them.

Cooking Oils: A fruity extra-virgin olive oil is a good choice for soups and stews but I often use a mix of unsalted butter and olive oil, particularly in northern Italian recipes. For Asian recipes I prefer peanut oil with perhaps a dash of toasted sesame seed oil, and for all-purpose recipes, a largely unsaturated blended vegetable oil with a high smoke point that's good for searing meats quickly.

Eggs: Large eggs are used in this book; do not substitute any other size unless a recipe specifies a different size. A number of recipes in this book call for hard-cooked eggs. Here's a foolproof way to hard-cook eggs:

- Choose eggs nearing their "sell-by date"—they're easier to peel.
- Place eggs in a heavy saucepan large enough to accommodate them in a single layer, cover by at least three inches of cold water, set uncovered over moderately high heat, and bring to a boil.
- Take pan off the heat, cover, and let eggs stand exactly 15 minutes (use a timer).
- Drain, fill pan with ice cubes and cold water, and let stand about 10 minutes.
- Take eggs up one by one, crack the butt or large end, then roll egg on the counter to craze the shell, and peel under cool running water. Blot dry on paper toweling and repeat until all eggs are peeled. *Tip: A colleague passed along this piece of advice: Add a little vinegar to the egg cooking water. She swears it makes the eggs a snap to peel.*
- Use immediately to prevent that ugly dark green ring from forming between the yolk and white.

Flour: All-purpose is the flour to use; recipes specify whether it's to be sifted before it's measured or not.

In this book, flour is used mainly to dredge meats before they're browned or to thicken gravies and sauces so there is no need to sift.

Fresh Herbs: Not so long ago, the only herbs available to us were dried and most, alas, quickly lost color and flavor. Today, farmer's markets sell fresh herbs in little pots and supermarkets in small, flat plastic containers—everything from chives and chervil to rosemary, sage, and thyme. By all means use them in the recipes that follow. Speaking of thyme, lemon thyme to my mind, is the best thyme of all—a perennial easily grown indoors or out. Its flavor is delicate, faintly lemony, glorious with mushrooms (one of those made-in-heaven combinations). Whenever I call for freshly chopped herbs, I mean leaves only unless the herb is so tender smaller stems can be included (as with chervil and cilantro). In every recipe specifying fresh herbs, I also give the dried herb equivalent. Rule of thumb: 1 tablespoon freshly chopped herb = 1 teaspoon crumbled dried herb. There are exceptions, however: For unusually strong herbs like rosemary and sage, I generally substitute ½ to ¾ teaspoon crumbled dried herb for each tablespoon of freshly chopped. *TIP: When using dried herbs, always crumble as you add—the warmth of your hands releases and increases their flavor.*

Garlic: In long-simmering soups and stews, garlic virtually melts, spreading its goodness, and that's why I so often call for a certain number of cloves, "smashed and skins removed." So much easier than crushing, mincing, or slicing. Moreover, the effect's the same. *TIP: Use a cutlet bat, a heavy saucepan, or a rolling pin sleeved in plastic to smash the garlic.*

Ghee: See Butter.

Lard: Rendered hog fat, not vegetable shortening. If unavailable at your butcher, grocery, or supermarket, head for the nearest Latino grocery. Most routinely carry it.

Leeks: Who, ten years ago, would have found leeks in a supermarket beyond the large metropolitan areas?

Today they're commonplace, still not everyone knows how to clean them. Here's how:

- Remove coarse green tops and roots, carefully leaving root ends intact.
- Lay leeks on a cutting board and quarter lengthwise, cutting to but not through the root end.
- Holding leeks one by one under cool running water, flush out all grit.
- Pat leeks dry on paper toweling before slicing or chopping.

Other Onions: Each recipe specifies which type of onion to use—yellow, red, Spanish, etc. Whenever onions are to be chopped, halve them lengthwise, slip off the skins, then quarter each half or if large, cut into sixths. Drop chunks into a food processor, distributing evenly, then alternately pulse and churn to just the right texture. *TIP: If a recipe calls for both chopped garlic and chopped onions, snap on the processor and drop the peeled garlic cloves down the feed tube into the whirring blade. Scrape the work bowl, add onion chunks, and pulse and churn until as finely chopped as needed.*

Parmigiano Reggiano: This imported Italian parmesan is the cheese of choice if you can afford it. Otherwise, go for a Wisconsin or Argentine parmesan. Do not settle for grated cheese; you'll save a little money if you buy it by the chunk and grate it yourself. Here's how: Using a cheese wedger, break the parmesan into chunks of about 1 inch, snap on the food processor, and drop the chunks down the feed tube into the spinning blade. A 30- to 40-second pulse-and-churn is all it takes to grate the cheese.

Parsley: Across much of the country, Italian or flat-leafed parsley is now as ubiquitous as the curly kind our mothers used to garnish everything from aspic to pot roast. I prefer the more flavorful Italian parsley and like to keep it on hand. Properly stored, it keeps for nearly two weeks. Here's how to prep:

- Unband the parsley as soon as you get home from the store and discard any softening or discolored stalks.

- Do not wash the parsley. Instead, half-fill a wide-mouth 1-pint preserving jar (or large old-fashioned glass) with cold water.
- Cut end off each parsley stem, slicing slightly on the bias just as you would when arranging roses, and stand parsley in the jar of water.
- Slip a soft plastic bag (the tear-off kind you get at produce counters) loosely over the parsley; do not secure around the bottom.
- Stand the jar in the refrigerator (the slightly warmer top shelf seems best because there's less chance of the leaves freezing).
- Whenever a recipe calls for fresh parsley, remove the number of sprigs you need, then re-cover the remaining parsley and return to the refrigerator

Pork: Today's lean pork, heavily promoted as "The Other White Meat," has had so much flavor and succulence bred out of it, it doesn't make very good stew. The solution is to buy locally grown pork from a small farm (organic or otherwise) or to use a boutique brand like Niman Ranch. Also see Sources at the end of this book for names of additional pork growers who pack and ship.

Potatoes: Scores of stews either contain potatoes or are served with them. In the old days, that meant all-purpose (Maine or Eastern potatoes), peeled and chunked. Now that sweet, nutty redskins, fingerlings, and Yukon golds are widely available, I've made them my all-purpose "stew" potatoes. They're small enough to cook or serve whole (a decided advantage), they hold their shape, and in developing recipes for this book, I discovered that they needn't be peeled; the skins don't slake off. Another time-saver. All that's needed is a good cool-water scrub. *NOTE: Be sure to remove any green patches. These—and to a lesser extent the "eyes"—are not only bitter but also contain solanine, a compound the body converts into toxic solanidine, which can make you sick. TIP: When adding whole redskins to stew, make sure they're more or less the same size so they'll all be done at the same time. Redskins are also the potatoes I serve alongside many* *stews—sometimes boiled in their skins but more often roasted. To Roast Potatoes:*

Allowing two to three redskins per person, scrub and arrange in a single layer in a small shallow pan (I often use a 9-inch pie pan), slide onto the middle shelf of a 400°F oven, and roast uncovered until a small skewer or poultry pin will pierce them easily—about 1 hour. What could be easier?

Rice: My all-purpose rice is converted rice, meaning parboiled (Uncle Ben is the best-known) because it's the rice we used for recipe testing and food photography at *The Ladies' Home Journal*—my first New York job. A few years later, a Chinese friend taught me his nearly fool-proof method (it makes enough rice for six to eight people). To cook rice:

- Place 1 inch rice in the bottom of a large heavy saucepan and add enough cold water to cover it by about 1¼ inches.
- Set uncovered over high heat and bring to a boil. Adjust heat so the water barely bubbles and cook the rice uncovered (no stirring!) until the surface dimples and water is absorbed— about 20 minutes. The rice will be slightly al dente.
- For softer rice, cover and let stand 5 minutes.

Salt: Uniodized table salt was used in testing these recipes, but feel free to substitute sea salt, coarse or kosher salt—you'll need slightly more of each. Taste-as-you-go is the best policy

Silverskins: Once second in popularity to all-purpose yellow onions, these Ping-Pong ball–size white onions seem to have fallen from favor. They're the ones we creamed every Thanksgiving, the ones we peeled and slipped whole into all manner of stews. *TIP: To peel zip-quick, blanch the onions in boiling water 20 to 30 seconds and remove to paper toweling with a slotted spoon. When cool enough to handle, slip the skins off. Use the same technique to peel Cippolini (see above).*

MEASURING TIPS

Lard, mayonnaise, mustard, sour cream, crème fraîche and other ingredients of similar texture are, unless specified to the contrary, measured tightly packed—small amounts in measuring spoons, larger ones in "dry" cup measures (the nested cups used to measure flours and sugars). Here's the technique: Scoop up a rounded tablespoon of the ingredient, drop into the measure, then pack with the bowl of the spoon. Repeat until the cup is full, level off the top with the broad side of a small thin-blade spatula. Recipes specify how these ingredients should be measured.

Light and Dark Brown Sugar: Measure just as you would lard (see above) unless a recipe directs otherwise

Molasses, Honey, Corn Syrup, and Other Sticky Liquids: They'll slide out of measuring cups and spoons more cleanly if these have been spritzed with nonstick cooking spray.

A FEW SHORT-CUTS

Like most busy cooks, I have no problem using prepared or partially prepared foods if they're top-quality. Here are a few time-savers that I call for in the recipes that follow:

Broths: Supermarket shelves bulge with every kind of broth—beef, chicken, vegetable, low-sodium, low-fat, and so on. I find them excellent for soups and stews and specify exactly which type to use in each recipe.

Carrots: Bagged baby carrots beckon from produce counters and I often use them in place of chunked or diced carrots. These, you should know, are not baby carrots. They're misshapen mature carrots peeled and cut small. Before buying, inspect the carrots carefully through their see-through plastic bag and reject any that seem slimy or wizened or cracked. Because there have been recalls due to bacterial contamination, I use baby carrots for cooking only. *NOTE: It's been said that baby carrots are given a chlorine bath before they're bagged. Not true, my research tells me. They are washed in tap water, which of course is chlorinated. But that hardly amounts to a chlorine bath.*

Mushrooms: Not so long ago the only mushrooms supermarkets sold were little white ones. Then came brown creminis (baby portabellas), then big fleshy portabellas, and now 8-ounce packages of each. I don't hesitate to use the pre-sliced if they look fresh (no sign of withering, discoloring, or softening). On my latest trip to my local high-end grocery, I saw ready-to-use gourmet mushroom blends—4-ounce packets of sliced baby bellas, shiitakes, and oyster mushrooms. Not cheap but a significant time-saver— no tedious wiping with a damp cloth, no slicing.

Pie Crusts: Few people bother to make their own pie crusts these days and to be accommodating, my pot pies call for unroll-and-fill pie crusts. These come two to the 15-ounce package, they're displayed near the ready-to-bake biscuits in refrigerated supermarket counters, and I find them surprisingly good. To add a homey touch, crimp the crust into a high, fluted edge—for looks, yes, but also to reduce the risk of boil-overs, a common problem with pot pies. Crimping takes less than a minute: Simply move around the edge of the crust making a zigzag pattern by pinching the dough between the thumb of one hand and the index finger and thumb of the other.

Tomatoes: With tomato season so short, few supermarkets sell local, sun-ripened tomatoes. Moreover, their season is not soup or stew season. Fortunately, the variety of canned tomatoes is virtually endless: stewed whole tomatoes (with or without any number of herbs), fire-roasted tomatoes, tomatoes with green chilies (from tepid to torrid), tomatoes packed in sauce, in water—but alas, fewer cans of crushed tomatoes, until recently my choice for soups and stews. I've switched to canned diced tomatoes and find them equally good. Sometimes I drain them, sometimes not. Each recipe specifies.

A FEW ADDITIONAL TIME-SAVERS

Some recipes must be cooled (brought to room temperature) or chilled (made refrigerator-cold) mid-recipe and that often takes time.

- To Cool Food Faster: Spread the food in a large shallow pan and either refrigerate or immerse in an ice bath. Either way, the food will cool two to three times faster than it would if set on a counter.
- To Chill Food Faster: Spread the food in a large shallow pan and set in the freezer for 30 to 40 minutes or until the food feels uniformly cold.

Make-Aheads: Soups and stews freeze well and there's no better way to short-cut party (or family dinner) prep than by making a recipe when you have a little time to spare, then stashing it in the freezer for future enjoyment. It couldn't be easier.

To Freeze: Cool soup or stew to room temperature and ladle into 1-quart freezer containers, filling each to within ½ inch of the top. Snap on lids, label, date, and set in a 0°F freezer. When ready to serve, thaw overnight in the refrigerator, then reheat slowly in a covered large heavy Dutch oven over moderately low heat, stirring now and then. *NOTE: If a soup or stew gets a last-minute sprinkling of chopped parsley or other fresh herb, add it just before serving, not before freezing.* Storage time: About three months.

POTS AND PANS

Pan sizes, shapes, and types are key to a recipe's success, so never substitute one pan for another unless recipes suggest alternatives.

Many recipes that follow call for nonreactive containers, ones that do not react with the ingredients put into them—particularly acidic ones like lemon juice, tomatoes, and vinegar—all common to many marinades, soups, and stews. The best nonreactive pots and pans are made of porcelain-clad metal (Le Creuset, to name one brand). Second best: stainless steel. When it comes to mixing bowls, choose glass or ceramic. Reactive pans (cast iron, aluminum, tin, etc.) often infuse the foods cooked in them with unpleasant metallic flavors.

Slow Cookers: No need to buy an expensive brand with all the bells and whistles. My modestly priced 4-quart Crock Pot® has served me well over the years. It has a removable, dishwasher-safe ceramic pot and see-through glass lid for at-a-glance monitoring. The heating elements are in the walls of the slow cooker (next time I'd like a bottom unit as well) and there are two degrees of heat: High (to jump-start cooking) and Low (for long simmering). Best all-round size: 4 to 6 quarts.

GADGETRY

Food Processors: What did we do before these miracle workers forever changed the way we cook? I bought one of the very first models (can it be?) 30 years ago. Today I keep three food processors at-the-ready—large, medium, and small—and use them to chop, slice, and purée all manner of things. If you've never owned a food processor, look for one with:

- A powerful motor that won't stall under duress.
- Enough heft to anchor the machine when processing heavy loads.
- A large work bowl (3½ quarts or 14 cups is the size I like) made of sturdy clear plastic with a feed tube large enough to swallow small potatoes and onions whole.
- A pulse button, preferably one you can engage while churning. Some processors lack this handy feature, forcing you to stop the churning before pulsing. No effortless switching back and forth.

Spice Grinders/Mini Choppers: My mini food processor both grinds and chops. It's a sturdy little machine with plenty of power though it sounds like an angry wasp. I use it to pulverize aromatic seeds, grind whole nutmegs, and chop small amounts of parsley, dill, cilantro, and other fresh herbs. Like my full-sized food processors, it can be put through the dishwasher.

Electric Blenders: Whenever a sauce or mixture must be liquefied, I use a blender because it's faster and more thorough than a food processor. For me, a simple but powerful two-speed (fast/slow) blender is perfectly adequate. No need for half a dozen push buttons with incremental speeds.

Immersion Blenders: Many soups and sauces must be puréed and if done in a food processor, it's a three- or four-step job. With an immersion blender, you can purée hot mixtures right in the pan. Choose a powerful model with a shaft long enough to work well in deep pots. But before buying, do your homework (there are half a dozen or more brands, some with prices approaching $200). Query friends who own immersion blenders for recommendations and survey the different brands online. Plenty of information there about specific models and no shortage of user comments—pro and con.

Microplanes: These hand-held rasps grate citrus zest, nutmeg, and hard cheese in jig time. For most jobs, I use a long-handled Microplane of moderately fine texture that can be laid straight across a bowl or pot. Saves time whenever a recipe calls for the grated zest of one lemon or half a grated nutmeg or several ounces of grated Parmigiano Reggiano.

Egg Slicers: Before pre-sliced mushrooms hit the supermarket, I sliced mushroom caps in an egg slicer and often still do. A terrific time-saver if slices of uniform thickness are needed.

Swivel-Bladed Vegetable Peelers: They're not just for peeling carrots and potatoes, apples and pears. These versatile gadgets are also perfect for removing long thin strips of citrus zest or shavings of cheese.

BEEF

BEEF

BRISKET, CHUCK (SHOULDER), FLANK, OXTAIL, PLATE/SHORT RIBS, ROUND, RUMP, SHANKS, AND SUCH

Beef may be America's Number One meat today, but until the turn of the 20th century, that distinction belonged to pork. For good reason; beef was a jaw-buster.

The cattle Spanish conquistadors brought to the Southwest back in the mid-16th century were lean, rangy animals. Soon dubbed Texas longhorns, they foraged so far and wide their meat was barely chewable. Even T-bones.

Late in the 19th century things began to change. Bony longhorns were cross-bred with meatier British stock (Angus and Herefords) and coast-to-coast rail service ended the days of cattle drives. More important, Gustavus Swift's refrigerated railroad car meant that sides of beef could be loaded at stockyards across the Middle West and "aged" (held at low temperature) while being shipped cross country. If beef is held at about 35°F for seven to ten days after slaughter, its enzymes go to work softening muscle and improving flavor. But, make a note, only beef is aged. Not veal, not lamb, not pork.

Equally responsible for turning America into a beef-and-potatoes nation was the new practice of pampering steers (males castrated while young) and fattening them on rations of grain instead of pasture grass. Steers matured faster and younger animals meant more tender meat.

Typically beef cattle are slaughtered between nine and thirty months of age. Those less than a year old are marketed as baby beef, the implication being that their meat is beyond tender. For me, however, these adolescents lack the flavor, marbling, and juiciness of animals a few months older.

Still, no matter how young the animal meat from any of its well exercised areas—brisket, chuck (shoulder), flank, round, rump, shanks, short-ribs, and so on—requires slow cooking in the presence of liquid (broth, wine, tomato juice, vinegar, etc.) to render it into submission.

It's a lesson our grandmothers learned early on but one few in today's steak-obsessed society ever do. Sadly, they're missing the most succulent, most flavorful, most economical beef of all.

BEEF NUTRITIONAL PROFILE

A first-rate source of protein with impressive amounts of vitamin B12, iron, and zinc (three nutrients vegetarians tend to lack) and a moderate source of three additional B vitamins—thiamin (B1), riboflavin (B2), and niacin. No fiber. Fat, calories, and cholesterol vary from grade to grade (Prime being the fattest); cut to cut (chuck's fatter than round or rump) and needless to add, according to how much fat is trimmed off. For comparison, here are approximate counts of two popular cuts:

- Braised Beef Round (4 ounces) = 237 calories, 8 grams fat, 109 milligrams cholesterol

- Braised Trimmed Chuck (4 ounces) = 246 calories, 9 grams fat, 115 milligrams cholesterol

USDA GRADES OF BEEF (IN DESCENDING ORDER)

- **Prime:** This pricey top grade has a thick blanket of fat and is velvety lean richly marbled (flecked) with fat. Used mostly by restaurant chefs, it is often available at fancy big-city butchers but rarely anywhere else. NOTE: *The heavier the marbling, the juicier the steak and prime ribs.*
- **Choice:** The highest grade most butchers and upscale groceries sell; fine-textured lean but less well-marbled than Prime.
- **Select:** The grade formerly called Good, this supermarket staple is leaner than Prime or Choice. Since the US Department of Agriculture (USDA) changed the terminology some 20 years ago, sales of this third grade of beef have quintupled.
- **Lower Grades:** Standard and Commercial are often sold as "store brands" and those lower still (Utility, Cutter, and Canner) are primarily used in processed meats though now and then may show up in the supermarket as pre-packaged ground beef.

SHOPPING TIPS

Because the grade (a purple shield stamped on the outer layer of fat) isn't always visible, it's important to know the hallmarks of quality:

- Beef lean should be bright cherry red and nicely marbled, but if you watch a butcher cut something from a carcass he's brought from his cooler, it will be brownish-maroon; only when meat is exposed to the air does it turn bright red. I once saw a woman berate a butcher when the meat he cut off a carcass was dark. "It's spoiled," she shrieked. "How dare you!" I happily bought the Swiss steak she'd rejected and it was delicious.
- Beef fat should be firm and snowy white. Yellowing fat indicates that the animal may be old and/or range-fed; either way the meat is likely to be tough.

STORAGE TIPS

Fresh meat is highly perishable so if you can't cook it the day you bought it, remove from the store wrapper, spread in a single layer on a large plate, cover loosely with plastic wrap, and store in the coldest part of the refrigerator. Cook and serve within two days.

FREEZER TIPS

Cast off the store package, then wrap the various cuts in foil or plastic freezer wrap this way:

- **Large Steaks and Pot Roasts:** Package each individually.
- **Smaller Steaks, Chops, and Cutlets:** Do not stack. Instead, arrange side-by-side, allowing no more than two or three per package.
- **Stew Meat:** Spread in a single layer—easier if you first line a shallow pan (9 x 9 x 2 inches is a good size) with foil—then fold ends in securely over meat. Once meat freezes, remove pan and, if necessary, over-wrap with plastic freezer wrap or additional foil. The point is to seal out all air and prevent "freezer burn."
- **Ground Beef:** Flatten into a round no more than two inches thick and wrap as snugly as possible. Or shape into burgers and wrap individually.

In each case, press all air from package, label, date, and set directly on the freezing surface of a 0°F freezer. *MAXIMUM STORAGE TIME: Three months for ground beef and stew meat, six months for larger cuts.*

RECYCLING LEFTOVERS

If I have a small amount of soup or stew left, I'll reheat with freshly cooked white or brown rice, macaroni or fusilli—a good way to stretch one serving as far as four. I may add curry powder if teaming with rice or top with freshly grated Parmigiano Reggiano when mixing with pasta. Leftover pot roast or Swiss steak can be hashed with potatoes or turned into curry or chili. It can be ground, mixed with chopped onion and garlic along with dried marjoram, basil, and/or thyme to taste, softened with a little canned gravy or tomato sauce, stuffed into scooped-out peppers, tomatoes, or onions, and baked uncovered at 350°F for about 45 minutes. Let your imagination be your guide.

BEEF CUTS

(WHERE THE TOUGH CUTS ARE)

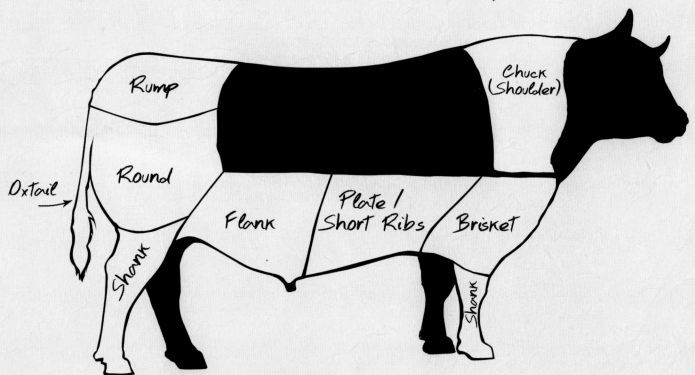

Rump

Chuck (Shoulder)

Round

Oxtail

Flank

Plate / Short Ribs

Brisket

Shank

Shank

BRISKET

Flat, fibrous slab above and behind the fore-shank; lean muscle with easily trimmed outer layer fat

USES
- CORNED BEEF
- POT ROAST

CHUCK (SHOULDER)

Hugely versatile; well-marbled lean plus enough sinew for succulence

USES
- POT ROAST
- POT PIE
- SWISS STEAK (NOTABLY BLADE STEAK WITH A KNIFE-LIKE BONE) AND MEATIER ARM STEAK (SINGLE ROUND BONE)
- BEST CUT FOR STEWS, MEATLOAVES, AND MEATBALLS

FLANK

Long, lean, boneless steak with muscle fibers running the length of it. Also called London broil.

USES
- SWISS STEAK
- ALSO STUFFED, ROLLED, AND BRAISED
- BROILED "RARE" AND SLICED THIN ACROSS THE GRAIN

OXTAIL

Bony, sinewy, gamy, gelatinous

USES
- SOUP
- STEW

PLATE/ SHORT RIBS

Fairly fat belly meat whence short ribs (the succulent rib ends) come

USES
- SOUP
- BRAISED SHORT RIBS

ROUND

Blocky, boneless cut; fine-textured lean; little or no fat

USES
- POT ROAST
- ROULADEN
- STUFFED, ROLLED, AND BRAISED

RUMP

Another blocky cut bone-in or out; less lean than round

USES
- POT ROAST

SHANKS

Lean, gristly, round cuts with central leg bone. Fore shanks best; hind shanks go into hamburger and hotdogs.

USES
- SOUP
- BRAISED SHANKS

my illinois grandmother's hearty beef and vegetable soup

My mother's mother always visited us in Raleigh, North Carolina, when Illinois winters turned fierce and at least once every visit, she'd make this old family recipe. I looked forward to that day even though I was drafted to prepare the vegetables. How Grandma Johnson would have loved the labor savers supermarkets now sell: peeled baby carrots and slaw mixes (why core and shred cabbage?), not to mention the amazing variety of canned broths and tomatoes. Note: I've slipped some garlic into Grandma's soup because I think it improves the flavor. She, who never used garlic, perhaps never tasted it, would disagree.

3 tablespoons bacon drippings or vegetable oil

1½ pounds boneless beef chuck, trimmed of excess fat and cut in 1-inch cubes

2 large yellow onions, halved lengthwise and each half sliced ¼ inch thick

4 medium celery ribs, trimmed and sliced ¼ inch thick (include some tops)

4 large garlic cloves, smashed and skins removed

2 large whole bay leaves (preferably fresh)

1 quart (4 cups) beef, vegetable, or chicken broth

1 can (14½ ounces) diced tomatoes, with their liquid

1 cup cold water (about)

1 teaspoon salt, or to taste

½ teaspoon freshly ground black pepper, or to taste

4 medium all-purpose potatoes, peeled and cut in ½-inch cubes

½ pound peeled baby carrots

2 cups packaged slaw mix (from supermarket produce counter)

¼ cup coarsely chopped fresh parsley

1. Heat drippings in a large heavy Dutch oven over moderately high heat until ripples appear on pan bottom—1½ to 2 minutes. Brown beef in two batches in drippings, allowing about 10 minutes per batch and lifting each to a bowl as it browns. Add onions, celery, garlic, and bay leaves to pot and sauté, stirring often, until limp—6 to 8 minutes.

2. Return beef to pot along with accumulated juices, add broth, tomatoes, water, salt, and pepper, and bring to a boil. Adjust heat so liquid bubbles slowly, cover, and simmer 1½ hours. Add potatoes, carrots, slaw mix, and if liquid seems skimpy, a little more water. Cover and simmer until meat and vegetables are tender—40 to 45 minutes. Discard bay leaves, taste for salt and pepper, and adjust as needed.

3. Mix in parsley, ladle into heated large soup plates, and serve with chunks of crusty country bread.

MAKES 6 SERVINGS

root soup

There's beef in this recipe but only enough to add body and flavor. Chuck is the cut to use because of its succulence and ability to complement the vegetables: golden beets, carrots, parsnips, and turnips along with onions, garlic, celery, and tomatoes. Now that every supermarket sells fresh herbs, do use them here. Your soup will be more fragrant and flavorful. Tip: Coarsely chopped chuck is a better choice for this recipe than ground and if your butcher won't do the chopping for you, your food processor will IF it's a sturdy one. First trim away as much connective tissue as possible, cut meat into one-inch cubes, and once it's firmed up in the freezer for 45 minutes, pulse briskly in three batches until the size of peas.

2 tablespoons extra-virgin olive oil

¾ pound coarsely chopped or ground
lean beef chuck (see Tip above)

2 medium yellow onions, coarsely chopped

2 large garlic cloves, finely chopped

3 small carrots, peeled and sliced ¼ inch thick

3 small parsnips, peeled and sliced ¼ inch thick

3 small golden beets, peeled, halved lengthwise,
and each half sliced ¼ inch thick

2 small white turnips, peeled, halved lengthwise,
and each half sliced ¼ inch thick

3 small celery ribs, trimmed and sliced
¼ inch thick (include some leaves)

1 can (14½ ounces) diced tomatoes, with their liquid

1¾ cups beef broth plus enough water to total 2 cups

⅓ cup dry white wine such as Chardonnay,
Riesling, or Pinot Grigio

2 large whole bay leaves tied in cheesecloth with
1 small sprig each rosemary and thyme (spice bag)

1 teaspoon salt, or to taste

½ teaspoon freshly ground black pepper, or to taste

¼ cup coarsely chopped fresh Italian parsley

1. Heat olive oil in a large heavy nonreactive soup kettle over moderately high heat until ripples appear on pan bottom—1½ to 2 minutes.

2. Add beef, onions, and garlic and stir-fry until beef is no longer red—5 to 8 minutes. Add all but last ingredient (parsley), wringing spice bag gently to release flavors, and bring to a boil.

3. Adjust heat so soup barely bubbles, cover, and simmer slowly until flavors have mellowed and married—about 2½ hours. Note: If heat is low enough, there's little danger of the kettle boiling dry, but check occasionally and if liquid seems skimpy, add a little water. Discard spice bag, taste for salt and pepper, and adjust as needed.

4. Mix in parsley, ladle into heated large soup plates, and serve with wedges of chewy yeast bread.

MAKES 6 SERVINGS

joe booker

More soup than stew, this economical Down East classic is said to have originated in the vicinity of Booth-bay Harbor, Maine. No one knows who Joe Booker was—the man who first bubbled up this muddle of beef, potatoes, carrots, and turnips or someone else for whom it was named. What is known is that Joe Booker is the take-the-chill-off meal men craved after a day of cutting ice or chopping wood. Note: Old recipes make dumplings optional but I find them a welcome addition given the stew's copious broth. Use your favorite recipe for drop biscuits, halving all ingredients or—even easier—substitute one package (6 ounces) containing five ready-to-bake refrigerated buttermilk biscuits. Snip each in half before dropping into the bubbling stew. Tip: Whenever you want to enrich a soup or stew, begin with cold liquid or water, as I do here. Cold liquids absorb and spread the flavors of other ingredients, particularly those of meats and vegetables. Boiling liquids do not.

½ pound salt pork, cut in ¼-inch dice

2 pounds boneless beef chuck,
trimmed of excess fat and cut in 1-inch cubes

2 large yellow onions, halved lengthwise
and each half sliced ¼ inch thick

2 quarts (8 cups) cold water (see Tip above)

1½ teaspoons salt, or to taste

½ teaspoon freshly ground black pepper,
or to taste

4 medium carrots,
peeled and sliced 1 inch thick

4 medium all-purpose potatoes,
peeled and cut in 1-inch cubes

4 medium turnips, peeled and cut in 1-inch cubes,
or 4 medium parsnips, peeled and sliced 1 inch thick

Dumplings (optional; see Note above)

1. Cook salt pork in a large heavy Dutch oven over moderate heat, stirring often, until drippings render out and only crisp brown bits remain—8 to 10 minutes. Using a slotted spoon, lift brown bits to paper toweling to drain, then bag in plastic and freeze to use another day for soup or stew.

2. Brown beef in two batches in drippings over moderately high heat, allowing 8 to 10 minutes per batch and lifting each to a large bowl as it browns.

3. Add onions to pot and stir-fry until limp and touched with brown—5 to 6 minutes.

4. Return beef to pot along with accumulated juices, add water, salt, and pepper, and bring to a boil.

5. Adjust heat so water barely bubbles, cover, and cook until meat is nearly tender—about 1½ hours. Note: If mixture boils, beef will toughen, so if necessary to keep stew at a slow simmer, slide a diffuser underneath pot. Add carrots, potatoes, and turnips, cover, and simmer slowly until almost tender—about 30 minutes.

6. If you decide to add dumplings, ease into bubbling stew allowing plenty of space between them (drop from-scratch dumplings by rounded teaspoons). Cover and simmer 15 minutes—no peeking. Taste broth for salt and pepper and adjust as needed.

7. To serve, ladle into heated large soup plates, making sure each person gets plenty of everything.

MAKES 6 TO 8 SERVINGS

oxtail soup

The easiest way to prepare oxtails is to simmer them in soup, the point being to cook them until the meat drops from the bones, then to return that meat to the pot along with any vegetables you fancy. Potatoes and carrots are traditional, ditto onions. I like to use scallions or green onions—easier to prep than yellow onions because you can bunch them and trim, bunch them and slice.

3 pounds oxtails, cut in 2-inch lengths

2 quarts (8 cups) cold water (about)

2 large whole bay leaves (preferably fresh)

2 teaspoons salt, or to taste

½ teaspoon freshly ground black pepper, or to taste

2 tablespoons bacon drippings or vegetable oil

4 bunches large scallions, washed, trimmed, and thickly sliced (include some green tops) or 1 large yellow onion, coarsely chopped

3 large garlic cloves, finely chopped

2 large all-purpose potatoes, peeled and cut in ½-inch dice

2 medium carrots, peeled and thickly sliced

2 medium celery ribs, trimmed and thickly sliced (include some leaves)

1 can (14½ ounces) diced tomatoes, with their liquid

¼ cup coarsely chopped fresh Italian parsley

1. Place oxtails, water, bay leaves, salt, and pepper in a large heavy nonreactive Dutch oven and bring to a boil over high heat. Adjust heat so mixture bubbles lazily, cover, and simmer slowly until meat almost falls from bones—4½ to 5 hours.

2. Using a slotted spoon, lift oxtails to a cutting board, strip meat from bones, and reserve; discard bones. Pour cooking mixture into a large bowl, skim fat from surface, and discard.

3. Rinse and dry Dutch oven and return to heat. Heat bacon drippings over moderately high heat until ripples appear on pan bottom—1½ to 2 minutes. Add scallions and garlic and stir-fry until limp and golden—3 to 5 minutes.

4. Add potatoes, carrots, and celery and turn until nicely coated. Return meat to pot along with reserved cooking mixture (and that includes bay leaves). Note: If liquid seems skimpy—it should not quite cover ingredients—add a little more water. Bring to a boil, adjust heat so mixture bubbles gently, cover, and simmer until vegetables are tender—about 45 minutes.

5. Mix in tomatoes and parsley and simmer uncovered just long enough for flavors to marry—15 to 20 minutes. Discard bay leaves, taste for salt and pepper, and adjust as needed.

6. To serve, ladle into heated large soup plates and accompany with crusty chunks of bread.

MAKES 6 SERVINGS

best-ever borsch

During my many winters in New York, I'd warm my southern bones by ordering a steaming bowl of borsch at the Russian Tea Room on West 57th Street—"slightly to the left of Carnegie Hall," as long-time owner Faith Stewart-Gordon liked to say. We all mourned when Tavern-on-the-Green owner Warner LeRoy bought and closed the RTR in '96, but cheered when he reopened it after a glitzy multi-million-dollar renovation. But neither the restaurant nor its food was the same. In 2002, bankruptcy forced another shut-down. Four years later new owners re-opened the Russian Tea Room with LeRoy's over-the-top décor untouched. I've yet to dine there and pray the winter borsch remains unchanged. This is my approximation of it. Note: For directions on cleaning leeks, see Leeks, How to Use This Book (page xiii).

¾ pound boneless beef chuck, trimmed of excess fat and cut in 1-inch cubes

6 ounces boneless pork shoulder, cut in 1-inch cubes

4 ounces kielbasa, coarsely chopped

6 cups beef broth

1½ cups water

2 large bay leaves (preferably fresh)

½ teaspoon salt, or to taste

½ teaspoon freshly ground black pepper, or to taste

3 large leeks, trimmed, washed, and thinly sliced (see Note above)

2 medium carrots, peeled and finely diced

2 medium parsnips, peeled and finely diced

2 medium celery ribs, trimmed and thinly sliced (include a few leaves)

¼ small cabbage, trimmed, cored, and sliced about ½ inch thick

½ cup coarsely chopped fresh Italian parsley

2 large garlic cloves, coarsely chopped

2 cans (14½ ounces each) sliced beets (beets from 1 can puréed with liquid from both cans and reserved)

1 can (14½ ounces) diced tomatoes, with their liquid blended with 2 tablespoons tomato paste

1 cup sour cream (use "light," if you like)

6 small sprigs fresh dill

1. Bring beef and next seven ingredients (pork through black pepper) to a boil in a large heavy nonreactive Dutch oven over moderately high heat. Adjust heat so liquid barely bubbles, set lid on askew, and simmer 1 hour, occasionally skimming off any froth that accumulates.

2. Add next seven ingredients (leeks through garlic) along with sliced beets and tomatoes. Set lid on askew and simmer until meat and vegetables are tender—about 1 hour.

3. Mix in reserved beet purée and heat uncovered just until mixture steams—8 to 10 minutes. Discard bay leaves, taste for salt and pepper, and adjust as needed.

4. To serve, ladle into heated large soup plates, drift each portion with sour cream, and sprig with dill.

MAKES 6 SERVINGS

beef shank soup with meatballs and vegetables

Nothing enriches a soup like a meaty bone—in this case beef shank. If unavailable, substitute veal shank, even a ham hock or two. Just make sure what you buy has plenty of meat attached. Like many soups, this one is a two-day affair, but don't let that put you off. This soup virtually cooks itself and a night in the fridge significantly improves its flavor. Note: The meatballs can be made in advance and frozen. Moreover, they needn't be reserved exclusively for this soup. Simmer them in your favorite pasta sauce or warm in cream sauce and serve as Swedish meatballs.

1 pound beef shank, cut in 2-inch chunks

2 quarts (8 cups) water (about)

2 large whole bay leaves (preferably fresh)

1½ teaspoons salt, or to taste

¼ teaspoon freshly ground black pepper, or to taste

1 medium yellow onion, halved lengthwise and each half thinly sliced

2 small carrots, peeled and thinly sliced

2 small parsnips, peeled and thinly sliced (optional)

2 small celery ribs, trimmed and thinly sliced (include some leaves)

1 medium all-purpose potato, peeled and thinly sliced

1½ cups packaged slaw mix (from supermarket produce counter)

1 can (14½ ounces) diced tomatoes, with their liquid

1 tablespoon raw sugar (if needed to mellow soup)

MEATBALLS

1 pound ground lean beef chuck

1½ cups fine soft breadcrumbs (3 slices firm-textured white bread)

4 medium scallions, trimmed and finely minced (white part only)

2 tablespoons finely minced fresh parsley

1 small garlic clove, finely minced

1 large egg

1 teaspoon salt

¼ teaspoon freshly ground black pepper

2 tablespoons cold water

¼ cup vegetable oil (for browning meatballs)

1. Place shank, water, bay leaves, salt, and pepper in a large nonreactive soup pot and bring to a boil over high heat. Adjust heat so water bubbles lazily, cover, and simmer very slowly until meat falls from bones—4 to 4½ hours.

2. When soup has simmered 4 to 4½ hours, discard bones. Cool broth and meat to room temperature, cover, and refrigerate overnight.

3. When ready to proceed, scoop fat from surface of broth and discard. Set pot over moderate heat, add onion, carrots, parsnips, if desired, celery, and potato, cover, and cook 45 to 50 minutes.

4. Meanwhile, prepare Meatballs: Mix all but last ingredient (vegetable oil) thoroughly and shape into balls about 1¼ inches in diameter. Arrange in a single layer on a foil-lined baking sheet and set in freezer until ready to cook. This will firm the meatballs up a bit.

5. Heat vegetable oil in a large heavy skillet over moderately high heat until ripples appear on pan bottom—1½ to 2 minutes. Add meatballs and brown on all sides—8 to 10 minutes. Drain on paper toweling.

6. Add meatballs and slaw mix to soup, and if liquid seems skimpy, a little more water. Cover and cook 25 minutes.

7. Add tomatoes, cover, and cook until meatballs are done—15 to 20 minutes more. Discard bay leaves, taste for salt and pepper, and adjust as needed, and if soup seems tart, mix in raw sugar.

8. Ladle into heated large soup plates and serve.

MAKES 6 SERVINGS

onion-smothered beef

Such a simple old-fashioned recipe, a fricassee with five ingredients only if you don't count the last-minute sprinkling of parsley. It's optional. You can braise bottom round this way as well but you'll be happier with chuck because of its greater succulence.

3 pounds boneless beef chuck,
trimmed of excess fat and cut in ½-inch cubes

1 cup unsifted all-purpose flour
mixed with 2 teaspoons salt and
½ teaspoon freshly ground black pepper
(seasoned flour)

4 tablespoons bacon drippings or
vegetable oil or a 50/50 mix (about)

2 large yellow onions, halved lengthwise
and each half sliced about ½ inch thick

1½ cups beef broth or water

2 tablespoons coarsely chopped
fresh parsley (optional)

1. Dredge beef, a few pieces at a time, by shaking in a large plastic zipper bag with seasoned flour and set aside.

2. Heat drippings in a large heavy Dutch oven over moderately high heat until ripples appear on pan bottom—1½ to 2 minutes. Brown dredged beef in several batches in drippings, allowing about 10 minutes per batch and lifting each to a bowl as it browns.

3. Add onions to pot and another tablespoon or so of drippings if they seem skimpy. Sauté, stirring often, until browned—12 to 15 minutes.

4. Return beef to pot along with accumulated juices, add broth, and bring to a boil. Adjust heat so liquid barely bubbles, cover, and simmer slowly until beef is fork-tender—1¼ to 1½ hours. Note: Check pot occasionally and if mixture threatens to scorch, add a little water, turn heat to lowest point, and slide a diffuser underneath pot.

5. Remove lid and if gravy seems thin, boil uncovered 20 to 30 minutes, stirring occasionally. Taste for salt and pepper and adjust as needed.

6. Serve over boiled or mashed potatoes and, for additional color, if desired, scatter a little parsley over each portion.

MAKES 6 SERVINGS

beef braised with vegetables of the vines

Vegetables of the vines? You know them as beans, peas, cucumbers, tomatoes, bell peppers, chilies, pumpkins, and summer and winter squash—New World gifts to the world table that sustained the native farming tribes of the East, South, and Southwest for centuries. This recipe is popular among the Pueblo Indians living along the "Great River of Life" (Rio Grande). With only a pound and a half of meat, it's a frugal stew, though it tastes anything but thanks to the tomatoes, summer squash, and corn it contains.

3 tablespoons bacon drippings, lard, or vegetable oil

1½ pounds boneless beef chuck, trimmed of excess fat and cut in ½-inch cubes

2 large yellow onions, coarsely chopped

2 large garlic cloves, finely chopped

1 teaspoon crumbled dried leaf oregano (preferably Mexican oregano)

1 teaspoon salt, or to taste

¼ teaspoon freshly ground black pepper, or to taste

1 can (14½ ounces) diced tomatoes, with their liquid

1 cup beef broth

2 cups fresh or frozen yellow corn kernels

4 small yellow squash or zucchini, trimmed and sliced ½ inch thick

1. Heat drippings in a large heavy deep nonreactive skillet over high heat until ripples appear on pan bottom—about 1½ minutes. Add beef and stir-fry until richly browned—about 10 minutes.

2. Push to one side of skillet and reduce heat to moderate. Add onions, garlic, oregano, salt, and pepper and sauté, stirring often, until onions are touched with brown—about 10 minutes.

3. Add tomatoes and broth and bring to a boil. Adjust heat so mixture simmers lazily, cover, and cook until beef is almost tender—about 1½ hours.

4. Add corn, cover, and cook until corn no longer tastes raw—20 to 25 minutes. Add squash, pushing down into mixture, cover, and simmer until tender—20 to 25 minutes. Taste for salt and pepper and adjust as needed.

5. To serve, ladle into heated large soup plates and accompany with a sturdy country bread.

MAKES 6 SERVINGS

beef stew with carrots, corn, and potatoes

Not the usual beef stew, this one contains sweet corn and fresh rosemary. Tips: To trim prep time, substitute 1½ cups peeled baby carrots (bagged in plastic at supermarket produce counters) for chunked carrots and frozen whole-kernel corn for fresh. Corn is a vegetable that freezes well and the frozen is often sweeter than what you would buy at the farmer's market.

2½ pounds boneless beef chuck,
trimmed of excess fat and cut in 1-inch cubes

¾ cup unsifted all-purpose flour
mixed with 1 teaspoon salt and
½ teaspoon freshly ground black pepper
(seasoned flour)

3 tablespoons bacon drippings or vegetable oil

1 large yellow onion,
halved lengthwise and each half thinly sliced

1 large whole bay leaf (preferably fresh)

1 small sprig fresh rosemary
or ½ teaspoon crumbled dried leaf rosemary

2 cups beef broth (about)

6 golf-ball-size redskin potatoes,
peeled or unpeeled

4 medium carrots, peeled and
cut in 1-inch chunks (see Tips above)

2 medium celery stalks, trimmed and
thinly sliced (include a few leaves)

1½ cups fresh or frozen yellow corn kernels
(see Tips above)

1. Dredge beef, a few pieces at a time, by shaking in a large plastic zipper bag with seasoned flour and set aside.

2. Heat drippings in a large heavy Dutch oven over moderately high heat until ripples appear on pan bottom—1½ to 2 minutes. Brown dredged beef in several batches in drippings, allowing about 10 minutes per batch and lifting each to a bowl as it browns.

3. Add onion, bay leaf, and rosemary to pot and sauté, stirring often, until onion is lightly browned—8 to 10 minutes.

4. Return beef to pot along with accumulated juices, add broth, and bring to a boil. Adjust heat so liquid bubbles gently, cover, and simmer until beef is nearly tender—about 1½ hours.

5. Add potatoes, carrots, and celery, and if broth seems skimpy, a little more broth or water. Cover and simmer until beef and carrots are tender—40 to 45 minutes more.

6. Add corn, cover, and simmer just until corn no longer tastes raw and flavors mellow—about 20 minutes. Discard bay leaf and rosemary sprig, taste for salt and pepper, and adjust as needed.

7. Ladle into heated large soup plates and serve—no accompaniments necessary for this dinner-in-a-dish.

MAKES 6 SERVINGS

mulligan stew

Not quite Irish stew (though sometimes called that), this one-kettle catch-all is more appropriately known as "hobo stew" because it contains very little meat and was originally bubbled up out of odds and ends. The version here is fairly classic. Note: Once made with finely diced sinewy meat, today's mulligan stews usually begin with ground beef. I offer both options. Tip: If you choose to dice the beef, you'll find that it cuts more cleanly if set in the freezer just long enough for the meat to firm up—about 45 minutes. Needless to add, use your sharpest knife to do the dicing.

3 tablespoons bacon drippings or vegetable oil

1 pound finely diced or coarsely ground bottom round (see Tip above)

3 medium all-purpose potatoes, peeled and cut in ¾-inch cubes

2 medium yellow onions, coarsely chopped

2 medium celery ribs, trimmed and thickly sliced (include some leaves)

2 medium carrots, peeled and thickly sliced

1 large white turnip, peeled and cut in ¾-inch cubes or 2 cups cubed rutabaga

¼ small cabbage, trimmed, cored, and sliced crosswise about ½ inch thick

1 quart (4 cups) water or for a richer stew, beef or vegetable broth (about)

1½ teaspoons salt, or to taste

¼ teaspoon freshly ground black pepper, or to taste

½ cup solidly frozen baby green peas

1. Heat drippings in a large heavy soup pot over high heat until ripples appear on pan bottom—about 1½ minutes. Brown beef in two batches in drippings, allowing about 10 minutes per batch and lifting each to a bowl as it browns.

2. Return beef to pot along with accumulated juices, add all but the final ingredient (frozen peas), and bring to a boil. Adjust heat so mixture barely bubbles, cover, and cook 1½ hours.

3. Uncover and simmer over lowest heat, stirring now and then, until meat and vegetables are very tender—30 to 40 minutes more. If stew threatens to scorch, add a little more water and slide a diffuser underneath the pot.

4. Add frozen peas and stir to break up clumps. Cook uncovered 10 minutes more, then taste for salt and pepper and adjust as needed.

5. Ladle into heated large soup plates and serve—no accompaniments needed.

MAKES 6 SERVINGS

gandy dancer's spiced kettle of beef

Gandy dancers were the crews who maintained America's railroads during the late 19th and early 20th centuries, often camping out and cooking their own meals. For obvious reasons, soups and stews were popular. Almost anything could be tossed into them, they fed an army and were virtually fail-safe. Moreover, leftovers could be reheated and plumped up with additional vegetables, even bits of leftover bread. Like Mulligan Stew, which precedes, this one welcomes improv.

2 pounds boneless beef chuck,
trimmed of excess fat and cut in 1-inch cubes

¾ cup unsifted all-purpose flour mixed with
1 tablespoon sweet paprika, 1 teaspoon salt,
and ½ teaspoon freshly ground black pepper
(seasoned flour)

3 tablespoons bacon drippings or vegetable oil

1 large yellow onion,
halved lengthwise and each half thinly sliced

6 cups water or beef or vegetable broth (about)

1 can (14½ ounces) diced tomatoes,
with their liquid

2 whole bay leaves and 2 teaspoons pickling spices
tied in cheesecloth (spice bag)

2 medium all-purpose potatoes,
peeled and cut in ¾-inch cubes

2 medium parsnips,
peeled and sliced ½ inch thick

2 medium carrots,
peeled and sliced ½ inch thick

3 tablespoons cornstarch
blended with ¼ cup cold water (thickener)

1. Dredge beef, a few pieces at a time, by shaking in a large plastic zipper bag with seasoned flour and set aside.

2. Heat drippings in a large heavy nonreactive Dutch oven over moderately high heat until ripples appear on pan bottom—1½ to 2 minutes. Brown dredged beef in several batches in drippings, allowing about 10 minutes per batch and lifting each to a bowl as it browns.

3. Add onion to pot and sauté, stirring often, until lightly browned—8 to 10 minutes.

4. Return beef to pot along with accumulated juices, add water, tomatoes, and spice bag, and bring to a boil. Adjust heat so liquid bubbles gently, cover, and simmer until beef is nearly tender—about 1½ hours.

5. Add potatoes, parsnips, carrots, and if stew seems thick, add a little more water. Cover and simmer until beef and vegetables are tender—30 to 35 minutes more. Discard spice bag, taste for salt and pepper, and adjust as needed.

6. Blend about 1 cup hot stew liquid into thickener, stir back into pot, and cook, stirring constantly, until gravy thickens and clears—3 minutes maximum. Note: Cooked longer than 3 minutes, cornstarch-thickened gravies will thin out.

7. Ladle into heated large soup plates and serve.

MAKES 6 SERVINGS

prairie stew

Chock-full of carrots, potatoes, and onions, this rib-sticking stew requires less meat than most. I wouldn't exactly call it a "hard times stew," but it is the sort that bubbled over campfires during America's westward push. Because it invites improvisation, Prairie Stew gracefully accepts add-ons: turnips, tomatoes, rutabaga, cabbage, greens (turnip or beet tops, collards, dandelions, and so on). Play around with different combos to see what you like best. Note: In frontier days, the meat and vegetables would have simmered in water, but I like to boost the flavor with beef broth. It's also likely that game would have supplied the meat—venison, perhaps even buffalo. Tip: If you blanch silverskin onions 20 to 30 seconds in boiling water, their skins will slip right off.

3 tablespoons bacon drippings or vegetable oil

1½ pounds boneless beef chuck,
trimmed of excess fat and cut in 1-inch cubes

1 quart (4 cups) beef broth plus 2 cups water

2 large yellow onions, halved lengthwise
and each half thickly sliced

2 large garlic cloves, finely chopped

1 tablespoon sweet paprika

1½ teaspoons salt, or to taste

½ teaspoon freshly ground black pepper,
or to taste

⅛ teaspoon ground cloves

6 medium all-purpose potatoes,
peeled and cut in ¾-inch dice

6 medium carrots,
peeled and cut in ¾-inch dice

12 whole silverskin (small white) onions,
peeled (see Tip above)

¼ cup unsifted all-purpose flour
blended with ½ cup cold water
(thickener)

1. Heat drippings in a large heavy nonreactive Dutch oven over high heat until ripples appear on pan bottom—about 1½ minutes. Brown beef in several batches in drippings, allowing about 10 minutes per batch and lifting each to a bowl as it browns.

2. Return meat to pot along with accumulated juices, add next seven ingredients (broth through ground cloves), and bring to a boil. Adjust heat so stew simmers lazily, cover, and cook 1½ hours.

3. Add potatoes, carrots, and onions, cover, and cook until meat and vegetables are tender—about 1 hour more.

4. Blend about 1½ cups hot stew liquid into thickener, stir back into pot, and cook, stirring constantly, until gravy thickens and no longer tastes of flour—about 5 minutes. Taste for salt and pepper and adjust as needed.

5. Ladle into heated large soup plates, serve, and get ready for "May I have a little more?" The stew's that good and, fortunately, bountiful enough for seconds.

MAKES 6 SERVINGS

sweet-sour beef stew

Such an easy stew and for me, a dinner party favorite. I make it one day, refrigerate overnight, and reheat shortly before serving. I vary the accompaniment, sometimes pairing with boiled unpeeled redskin potatoes, sometimes with steamed rounds of sweet potato, or boiled brown or white rice. Note: To save time, I use the bagged-in-plastic peeled baby carrots now sold at most supermarkets.

**3 pounds boneless beef chuck,
trimmed of excess fat and cut in 1½-inch cubes**

**1 cup unsifted all-purpose flour
mixed with 1 teaspoon salt and
½ teaspoon freshly ground black pepper
(seasoned flour)**

⅓ cup bacon drippings or vegetable oil

2 large yellow onions, coarsely chopped

2 large garlic cloves, finely chopped

1 tablespoon finely minced fresh ginger

2 large whole bay leaves (preferably fresh)

1 teaspoon crumbled dried leaf thyme

**1 can (14½ ounces) diced tomatoes,
with their liquid**

¼ cup red wine vinegar

2 tablespoons molasses (not too dark)

2 tablespoons tomato paste

2 cups peeled baby carrots (see Note above)

1. Dredge beef, a few pieces at a time, by shaking in a large plastic zipper bag with seasoned flour and set aside.

2. Heat drippings in a large heavy nonreactive Dutch oven over moderately high heat until ripples appear on pan bottom—1½ to 2 minutes. Brown dredged beef in several batches in drippings, allowing about 10 minutes per batch and lifting each to a bowl as it browns.

3. Add onions, garlic, ginger, bay leaves, and thyme to pot and sauté, stirring often, until lightly browned—10 to 12 minutes.

4. Return beef to pot along with accumulated juices, add tomatoes, vinegar, molasses, and tomato paste, and bring to a boil. Adjust heat so liquid bubbles gently, cover, and simmer until beef is nearly tender—about 1½ hours.

5. Add carrots, cover, and simmer until beef and carrots are tender—30 to 35 minutes more. Discard bay leaves, taste for salt and pepper, and adjust as needed.

6. Dish up and serve with the carbohydrate of your choice (see headnote).

MAKES 6 SERVINGS

ragout of beef with cranberries and wild mushrooms

Some years ago when little packets of dried wild mushrooms showed up in my supermarket, I began experimenting with them and discovered that when added to soups and stews, they need not be reconstituted in water. I've taken a few other short-cuts here—using packaged sliced cremini (baby bella) mushrooms as well as canned cranberry sauce. It does double duty here, first helping tenderize the meat and second, adding welcome tartness. Note: Good butchers sell double-smoked bacon and will cut it to order. Failing that, substitute diced hickory-smoked bacon.

¼ cup (½ stick) unsalted butter or vegetable oil

3 pounds boneless beef chuck, trimmed of excess fat and cut in 1-inch cubes

4 large shallots or scallions, coarsely chopped

2 large yellow onions, coarsely chopped

2 packages (8 ounces each) sliced cremini or white mushrooms

¼ pound double-smoked slab bacon, finely diced, blanched 10 minutes in boiling water, and drained well (see Note above)

2 small sprigs fresh thyme (preferably lemon thyme) or ½ teaspoon crumbled dried leaf thyme

1 small sprig fresh rosemary or ½ teaspoon crumbled dried leaf rosemary

2 cups dry red wine such as Pinot Noir or Cabernet

1¾ cups beef broth

1 cup whole cranberry sauce

2 packages (¼ ounce each) dried porcini or chanterelles

1 teaspoon salt, or to taste

¼ teaspoon freshly ground black pepper, or to taste

1 cup heavy cream

1. Melt butter in a large heavy nonreactive Dutch oven over moderately high heat and as soon as it froths and subsides, brown beef in several batches in melted butter, allowing about 10 minutes per batch and lifting each to a bowl as it browns.

2. Add shallots, onions, sliced mushrooms, bacon, thyme, and rosemary to pot and sauté, stirring often, until lightly browned—10 to 12 minutes.

3. Return beef to pot along with accumulated juices, add wine, broth, cranberry sauce, dried mushrooms, salt, and pepper, and bring to a boil. Adjust heat so liquid bubbles gently, cover, and simmer until beef is fork-tender and flavors mellow—2 to 2½ hours.

4. Mix in cream and simmer uncovered until liquids reduce to a nice gravy consistency—about 30 minutes. Discard thyme and rosemary sprigs, taste for salt and pepper, and adjust as needed.

5. Serve hot with boiled potatoes, buttered broad egg noodles, or spätzle.

MAKES 6 SERVINGS

chunks of beef fricaseed with fresh basil and wine

I've been making this easy stew for years and serving it at dinner parties where even picky eaters seldom refuse seconds. The beauty of this stew is that it freezes beautifully and can be thawed and reheated as needed. It's even better (read *more tender*) after a stay in the freezer (a night in the fridge improves this stew, too, so if you don't plan to freeze it, prepare a day in advance). It may seem odd to fricassee beef in white wine instead of red. Not at all. Note: Please use fresh herbs for this stew—every supermarket sells them. Better yet, grow your own—a sunny windowsill is all you need.

2 tablespoons extra-virgin olive oil

1 tablespoon unsalted butter

3 pounds boneless beef chuck, trimmed of excess fat and cut in 1½-inch cubes

1 large yellow onion, coarsely chopped

1 large garlic clove, finely chopped

¾ cup dry white wine

1 cup canned diced tomatoes, with their liquid

1 cup coarsely chopped fresh basil (plus a little extra for garnishing, if you like)

1 teaspoon coarsely chopped fresh thyme (preferably lemon thyme)

1 teaspoon salt, or to taste

¼ teaspoon freshly ground black pepper, or to taste

1. Heat oil and butter in a large heavy nonreactive Dutch oven over high heat until ripples appear on pan bottom—about 1½ minutes.

2. Add beef and brown in several batches, allowing about 10 minutes per batch and lifting each to a bowl as it browns.

3. Reduce heat to low, add onion and garlic and sauté, stirring often, until soft but not brown—10 to 12 minutes. Add wine and simmer uncovered until slightly reduced—8 to 10 minutes. Add all remaining ingredients—but only half the basil—and simmer uncovered 5 minutes.

4. Return beef to pot along with accumulated juices and spoon pan mixture on top. Adjust heat so liquid bubbles gently, cover, and simmer until beef is fork-tender—about 2 hours. Stir in remaining ½ cup chopped basil, taste for salt and pepper, and adjust as needed.

5. Serve at once, sprinkling each portion with a little more chopped basil, if you like. Accompany with boiled rice or potatoes.

MAKES 6 SERVINGS

easy oven dinner

Like many good recipes, this one was born of desperation—scouring freezer, fridge, and pantry for something to feed unexpected guests. And do try the lamb and pork variations that follow. They're equally delicious.

2 large (softball-size) yellow onions,
halved lengthwise and each half sliced ¼ inch thick

6 large garlic cloves,
smashed and skins removed

1 tablespoon extra-virgin olive oil

2 large whole bay leaves (preferably fresh)

½ teaspoon crumbled dried leaf thyme

½ teaspoon salt, or to taste

½ teaspoon freshly ground black pepper,
or to taste

2 pounds boneless beef chuck,
trimmed of excess fat and cut in 1½-inch cubes

½ cup canned condensed beef consommé

½ cup dry white wine (from whatever bottle's open)
or ¼ cup dry vermouth

12 golf-ball-size redskin or Yukon gold potatoes,
scrubbed but not peeled

8 medium carrots,
peeled and cut in 2-inch chunks

1. Preheat oven to 350°F.

2. Combine first seven ingredients (onions through pepper) in a heavy medium-size nonreactive Dutch oven and toss well. Arrange beef on top in a single layer. Bake uncovered on middle oven shelf for 30 minutes.

3. Add consommé and wine, stir well, cover, and braise 1 hour.

4. Lay potatoes and carrots on top, cover, and braise until meat and vegetables are tender— about 1½ hours more. Discard bay leaves, taste for salt and pepper, and adjust as needed.

5. Ladle into heated large soup plates and serve, making sure that everyone gets plenty of meat, vegetables, and savory pan juices.

Variations:

EASY LAMB DINNER: Prepare as directed, substituting boneless lamb shoulder for beef, dried leaf rosemary for thyme, and 4 medium parsnips for 4 carrots. Sprinkle with 2 tablespoons coarsely chopped Italian parsley or mint just before serving. Makes 4 to 6 servings.•

EASY PORK DINNER: Prepare as directed, substituting bacon drippings for olive oil, boneless pork shoulder (not too lean) for beef, and chicken broth for beef consommé. Also add ¼ teaspoon rubbed sage or poultry seasoning along with thyme, salt, and pepper. Makes 4 to 6 servings.

MAKES 4 TO 6 SERVINGS

beef dinner-in-a-dish with rice and vegetables

Beef simmered with onions, carrots, bell pepper, and rice—an all-in-one dinner as colorful as it is easy and nutritious. Who could ask for more?

3 tablespoons extra-virgin olive oil or vegetable oil

2½ pounds boneless beef chuck,
trimmed of excess fat and cut in 1½-inch cubes

2 large yellow onions, coarsely chopped

2 medium carrots, peeled and coarsely chopped

1 medium red bell pepper, cored,
seeded, and coarsely chopped

2 large garlic cloves, finely chopped

2 large whole bay leaves (preferably fresh)

1 teaspoon crumbled dried leaf marjoram or oregano

1¾ cups beef or vegetable broth

¼ cup dry red or white wine mixed with
2 tablespoons tomato paste

1 teaspoon salt, or to taste

¼ teaspoon freshly ground black pepper,
or to taste

1 cup uncooked converted rice sautéed 2 minutes
in 2 tablespoons extra-virgin olive oil

⅓ cup coarsely chopped fresh Italian parsley

1. Heat oil in a large heavy nonreactive Dutch oven over high heat until ripples appear on pan bottom—about 1½ minutes. Brown beef in several batches in oil, allowing 8 to 10 minutes per batch and lifting each to a bowl as it browns.

2. Add onions, carrots, bell pepper, garlic, bay leaves, and marjoram to pot and sauté, stirring often, until lightly browned—10 to 12 minutes.

3. Return beef to pot along with all accumulated juices, add broth, wine mixture, salt, and pepper. Adjust heat so mixture bubbles gently, cover, and simmer until beef is nearly tender—about 1½ hours.

4. Stir in rice, cover, and simmer until rice and beef are tender—about 30 minutes more. Remove bay leaves, taste for salt and pepper, and adjust as needed.

5. Mix in parsley and serve as the centerpiece of a family or casual company supper. Nothing more needed other than a dessert of fresh fruit.

MAKES 6 SERVINGS

that fiery beef bowl of red

Is this the original chili? Some food historians say so, adding that it's a campfire stew concocted by Texas cowboys who carried, as a sort of K-ration, a beef-and-chili pemmican that could be boiled in a bucket of water. No beans in their bowl of red, no tomatoes or onions, just gristly beef coarsely chopped (usually bottom round, rump, or chuck, which I prefer because of its greater succulence), garlic whenever available, oregano, cumin, and enough chilies to blow a safe. Note: Can't take the heat? No problem. Simply add the chili powder and cayenne in small increments, tasting as you go. Tip: If you have a big, powerful food processor, use it to chop the meat. But first trim away as much connective tissue as possible, cut the meat into one-inch cubes, and firm up by setting in freezer for 45 minutes or so. Finally, pulse the meat briskly in three batches until the size of small peas. Or to save time, use coarsely ground beef chuck (have your butcher trim and grind it to your specification instead of settling for pre-packaged hamburger meat).

2 tablespoons melted beef fat (suet), bacon drippings, or vegetable oil

2½ pounds coarsely chopped or ground beef chuck (see Tip above)

⅓ to ½ cup chili powder, depending on how "hot" you like things

3 large garlic cloves, finely chopped

1 tablespoon crumbled dried leaf oregano (preferably Mexican oregano)

2 teaspoons ground cumin

6 cups water (about)

2 tablespoons cornmeal (preferably stone-ground)

1½ teaspoons salt, or to taste

½ to 1 teaspoon ground hot red pepper (cayenne), or to taste

1. Heat suet in a small heavy Dutch oven over moderately high heat until ripples appear on pan bottom—1½ to 2 minutes. Add beef, ⅓ cup chili powder, garlic, oregano, and cumin and cook, stirring often, until beef is no longer red—about 5 minutes; do not brown.

2. Add water and bring to a boil. Adjust heat so chili bubbles lazily, and simmer uncovered—very slowly—for 1 hour, stirring now and then. Note: If at any time the chili threatens to scorch, mix in a little more water and slide a diffuser underneath the pot.

3. Mix in cornmeal, salt, and ½ teaspoon cayenne. Cover and simmer slowly 30 minutes.

4. Taste for chili powder, salt, and cayenne, adjusting each as needed.

5. Cook and stir 5 minutes more, then ladle into heated large soup bowls, and serve with good yeasty country bread or fresh-baked corn bread.

MAKES 6 SERVINGS

jugged beef

"Jugged" is just another way of saying "oven stew." Its advantage, of course, is that there's less danger of the pot's boiling dry and everything in it scorching. Most jugged meats are simmered with wine and this one calls for two—a dry table red plus a sweeter fortified port or Madeira. To trim prep time, I use two handy supermarket items: packaged sliced mushrooms and bagged, peeled baby carrots. In a slow-simmering stew, both work well.

2½ pounds boneless beef chuck,
trimmed of excess fat and cut in 1-inch cubes

½ cup unsifted all-purpose flour
mixed with 1 teaspoon salt and
½ teaspoon freshly ground black pepper
(seasoned flour)

6 thick slices bacon,
snipped crosswise at ½-inch intervals

3 large yellow onions, coarsely chopped

2 packages (8 ounces each) sliced cremini
or white mushrooms

1 package (1 pound) peeled baby carrots

2 large whole bay leaves (preferably fresh)

3 small sprigs fresh thyme (preferably lemon thyme)
or ½ teaspoon crumbled dried leaf thyme

1-inch-long cinnamon stick

1 cup dry red wine mixed with
¼ cup medium-dry Madeira or port

½ cup tart red currant jelly

3 tablespoons coarsely chopped fresh Italian parsley

1. Preheat oven to 300°F. Dredge beef, a few pieces at a time, by shaking in a large plastic zipper bag with seasoned flour and set aside.

2. Sauté bacon in a large heavy nonreactive Dutch oven over moderately high heat, stirring often and adjusting heat as needed, until all drippings render out and only brown bits remain—8 to 10 minutes. Using a slotted spoon, lift brown bits to paper toweling to drain and reserve.

3. Drain all drippings from pot, stir 3 tablespoons back in, and heat until ripples appear on pan bottom—1½ to 2 minutes. Add dredged beef in several batches and brown in drippings, allowing about 10 minutes per batch and lifting each to a bowl as it browns.

4. Spoon remaining drippings into pot, add onions, mushrooms, carrots, bay leaves, thyme, and cinnamon, and sauté, stirring often, until onions and mushrooms are lightly browned—10 to 12 minutes.

5. Return beef to pot along with accumulated juices, add combined wines and jelly, and bring to a boil over high heat. Slide pot onto middle oven shelf, cover, and braise until meat is fork-tender and flavors marry—2 to 2½ hours. Discard cinnamon stick, bay leaves, and thyme sprigs, if used. Taste for salt and pepper and adjust as needed.

6. Ladle jugged beef into a heated deep platter or tureen, scatter parsley and reserved bacon on top, and serve with boiled potatoes, buttered broad egg noodles, or spätzle.

MAKES 6 SERVINGS

green chili with pinto beans

In Santa Fe they call it "a Christmas," two portions of chili—one red, one green side by side in a bowl. This isn't "a Christmas" though it contains both green chili peppers and red. I first tasted it some twenty-five years ago while attending the Corn Dance at San Ildefonso Pueblo between Santa Fe and Los Alamos. Cauldrons of green chili bubbled all day along with separate pots of pinto beans—San Ildefonso's staff of life. I've combined the two in a single Dutch oven and taken a few other shortcuts: substituting canned pinto beans for dried, which not only must be soaked overnight but also aren't as widely available. I also use canned diced tomatoes and green chilies in place of separate cans of each. This is a taste-as-you-go recipe—its chemical heat, i.e. the amount of chilies that go into it depending entirely on your tolerance for them. Note: Here's a lesson learned from an old Santa Fe friend: If your mouth's on fire, don't reach for a glass of ice water. Instead, cool your palate with a dish of sherbet (last time I was in Santa Fe, pineapple sherbet accompanied the bowl of chili I'd ordered). Tip: Coarsely chopped chuck is a better choice for this recipe than ground and if your butcher won't do the chopping for you, your food processor will as long as it's a sturdy one. First trim away as much connective tissue as possible, cut meat into one-inch cubes, and firm up by setting in freezer for 45 minutes. Finally, pulse meat briskly in three batches until the size of peas.

3 tablespoons bacon drippings, lard, or corn oil

1½ pounds coarsely chopped or ground
lean beef chuck (see Tip above)

2 medium to large yellow onions,
coarsely chopped

2 large garlic cloves, finely chopped

2 cans (10 ounces each) diced tomatoes
and green chilies, with their liquid
(the "regular," not the "hot")

1 cup water (about)

1 teaspoon salt, or to taste

¼ teaspoon chili flakes
(crushed dried hot red chili peppers), or to taste

2 cans (15½ ounces each) pinto beans,
rinsed and drained

1. Heat drippings in a heavy medium-size nonreactive Dutch oven over high heat until ripples appear on pan bottom—about 1½ minutes.

2. Add beef and fry, stirring often, until lightly browned—8 to 10 minutes. Push to one side of pot, reduce heat to moderate, add onions and garlic, and cook, stirring now and then, until limp and touched with brown—8 to 10 minutes.

3. Add all but the last ingredient (beans), turn heat down low, and simmer uncovered—very slowly, stirring now and then—until the consistency of pasta sauce and meat is tender—1 to 1½ hours. Note: If at any time the chili threatens to scorch, mix in a little more water and slide a diffuser underneath pot.

4. Add beans and simmer uncovered—slowly, stirring now and then—10 to 15 minutes more. Taste for salt and chili flakes and adjust as needed.

5. Ladle into heated large soup bowls and accompany with freshly baked corn bread.

MAKES 6 SERVINGS

picadinho de carne

Made the Brazilian way, this spicy meat-stretching dish with the consistency of chili contains finely diced bottom round, but as an alternative, I suggest coarsely ground beef chuck, a juicier cut. How do you serve picadinho? Over hamburger buns à la sloppy Joes, in omelets or scrambled eggs, over boiled rice, or baked into *empadas* (meat turnovers). You can also mound picadinho into scooped-out bell peppers, tomatoes, or zucchini halves. Take your pick. Tip: If you choose to dice the beef, you'll find that it cuts more cleanly if set in the freezer just long enough for the meat to firm up. Needless to add, only your sharpest knife will do.

3 tablespoons corn or peanut oil

2 large yellow onions, moderately finely chopped

2 large garlic cloves, finely chopped

1½ pounds finely diced bottom round or coarsely ground lean beef chuck (see Tip above)

½ teaspoon ground coriander

½ teaspoon crumbled dried leaf thyme

¼ teaspoon ground ginger

1 can (14½ ounces) diced tomatoes, with their liquid

½ cup finely chopped pimiento-stuffed green olives

½ cup seedless raisins

2 tablespoons tomato paste

2 tablespoons raw sugar

1 teaspoon salt, or to taste

½ teaspoon freshly ground black pepper, or to taste

1. Heat oil in a large heavy deep nonreactive skillet over moderately high heat until ripples appear on pan bottom—1½ to 2 minutes.

2. Add onions and garlic and sauté, stirring often, until limp and touched with brown—8 to 10 minutes. Push all to one side of skillet, add beef, and brown well, breaking up large chunks with a fork—10 to 12 minutes in all.

3. Mix in all remaining ingredients, adjust heat so mixture simmers very slowly (slide a diffuser underneath skillet, if necessary), and cook, stirring occasionally, until a little thicker than pasta sauce—1 to 1¼ hours. Taste for salt and pepper and adjust as needed.

4. Serve hot choosing any of the options suggested in the headnote. Note: I also think picadinho would be delicious tossed with fusilli, even ladled over split and pushed-up baked potatoes or sweet potatoes.

MAKES 6 SERVINGS

texas beef 'n' beans

Of the many chilis to come out of Texas, I prefer this one because it's spicy but not incendiary and makes enough for a party. The original chili, it's said, was the cowboy "bowl of red" (see page 29). Tip: Bottom round will dice more cleanly if set in the freezer just long enough for it to firm up. Needless to add, the knife you use should be honed to razor-sharpness. Easier still, use your food processor—if it's a big powerful one. You won't get a dice, only coarsely chopped meat, but that's acceptable. First trim off as much connective tissue as possible, cut meat into one-inch cubes, and firm up by setting in freezer 45 minutes or so. Finally, pulse meat briskly in three batches until the size of small peas.

1 pound dried red kidney beans, washed, sorted, and soaked overnight in cold water

2 quarts (8 cups) cold water (about)

4 tablespoons lard (not vegetable shortening), bacon drippings, or vegetable oil

2 pounds finely diced bottom round or coarsely ground lean beef chuck (see Tip above)

2 large Spanish or Vidalia onions, coarsely chopped

4 large garlic cloves, finely chopped

2 tablespoons chili powder

2 teaspoons salt, or to taste

1½ teaspoons crumbled dried leaf oregano (preferably Mexican oregano)

½ to 1 teaspoon ground hot red chili peppers (cayenne; depending on how "hot" you like things)

½ teaspoon ground cumin

2 large whole bay leaves (preferably fresh)

1 can (14½ ounces) diced tomatoes, with their liquid

1. Drain beans, rinse well in cold water, and place in a large saucepan. Add 6 cups cold water and bring to a boil over moderate heat. Adjust so water barely ripples, cover, and cook until beans are nearly tender—about 1 hour.

2. Meanwhile, heat lard in a large heavy nonreactive Dutch oven over high heat until ripples appear on pan bottom—about 1½ minutes. Brown beef in several batches in lard, allowing about 10 minutes per batch and lifting each to a bowl as it browns.

3. Add next eight ingredients (onions through bay leaves) to drippings and sauté, stirring often, until lightly browned—10 to 12 minutes. Return beef to pot along with accumulated juices and add tomatoes.

4. When beans have cooked 1 hour, add them and all cooking liquid to pot plus remaining 2 cups water or just enough to cover ingredients by about 1 inch. Bring to a boil over high heat, turn heat down low so chili barely bubbles, and simmer uncovered, stirring now and then, until fairly thick and flavors mellow—2 to 2½ hours. Note: If chili threatens to scorch, mix in a little more water and slide a diffuser underneath the pot. Remove bay leaves, taste for salt and cayenne, and adjust as needed.

5. Ladle into heated large soup bowls and accompany with plenty of soda crackers or crusty chunks of country bread. Or, if you prefer, cool to room temperature, cover, and refrigerate overnight. Reheated the next day, your chili will taste even better.

MAKES 8 TO 10 SERVINGS

beef bourguignon

I felt I owed it to today's busy cooks to develop a slow cooker beef bourguignon they'd be proud to serve. Note: Use bacon drippings, if possible, because their smoky/salty flavor improves the recipe. Tips: If you blanch silverskin or cippolini onions 20 to 30 seconds in boiling water, their skins will slip right off. Two more time-savers: Use packaged sliced mushrooms, preferably the thickly sliced ones sold as "steak mates" in high-end grocery chains. They're fleshy enough to hold their own during an extended stay in the slow cooker. Second, processor-chop the onion, carrots, and garlic. Remove chopping blade, but leave chopped vegetables in covered work bowl until needed. Saves on dishwashing.

3 pounds boneless beef chuck,
trimmed of excess fat and cut in 1½-inch cubes

3 tablespoons bacon drippings or vegetable oil
(see Note above)

1 large yellow onion, coarsely chopped
(see Tips above)

2 medium carrots, peeled and coarsely chopped

2 large garlic cloves, finely chopped

¼ cup unsifted all-purpose flour mixed with
1 teaspoon salt and ¼ teaspoon freshly ground black
pepper (seasoned flour)

½ cup canned condensed beef consommé
blended with 1 tablespoon tomato paste

½ cup red Burgundy wine

2 large bay leaves tied in cheesecloth
with 4 medium sprigs each lemon thyme
and Italian parsley (bouquet garni)

12 whole silverskin (small white) or cippolini onions,
peeled (see Tips above)

2 packages (12 ounces each)
thickly sliced mushrooms (see Tips above),
large ones halved lengthwise (cap through stem)

1. Let beef stand at room temperature 35 to 40 minutes. Meanwhile, preheat broiler.

2. Toss beef with 2 tablespoons bacon drippings and spread in a single layer on a foil-lined large, rimmed baking sheet. Slide into broiler, setting 4 inches from heat, and broil until touched with brown—6 to 8 minutes.

3. Transfer beef and accumulated juices to a large (4- to 6-quart) slow cooker. Scoop onion, carrots, and garlic on top of beef, drizzle with remaining bacon drippings, and stir well. Sprinkle with seasoned flour and stir again.

4. Add consommé mixture, wine, and bouquet garni, wringing it gently to release flavors. Cover and cook on HIGH 1 hour. Stir well, cover, and cook on LOW 2 hours.

5. Add silverskin onions and mushrooms, pushing underneath gravy, cover, and cook on LOW 1 hour.

6. Stir well, again pushing onions and mushrooms into gravy, set lid on askew so steam can escape, and cook on HIGH 1 to 1½ hours longer, stirring now and then, until beef and vegetables are tender. Discard bouquet garni, taste for salt and pepper, and adjust as needed.

7. Serve with small redskin or Yukon gold potatoes boiled in their jackets and spoon plenty of gravy over them.

MAKES 6 SERVINGS

slow 'n' easy austrian goulash

Soon after they married, my parents lived in Vienna where my father taught plant physiology at the university while my mother learned to make some of the recipes their landlady served, among them this luscious beef stew. Mother browned the meat the old-fashioned way—bit by bit in a large skillet; so, too, the mushrooms, onions, and garlic. I've reworked Frau Berringer's old family recipe for the slow cooker and find it both easier and better. This goulash owes much of its flavor to well-browned meat and to avoid dirtying a skillet, I broil the beef on a foil-lined pan to give it color, then let the slow cooker work its magic. Note: Broiling beef releases plenty of savory drippings. Drain these into a measuring cup, add ¼ cup to the goulash at the outset, and refrigerate the rest. You'll need another ¼ cup for the flour thickener, but skim off all fat before using. Tip: I also trim prep time by using the presliced mushrooms most supermarkets sell, snipping overly large slices in two as I drop them into the cooker.

3 pounds boneless beef chuck, trimmed of excess fat and cut in 1½-inch cubes

1 tablespoon clarified butter (melted butter from which milk solids have been skimmed; see Butter, page xii)

3 tablespoons sweet rose paprika

1 package (8 ounces) sliced white or cremini mushrooms (see Tip above)

2 medium yellow onions, coarsely chopped

1 large garlic clove, finely minced

1½ teaspoons salt, or to taste

½ teaspoon freshly ground black pepper, or to taste

½ teaspoon crumbled dried leaf thyme

½ cup beef broth

3 tablespoons all-purpose flour blended with ¼ cup cold broiler drippings, beef broth, or water (thickener)

1 cup sour cream (use "light," if you like), at room temperature

1. Preheat broiler. Sprinkle beef with clarified butter, toss well, then spread in a single layer on a foil-lined large, rimmed baking sheet. Slide into broiler, setting 4 inches from heat, and broil until touched with brown—6 to 8 minutes.

2. Transfer beef to a large (4- to 6-quart) slow cooker, reserving all drippings and sprinkle evenly with paprika. Add ¼ cup broiler drippings, mushrooms, onions, garlic, salt, pepper, and thyme; refrigerate remaining drippings; you'll need another ¼ cup for the gravy thickener. Mix goulash ingredients well, cover, and cook on HIGH 1 hour.

3. Stir well, mix in broth, cover, and cook on LOW 3 hours. Blend about ½ cup hot stew liquid into thickener, stir back into goulash, then cook and stir for about 1 minute.

4. Cover and cook on LOW until beef is fork-tender and flavors are well blended—about 30 minutes. Taste for salt and pepper and adjust as needed, then smooth in sour cream.

5. To serve, ladle goulash into a heated large deep platter and accompany with broad buttered noodles lightly sprinkled with poppy seeds.

MAKES 6 SERVINGS

hungarian goulash with sauerkraut

With three kinds of stew meat—beef chuck, veal and pork shoulder—Hungarian goulash differs from the Viennese version my mother used to make for special occasions. There's a hearty helping of sauerkraut in Hungarian Goulash, too (but no mushrooms), and as with my mother's goulash, more than a blush of paprika plus sour cream to bond and mellow the flavors. Note: Use fresh sauerkraut, if possible, because it's less salty than the canned and has superior flavor. Still, it should be rinsed well and squeezed dry before it goes into the pot.

¼ cup (½ stick) unsalted butter

1 large Spanish, Bermuda, or Vidalia onion,
moderately finely chopped

1 pound boneless beef chuck,
trimmed of excess fat and cut in 1½-inch cubes

1 pound boneless pork shoulder,
trimmed of excess fat and cut in 1½-inch cubes

1 pound boneless veal shoulder, cut in 1½-inch cubes

3 tablespoons Hungarian sweet rose paprika
blended with ¼ cup warm water, 1½ teaspoons salt,
and ¼ teaspoon freshly ground black pepper

¾ cup water or beef broth

2 cups sauerkraut (preferably fresh),
rinsed well and wrung fairly dry in a tea towel

1 cup sour cream (use "light," if you like),
at room temperature

1. Melt butter in a large heavy nonreactive Dutch oven over moderately high heat and as soon as it froths and subsides, add onion and sauté, stirring often, until limp and golden—6 to 8 minutes. Using a slotted spoon, lift to a large bowl and reserve.

2. Brown meat in Dutch oven in three batches in order listed, allowing about 10 minutes per batch and lifting each to bowl as it browns.

3. Return onion and meats to pot along with accumulated juices, paprika mixture, and water, and bring to a boil. Adjust heat so mixture barely ripples, cover, and simmer very slowly until meats are tender—about 2 hours. Note: Check pot occasionally and if mixture threatens to scorch, add a little more water, turn heat to lowest point, and slide a diffuser underneath pot.

4. Mix in sauerkraut, cover, and simmer 10 minutes, then smooth in sour cream and bring just to serving temperature—3 to 5 minutes. Do not boil or sour cream may curdle. Taste for salt and pepper and adjust as needed.

5. Serve hot with buttered poppy-seed noodles or boiled and peeled redskin, fingerling, or Yukon gold potatoes.

MAKES 6 SERVINGS

slow cooker carbonnade flamande

For several reasons, this Belgian classic is my favorite stew. First, it requires little prep other than slicing six onions and mincing two cloves of garlic, two jobs I do by food processor. Second, the beef simmers in beer—a brilliant combo. Third, the recipe's easily adapted for the slow cooker so there's no danger of scorching. Finally, slow cooking generates more liquid than stove-top stewing, so you need only half as much beer. Tip: To processor-mince garlic and processor-slice onions, drop whole peeled garlic cloves down feed tube into spinning blade and when finely minced, snap machine off and scrape work bowl, pushing bits of garlic to the bottom. Replace chopping blade with medium slicing disc. By hand, slice ends off each onion, halve unpeeled onions lengthwise, and slip off skins. Stack as many onion halves in feed tube as will fit, then exerting gentle pressure on plunger, pulse-slice the onions. Repeat until all onions are sliced, remove slicing disk, but leave onions and garlic in work bowl until needed. Saves on dishwashing. Note: Instantized flour is the shake-and-blend type you use to make lump-free gravies.

3 pounds boneless beef chuck,
trimmed of excess fat and cut in 1½-inch cubes

¼ cup (½ stick) unsalted butter, melted

6 medium-large yellow onions,
moderately thinly sliced (see Tip above)

2 large garlic cloves, finely minced

6 tablespoons instantized flour (see Note above)
mixed with 2 teaspoons salt, ½ teaspoon each freshly
ground black pepper, crumbled dried leaf thyme,
and freshly grated nutmeg (seasoned flour)

1 can (12 ounces) beer, at room temperature

1. Let beef stand at room temperature 35 to 40 minutes to take the chill off. Meanwhile, preheat broiler.

2. Toss beef with 2 tablespoons melted butter and spread in a single layer on a foil-lined large, rimmed baking sheet. Slide into broiler, setting 4 inches from heat, and broil until touched with brown—6 to 8 minutes.

3. Transfer beef and accumulated juices to a large (4- to 6-quart) slow cooker. Scoop onions and garlic on top of beef, drizzle with remaining butter, and stir well. Sprinkle with seasoned flour and stir again. Add beer, cover, and cook on HIGH 1 hour.

4. Stir well, cover, and cook on LOW until beef is fork-tender and flavors marry—3½ to 4 hours. Taste for salt and pepper and adjust as needed.

5. Serve with small redskin or Yukon gold potatoes (or a 50/50 mix) boiled in their jackets, allowing two potatoes per person.

MAKES 6 SERVINGS

braised steak and onions
with sour cream–mustard gravy

Steaks cut from the bottom round are too tough to broil. But cooked this way—low and slow—they emerge tender and juicy. Accompany with tartly dressed green salad and a rough country bread to sop up every drop of gravy. Note: Blade and arm steaks cut from the chuck are equally good prepared this way, but they contain bone so you'll need a 2¾- to 3-pound steak.

A 2½-pound bottom round steak,
1 inch thick (see Note above)

⅓ cup unsifted all-purpose flour
blended with 1 teaspoon salt and
½ teaspoon each freshly ground black pepper
and crumbled dried leaf thyme
(seasoned flour)

3 tablespoons bacon drippings or unsalted butter

3 large yellow onions,
halved lengthwise and each half thinly sliced

1 cup beef broth

1 cup sour cream, at room temperature

2 tablespoons Dijon mustard

1. Slash fat edges of steak all around at 1-inch intervals so it will lie flat as it cooks. Rub steak well on both sides with seasoned flour and set aside.

2. Heat drippings in a large heavy deep skillet over high heat until ripples appear on pan bottom—1½ to 2 minutes. Add steak and brown well on both sides—about 10 minutes in all. Lift steak to large plate and reserve.

3. Add onions to skillet, reduce heat to moderate, and stir-fry in drippings until limp and lightly browned—about 10 minutes.

4. Return steak to skillet, scooping onions on top, and add broth. Adjust heat so liquid bubbles gently, cover, and cook until you can pierce steak easily with a fork—about 1 hour.

5. Lift steak to a heated large platter, cover loosely with foil, and keep warm.

6. Boil skillet mixture over high heat, stirring often, until reduced by almost half—about 5 minutes. Smooth in sour cream and mustard and simmer—do not boil—2 to 3 minutes more. Taste for salt and pepper and adjust as needed.

7. Pour skillet mixture over steak and serve.

MAKES 6 SERVINGS

beef catalan

Popular in the Pyrenees, this spicy beef and bean stew aromatic of orange oven-simmers in wine and beef broth. Once the beef and onion are browned, the oven does the rest but—make a note—it's important that your Dutch oven have a tight-fitting lid. If not, your stew may boil dry. Tip: For stews this rich, I smash rather than chop the garlic so it "melts" into the juices. Moreover, smashing saves time. One good whack with the broad side of a chef's knife and the skin separates from the clove and can be discarded quickly. P.S. When I tested this recipe, the friend I invited to taste gave it an A+.

6 thick slices hickory-smoked bacon,
snipped crosswise at ½-inch intervals

3 pounds boneless beef chuck,
trimmed of excess fat and cut in 1½-inch cubes

2 large Spanish onions,
halved lengthwise and each half sliced ¼ inch thick

6 large garlic cloves,
smashed and skins removed (see Tip above)

2 large whole bay leaves (preferably fresh)
tied in cheesecloth with two 3-inch strips orange zest,
a 2-inch cinnamon stick, 2 large sprigs fresh thyme,
and 4 whole cloves (spice bag)

1 cup beef broth

1 can (14½ ounces) diced tomatoes, with their liquid

1 cup dry red wine such as a Spanish Rioja or
Portuguese wine from the Douro or Alentejo region

1 teaspoon salt, or to taste

½ teaspoon freshly ground black pepper, or to taste

½ pound peeled baby carrots

1 can (1 pound, 3 ounces) cannellini
(white kidney beans), rinsed and drained

¼ cup coarsely chopped fresh Italian parsley

1. Preheat oven to 325°F.

2. Sauté bacon in a large heavy nonreactive Dutch oven over moderately high heat, stirring often and adjusting heat as needed, until all drippings render out and only brown bits remain—8 to 10 minutes. Using a slotted spoon, scoop bacon to paper toweling and reserve.

3. Drain all drippings from pot, stir 4 tablespoons back in, and heat until ripples appear on pan bottom—1½ to 2 minutes. Brown beef in several batches in drippings, allowing 8 to 10 minutes per batch and lifting each to a bowl as it browns.

4. Add onions to pot and sauté, stirring often, until limp and beginning to brown—6 to 8 minutes. Return beef to pot along with accumulated juices, add next seven ingredients (garlic through pepper), wringing spice bag gently to release flavors as you drop it in, and bring to a boil.

5. Transfer to middle oven shelf, cover, and simmer 2 hours. Note: Check after 1 hour or so and if juices seem skimpy—they shouldn't if lid is snug—add a little water.

6. Add carrots, pushing down into liquid, cover, and simmer 30 minutes. Add cannellini, cover, and simmer 20 minutes more. Discard spice bag, taste for salt and pepper, and adjust as needed.

7. Sprinkle with parsley and reserved bacon, ladle onto heated large dinner plates, and serve with sturdy yeast bread.

MAKES 6 SERVINGS

beef-shank stew with pasta and vegetables

Few cuts of beef are as flavorful as the foreleg or shank and few make better stew though admittedly, this one is a two-day affair. Not as labor-intensive as it sounds because you simmer the shanks one day, refrigerate overnight, and finish the stew the next day. Tip: You'll note that tomatoes don't go into this stew until shortly before serving. There's good reason for this: their acid keeps the potato and macaroni, even the peas, from becoming as tender as we like.

2 pounds beef shanks, cut in 2-inch chunks

5 cups water

1 medium yellow onion,
halved lengthwise and each half thinly sliced

2 large whole bay leaves (preferably fresh)

1½ teaspoons salt, or to taste

¼ teaspoon freshly ground black pepper,
or to taste

2 small carrots, peeled and thinly sliced

1 medium all-purpose potato,
peeled and cut in ½-inch dice

¾ cup elbow macaroni

½ cup frozen green peas, thawed and drained

1 cup canned diced tomatoes,
with their liquid (see Tip above)

¼ cup coarsely chopped fresh Italian parsley

1. Place shanks, water, onion, bay leaves, salt, and pepper in a large nonreactive soup pot and bring to a boil over high heat. Adjust heat so water bubbles lazily, cover, and simmer until meat falls from shanks—4 to 4½ hours.

2. Discard bones, cool broth and meat to room temperature, cover, and refrigerate overnight in soup pot.

3. When ready to proceed, scoop fat from surface of broth and discard. Set pot over moderate heat, add carrots and potato, cover, and cook 30 minutes.

4. Add macaroni and peas, cover, and cook until pasta is al dente—20 to 25 minutes more.

5. Stir in tomatoes, cover, and cook 10 minutes more. Discard bay leaves, taste for salt and pepper, and adjust as needed.

6. Mix in parsley, ladle into heated large soup bowls, and serve.

MAKES 6 SERVINGS

swiss steak with tomato gravy

Few recipes are easier than this one. It takes a while to cook, true, but once in the oven, no attention needed until time to make the gravy. Serve with polenta or boiled or mashed potatoes.

A 3-pound bone-in chuck arm or blade steak, 2 inches thick

1 large garlic clove, crushed

1 large yellow onion, halved lengthwise and each half thinly sliced

2 cans (14½ ounces each) diced tomatoes, with their liquid

1 teaspoon crumbled dried leaf basil

½ teaspoon crumbled dried leaf thyme

1 teaspoon salt, or to taste

¼ teaspoon freshly ground black pepper, or to taste

Beef broth or tomato juice, as needed

¼ cup (½ stick) unsalted butter

4 tablespoons all-purpose flour

1. Preheat oven to 300°F.

2. Slash fat edges of steak all around at 1-inch intervals so it will lie flat as it cooks. Rub steak all over with garlic and lay flat in a heavy non-reactive Dutch oven just big enough to accommodate it.

3. Top with onion slices, add tomatoes, basil, thyme, salt, and pepper. Slide onto middle oven shelf, cover, and braise until meat is fork-tender—about 3 hours.

4. Lift steak to a heated large platter, cover loosely with foil, and keep warm. Measure pan liquids; you need 2½ cups, so round out measure, if needed, with beef broth or tomato juice.

5. Melt butter in a small heavy saucepan over moderate heat, blend in flour, add measured pan liquids, and cook, stirring constantly, until thickened, smooth, and no raw floury taste remains—about 5 minutes. Taste for salt and pepper and adjust as needed.

6. Remove bone from steak, then cut meat against the grain and slightly on the bias into slices about ½ inch thick.

7. To serve, overlap slices of steak down center of a heated large platter, spoon some of the gravy on top, and pass the rest.

MAKES 6 SERVINGS

swiss steak braised with portabellas and beer

"Belgian" steak is perhaps more appropriate because Belgians like to cook beef with beer (see Slow Cooker Carbonnade Flamande, page 40, an exquisite nut-brown stew that's a particular favorite of mine). Of course "Swiss steak" is as generic as "pot roast," a specific way of cooking tough steaks until tender. Sealed in foil, this one is unusually succulent. Note: Meaty portabella mushrooms make it possible to use a little less beef. Choose moist, smallish ones with caps no bigger than biscuits. Larger caps should be halved, then sliced. If portabellas are unavailable, substitute shiitakes, even cremini (baby portabellas) now sold—presliced—in eight-ounce packages.

A 2½- 2¾-pound bone-in chuck arm or blade steak 1½ inches thick

2 tablespoons vegetable oil

1 tablespoon unsalted butter

1 pound small portabella mushrooms, stemmed, wiped clean, and sliced ¼ inch thick (see Note above)

1 large Spanish or Vidalia onion, halved lengthwise and each half thinly sliced

⅓ cup unsifted all-purpose flour blended with ½ teaspoon each salt, freshly ground black pepper, and crumbled dried leaf thyme, and a pinch freshly grated nutmeg (seasoned flour)

1 cup stale beer

1 cup beef broth

1. Preheat oven to 350°F. Slash fat edges of steak all around at 1-inch intervals so it will lie flat as it cooks; set aside. Crisscross two long strips heavy-duty foil in a large shallow baking pan, adjusting so they intersect dead-center and foil ends overhang pan about 8 inches all around.

2. Heat oil and butter in a large heavy skillet over moderately high heat until ripples appear on pan bottom—1½ to 2 minutes. Add steak and brown well on both sides—about 10 minutes in all. Lift steak to foil-lined pan and center.

3. Sauté mushrooms and onion in skillet drippings, stirring often, until nicely browned—10 to 12 minutes. Blend in seasoned flour and cook and stir over moderate heat 2 minutes. Add beer and broth and cook, stirring constantly, until thickened—3 to 5 minutes.

4. Pour skillet mixture over steak, bring foil ends up, then roll down on top of steak forming a snug package. Slide onto middle oven shelf and braise until steak is fall-off-the-bone-tender—about 1½ hours.

5. To serve, carve steak across the grain and slightly on the bias into slices about ½ inch thick and overlap on a heated large deep platter. Taste mushroom mixture for salt and pepper, adjust as needed, then spoon over and around steak. Accompany with boiled redskin or fingerling potatoes. Good, too, with brown rice.

MAKES 6 SERVINGS

country-fried steak

My favorite aunt, my mother's older sister, married a farmer and I spent many happy summer vacations on their farm in central Illinois. They were "diversified farmers," raising beef and dairy cattle, sheep, hogs, chickens, geese, and ducks plus vast acreages of corn, soybeans, and wheat. Whenever I wasn't riding Duke, a retired circus pony they'd adopted, I'd be gathering eggs, milking cows, or helping Aunt Florence separate cream. Her big airy kitchen was my favorite room in their red brick farmhouse and my aunt, like my mother, welcomed me as sous-cook—*until* I broiled a steak and served it so rare her sons called me "cannibal" and fled from the dinner table. Aunt Florence country-fried every steak—even T-bones—to me a shocking extravagance! Down south where I grew up, only the cheaper, tougher steaks were country-fried (or chicken-fried) because that was the way to make them tender. Technically, country-fried steaks aren't fried, they're braised, that is quickly browned, then cooked slowly with a little liquid. Tip: To pound beef without tearing it, slide each steak between a double thickness of plastic wrap and flatten with a cutlet bat or rolling pin.

**2 pounds bottom round,
cut into 6 steaks about 4 inches long,
3 inches wide, and ¼ inch thick**

1 teaspoon salt, or to taste

½ teaspoon crumbled dried leaf thyme

**¼ teaspoon freshly ground black pepper,
or to taste**

½ cup unsifted all-purpose flour

4 tablespoons bacon drippings or vegetable oil

1 cup water or beef broth

1. Sprinkle both sides of each steak with salt, thyme, and pepper, then rub generously with flour—again, both sides. Pound each steak as thin as scaloppini (see Tip above), and let stand at room temperature 30 minutes; this helps the flour stick.

2. Heat drippings in a large heavy skillet over high heat until ripples appear on pan bottom—about 1½ minutes. Quickly brown steaks on both sides—8 to 10 minutes in all.

3. Reduce heat to low, add water, cover, and simmer slowly until steaks are tender enough to cut with a fork—about 40 minutes. Note: Check skillet occasionally and if liquid seems skimpy, add a little more water, turn heat to lowest point, and if necessary, slide a diffuser underneath skillet. Taste gravy for salt and pepper and adjust as needed.

4. Serve at once with mashed potatoes. I also like country-fried steak with brown or white rice, even fresh-baked biscuits (great for sopping up every drop of gravy).

MAKES 6 SERVINGS

country-fried steak with mushrooms and madeira

If you want to turn country-fried steak into a party dish, here's an easy way to do it. Note: When buying packaged, presliced mushrooms, choose those that look fresh and moist—*not wet*. If cremini (aka baby bellas—baby portabella mushrooms) are unavailable, use presliced white mushrooms, again selecting those that look absolutely fresh. Tip: To pound beef without tearing it, slide each steak between a double thickness of plastic wrap and flatten with a cutlet bat or rolling pin.

**2 pounds bottom round,
cut into 6 steaks about 4 inches long,
3 inches wide, and ¼ inch thick**

**½ cup unsifted all-purpose flour
mixed with 1 teaspoon salt, ½ teaspoon each
crumbled dried leaf marjoram and thyme, and
¼ teaspoon freshly ground black pepper
(seasoned flour)**

¼ cup (½ stick) unsalted butter

**2 packages (8 ounces each) sliced
cremini mushrooms (see Note above)**

1 large garlic clove, finely chopped

**1 cup beef broth mixed with ¼ cup Madeira wine
(preferably a semi-sweet Verdelho)**

1. Rub both sides of each steak generously with seasoned flour, pound as thin as scaloppini (see Tip above), and let stand at room temperature 30 minutes; this helps the flour stick.

2. Melt butter in a large heavy deep skillet over moderately high heat and as soon as it froths and subsides, add steaks and brown well on both sides—8 to 10 minutes in all. Lift steaks to a large plate and reserve.

3. Add mushrooms and garlic to skillet and sauté in drippings, stirring now and then, until mushrooms release their juices and these evaporate—about 10 minutes.

4. Return steaks to skillet along with accumulated juices and spoon mushrooms on top. Add broth mixture, cover, and simmer slowly until steaks are fork-tender—about 40 minutes. Note: Check skillet occasionally and if liquid seems skimpy, add a little more broth, turn heat to lowest point, and if necessary, slide a diffuser underneath skillet. Taste mushroom mixture for salt and pepper and adjust as needed.

5. To serve, overlap steaks on a heated large platter and smother with mushrooms and pan juices. Instead of serving with mashed potatoes, round out the main course with scalloped potatoes and crisp-tender asparagus spears drizzled with browned butter.

MAKES 6 SERVINGS

onion-smothered chicken-fried steak

What most Americans call "country-fried," Southerners call "chicken-fried," perhaps because the steak, like chicken, is heavily dredged in seasoned flour before it hits the skillet. But there similarities end because chicken-fried steaks brown in butter—and not much of that. This recipe is my jazzed-up version of the chicken-fried steak so popular down south, land of those big sweet Vidalia onions. If unavailable, substitute fawn-skinned Spanish onions, white-skinned Bermudas, or the biggest yellow onions you can find. Tip: To pound beef without tearing it, slide each steak between a double thickness of plastic wrap and flatten with a cutlet bat or rolling pin.

2 pounds bottom round, cut into 6 steaks about 4 inches long, 3 inches wide, and ¼ inch thick

½ cup unsifted all-purpose flour mixed with 1 teaspoon salt and ½ teaspoon each finely crumbled dried leaf thyme and freshly ground black pepper (seasoned flour)

¼ cup (½ stick) unsalted butter

2 large Vidalia onions, halved lengthwise and each half thinly sliced (see headnote)

1 cup chicken broth blended with 1½ tablespoons Dijon mustard

1. Rub both sides of each steak generously with seasoned flour, pound as thin as scaloppini (see Tip above), and let stand at room temperature 30 minutes; this helps the flour stick.

2. Melt butter in a large heavy deep skillet over moderately high heat and as soon as it froths and subsides, add steaks and brown well on both sides—8 to 10 minutes in all. Lift steaks to a large plate and reserve.

3. Add onions to skillet and sauté in drippings, stirring now and then, until lightly browned—10 to 12 minutes.

4. Return steaks to skillet along with accumulated juices and spoon onions on top. Add broth mixture, cover, and simmer slowly until steaks are fork-tender—about 40 minutes. Note: Onions exude a lot of liquid as they cook, so if skillet mixture seems "soupy," lift steaks to a heated platter, cover loosely with foil, and keep warm. Boil skillet mixture uncovered until consistency of gravy. Taste for salt and pepper and adjust as needed.

5. To serve, overlap steaks on heated large platter and smother with onions and pan gravy. Accompany with boiled, baked, or mashed potatoes. Good, too, with farro (an ancient hulled wheat said to have sustained Roman legions), white, brown, or wild rice.

MAKES 6 SERVINGS

shepherd's pie

Every good cook knows that the most effective way to tenderize a sinewy cut of meat is to chop it fine or better yet, grind it, which explains why ground meat is the foundation of so many homespun recipes. This beloved Irish classic not only proves the point but also offers a way to use up leftover cooked vegetables—green beans or peas, for example, broccoli or cauliflower florets, one-inch pieces of asparagus—but no more than one cup total. Note: Unless you have four cups leftover mashed potatoes to use as the topping, I'm afraid you'll have to boil and mash them—you'll need about two pounds all-purpose potatoes. Peel them, boil until tender, rice or mash, then season with 2 tablespoons each unsalted butter and milk plus salt and pepper to taste. Tip: By no means processor-mash the potatoes. They'll turn to "library paste."

2 tablespoons bacon drippings or vegetable oil

2 pounds ground lean beef chuck
shaped into one "monster burger"

1 large yellow onion, coarsely chopped

2 medium carrots,
peeled and moderately finely chopped

2 tablespoons all-purpose flour

1 cup beef broth
blended with 1 tablespoon tomato paste

1 cup leftover cooked vegetables (see headnote)

1 teaspoon salt, or to taste

¼ teaspoon freshly ground black pepper,
or to taste

4 cups hot seasoned mashed potatoes
(see Note above)

1. Preheat oven to 350°F. Lightly spritz a shallow 2-quart casserole with nonstick cooking spray and set aside.

2. Heat drippings in a large heavy skillet over high heat until ripples appear on pan bottom—about 1½ minutes. Add burger and brown well on both sides—6 to 8 minutes in all. Break burger into 1-inch chunks and push to one side of skillet.

3. Add onion and carrots and stir-fry over moderately high heat until limp and golden—about 5 minutes.

4. Mix in flour, then add broth mixture and cook, stirring constantly, until thickened—about 5 minutes. Mix in leftover vegetables along with salt and pepper.

5. Scoop all into casserole, spreading to edge all around, and frost with mashed potatoes, swirling into peaks and valleys.

6. Slide onto middle oven shelf and bake until bubbly and lightly browned—30 to 35 minutes.

7. Serve at table making sure that everyone gets plenty of meat, mashed potatoes, and gravy.

MAKES 6 SERVINGS

biscuit, beef, and vegetable pie

This is nothing more than a hearty stew baked *en casserole* under a biscuit topping. Use the recipe below or six cups of a favorite family stew or any one in this book as long as it has lots of gravy—Prairie Stew, for example, or Milwaukee "Brew" Stew (see Index for page numbers). Tip: If pressed for time it's okay to substitute refrigerated ready-to-bake biscuits, which every supermarket carries. Pop the can open, then space the unbaked biscuits about one inch apart on top of the stew. Baking time should be about the same, but watch closely and remove casserole from the oven as soon as the biscuits are puffed and lightly browned and the stew underneath bubbling.

2 pounds boneless beef chuck or lamb shoulder, trimmed of excess fat and cut in 1-inch cubes

¾ cup unsifted all-purpose flour mixed with 1 teaspoon salt and ½ teaspoon each crumbled dried leaf thyme and freshly ground black pepper (seasoned flour)

3 tablespoons bacon drippings or vegetable oil

1 large yellow onion, coarsely chopped

2 large whole bay leaves (preferably fresh)

3 cups beef or vegetable broth (about)

1 teaspoon cider vinegar

3 medium carrots, peeled and thinly sliced

3 medium all-purpose potatoes, peeled and cut in ½-inch cubes

2 tablespoons all-purpose flour blended with 3 tablespoons cold water (thickener)

BISCUIT TOPPING (SEE TIP ABOVE)

2 cups sifted all-purpose flour

4 teaspoons baking powder

½ teaspoon crumbled dried leaf thyme

4 tablespoons lard (not vegetable shortening) or unsalted butter

1 cup moderately coarsely grated sharp Cheddar cheese

⅔ cup milk

1. Dredge beef, a few pieces at a time, by shaking in a large plastic zipper bag with seasoned flour and set aside.

2. Heat drippings in a large heavy Dutch oven over moderately high heat until ripples appear on pan bottom—1½ to 2 minutes. Brown beef in several batches in drippings, allowing about 10 minutes per batch and lifting each to a bowl as it browns.

3. Add onion and bay leaves to drippings and sauté, stirring often, until lightly browned—8 to 10 minutes. Return beef to pot along with accumulated juices, add broth and vinegar, and bring to a boil. Adjust heat so stew bubbles gently, cover, and simmer until beef is nearly tender—about 1½ hours.

4. Add carrots, potatoes, and if stew seems dry, a little more broth or water. Cover and simmer until beef and vegetables are tender—30 to 35 minutes more. Discard bay leaves, taste for salt and pepper, and adjust as needed.

5. Blend about 1 cup hot stew liquid into thickener, stir back into pot, and cook, stirring constantly, until thickened, smooth, and no raw floury taste remains—about 5 minutes. Scoop stew into an ungreased 2-quart casserole and set aside. Preheat oven to 400°F.

6. For Biscuit Topping: Combine flour, baking powder, and thyme in a large bowl, add lard, and using a pastry blender, cut in until the texture of lentils. Mix in grated cheese, then fork in milk. As soon as a soft dough forms, turn onto a lightly floured surface and knead lightly 3 to 5 times.

7. Using a floured rolling pin, roll dough into a circle slightly larger than casserole. Ease on top of stew, cut off ragged edges, then turn edge of dough under on casserole rim that has been moistened with cold water, and crimp. Cut several decorative steam vents in biscuit topping.

8. Slide casserole onto middle oven shelf and bake until lightly browned—20 to 25 minutes.

9. Serve at table, spooning plenty of everything onto heated dinner plates.

MAKES 6 SERVINGS

old english steak and kidney pie

The English have always had a deft hand with beef be it a majestic standing rib or humble "pasty." Few recipes, however, are more deeply identified with Britain than this one, which renders sinewy beef chuck and kidney surprisingly succulent. Note: If, perish the thought, beef kidney puts you off or is unavailable, omit it and increase amount of beef chuck to 2¾ pounds.

3 tablespoons melted beef fat (suet),
bacon drippings, or vegetable oil

2 pounds boneless beef chuck, trimmed of excess fat
and cut in 1-inch cubes

A ¾-pound beef kidney, soaked 2 hours in
1 quart cold water mixed with 1½ teaspoons salt
(see Note above)

2 large yellow onions, coarsely chopped

3 tablespoons minced fresh parsley

2 large whole bay leaves (preferably fresh)

½ teaspoon crumbled dried leaf thyme

½ teaspoon salt, or to taste

¼ teaspoon freshly ground black pepper, or to taste

5 tablespoons all-purpose flour

2 cups beef broth (about)

1 unroll-and-bake pie crust
(from a 15-ounce package)

1 large egg yolk whisked until smooth with
1 tablespoon cold water (egg wash)

1. Heat suet in a medium-size Dutch oven over moderately high heat until ripples appear on pan bottom—1½ to 2 minutes. Brown beef in two batches in suet, allowing about 10 minutes per batch and lifting each to a bowl as it browns.

2. Meanwhile, drain kidney, halve lengthwise, then using a sharp knife, remove fatty core in center of kidney. Rinse kidney well, pat dry, and cut in 1-inch cubes. Brown in drippings—6 to 8 minutes in all—and add to beef in bowl.

3. Add onions, parsley, bay leaves, thyme, salt, and pepper to drippings and sauté, stirring often, until limp and touched with brown—8 to 10 minutes.

4. Return beef and kidney to pot along with accumulated juices, sprinkle with flour, add broth, and bring to a boil. Adjust heat so mixture barely bubbles, cover, and simmer very slowly until beef and kidney are tender—1½ to 2 hours. Note: Check pot occasionally, and if mixture seems dry, add a little more broth.

5. Using a slotted spoon, scoop beef and kidney into a 10-inch pie pan. Boil pan mixture uncovered over moderate heat, stirring often, until a good gravy consistency—about 10 minutes. Remove bay leaves, taste for salt and pepper, and adjust as needed. Pour evenly over meat in pie tin.

6. Preheat oven to 425°F. Moisten pie pan rim with cold water, unfurl pastry, fit over meat, then roll pastry edges under and onto pan rim. Crimp in a zig-zag pattern and make several decorative steam vents near center of pastry. Brush with egg wash, taking care to avoid steam vents.

7. Set pie on a rimmed baking sheet, slide onto middle oven shelf, and bake until filling bubbles and pastry is crisp and nicely browned—25 to 30 minutes.

8. Serve the pie at table, cutting into wedges just as you would a dessert pie.

MAKES 6 TO 8 SERVINGS

forfar bridies

The Scottish equivalent of Cornish pasties, these half-moon meat pies are remarkably easy. Everything—meat, onion, seasonings—goes into them raw eliminating the bother of an initial browning. Scottish cooks consider suet pastry essential for Forfar Bridies but in this age of cholesterol-consciousness, unroll-and-bake pie crusts (stocked near the ready-to-bake biscuits in the supermarket's refrigerated counter) are not only an acceptable substitute but also a major time-saver. Note: You can processor-chop the meat—if your machine's a sturdy one. Here's how: Trim away as much connective tissue as possible, cut meat into one-inch cubes, and once they've firmed up in the freezer for 45 minutes, pulse briskly in three batches until the size of small peas. Don't settle for hamburger meat; it will make the pies soggy. I'm afraid you'll have to hand-chop the suet (beef fat) but the amount is so small job's done in no time. Tip: If you don't trim the fat off the beef chuck, you can probably omit the suet but the filling won't be as juicy.

1½ pounds coarsely chopped lean beef chuck (see Note above)

⅓ cup moderately coarsely chopped beef fat (suet; see Tip above)

1 large yellow onion, finely chopped

2 tablespoons all-purpose flour

2 tablespoons minced fresh parsley

¾ teaspoon salt

¼ teaspoon freshly ground black pepper

Pinch freshly grated nutmeg

1 package (15 ounces) unroll-and-bake pie crusts (see headnote above)

2 tablespoons milk (for glazing pastry)

1. Preheat oven to 400°F. Mix all but last two ingredients (pastry and milk) in a large bowl and set aside.

2. Cut pastry into six 6-inch circles using a saucer as template, rolling pastry a bit thinner, if necessary, and re-rolling scraps as needed. Moisten edges of each circle all round with water, place about ½ cup meat mixture in center of each, fold in half, and crimp edges firmly with a fork. With same fork, prick decorative steam vents in top of each pie, then brush with milk taking care to dodge vents.

3. Arrange pies, not touching, on an ungreased baking sheet and bake on middle oven shelf 10 minutes. Reduce oven temperature to 325°F and bake until bubbly and nicely browned—40 to 45 minutes more.

4. Serve hot or at room temperature.

MAKES 6 SERVINGS

malaysian spiced beef

I've always thought "London broil" a euphemism for flank steak because truthfully, it's too tough to broil. What saves London broil is that it's sliced across the grain—almost tissue-thin—effectively severing those long chewy strands. Even better, this two-step way of tenderizing flank steak: First cut the steak into thin strips, then simmer in a heady mix of East Indian spices. "Simmer" is the operative word because the beef should never boil. Flank is lean, fibrous, and nearly devoid of the gristle that slow, moist cooking magically converts to gelatin. Boiling flank won't speed the cooking but it will definitely toughen the meat. So keep an eye on the skillet, turn the flame as low as it will go, and if necessary, slide a diffuser underneath it to keep liquids well below the boil. Tip: If you can persuade your butcher to cut the flank into strips, so much the better. If not, you'll find that it cuts more quickly and cleanly if firmed up in the freezer—45 minutes should do it.

3 tablespoons peanut oil or vegetable oil (about)

3 pounds flank steak, cut across the grain into strips about 3 inches long and ½ inch wide (see Tip above)

2 large yellow onions, coarsely chopped

3 large garlic cloves, finely chopped

A 1-inch cube fresh ginger, peeled and finely chopped

2 tablespoons sweet paprika blended with 2 tablespoons curry powder, 1 teaspoon salt, and ¼ teaspoon each ground cloves and ground hot red pepper (cayenne)

A 2-inch cinnamon stick

1 can (14 ounces) unsweetened Thai coconut milk plus enough water to total 2 cups

1½ tablespoons raw sugar

1. Heat oil in a large deep heavy skillet over high heat until ripples appear on pan bottom—about 1½ minutes.

2. Stir-fry steak in several batches in oil over high heat, allowing 5 to 6 minutes for each to brown and lifting each to a large bowl as it browns.

3. Add onions, garlic, and ginger to skillet and stir-fry in drippings until limp and golden—5 to 7 minutes, adding a little more oil, if needed.

4. Turn heat to lowest point, return steak to skillet along with accumulated juices, and add all remaining ingredients. Cover and simmer slowly, stirring occasionally, for 1 hour. Note: Slide a diffuser underneath skillet if liquid begins to boil. Discard cinnamon stick.

5. Cover skillet and continue simmering very slowly until meat is tender—1½ to 2 hours more. Using a slotted spoon, scoop meat to a large bowl.

6. Boil pan gravy uncovered over high heat, stirring constantly, until reduced by one-third—3 to 4 minutes. Return meat to skillet, stirring with gravy, and warm 1 to 2 minutes. Taste for salt and adjust as needed. Also, add a bit more cayenne if you like things "hot."

7. Ladle over boiled rice (preferably basmati) and serve.

MAKES 6 SERVINGS

morcon

This colorful Filipino rolled and stuffed flank steak demonstrates how versatile this long stringy cut from "the belly of the beast" actually is. For most of us, it's London broil, period. I'll admit that morcon takes a bit of doing, but oh my, the results! There's a Spanish flair to it—no surprise here; for 400 years, the Philippines belonged to Spain and its influence remains strong in island culture and cuisine. Tip: Sweet-talk your butcher into butterflying and pounding the steak for you. It's a job best done by pros.

A 1½- to 2-pound flank steak,
butterflied and pounded ⅜ inch thick
(see Tip above)

¼ cup fresh lime juice mixed with
2 tablespoons soy sauce and 1 crushed garlic clove
(seasoning)

2 slices richly smoked lean bacon

4 ounces pepperoni, cut in 6 x ¼ x ¼-inch strips

2 medium carrots, peeled and cut in 6 x ¼ x ¼-inch
strips

Two 4-inch dill pickles, cut in 4 x ¼ x ¼-inch strips

2 large hard-cooked eggs,
peeled and quartered lengthwise

4 tablespoons bacon drippings or olive oil

2 medium yellow onions, cut in slim wedges

2 large whole bay leaves (preferably fresh)

¼ teaspoon salt, or to taste

¼ teaspoon freshly ground black pepper, or to taste

2 cups beef broth

1 cup canned diced tomatoes, with their liquid

1. Spread steak flat on a double thickness of wax paper slightly longer than steak and brush well on both sides with seasoning.

2. Arrange bacon across steak 2 inches from one end, then lay pepperoni, carrot, and pickle strips, and quartered eggs across steak, shaping into a mound 2½ to 3 inches wide and leaving at least 1½ inches of steak exposed at each end.

3. Using wax paper to guide you, fold one end of steak in over strips, then opposite end, pulling tight to enclose filling and form a big roll. Tie round with string at 2-inch intervals, each time pulling tight to compact roll.

4. Heat drippings in a large heavy nonreactive Dutch oven over moderately high heat until ripples appear on pan bottom—1½ to 2 minutes. Add beef roll and brown well on all sides—10 to 12 minutes.

5. Push to one side, add onions, bay leaves, salt, and pepper and sauté, stirring often, until onions are glassy—8 to 10 minutes.

6. Add broth and tomatoes and bring to a boil. Adjust heat so mixture bubbles gently, cover, and simmer slowly until you can pierce beef easily with a fork—1½ to 2 hours.

7. Lift beef roll to a rimmed baking sheet, cover loosely with foil, and set in a keep-warm oven. Strain broth mixture, reserving both liquid and solids. Discard bay leaves.

8. Purée solids with 1 cup strained liquid in a food processor, return to pot along with remaining strained liquid and boil uncovered over high heat until reduced by one-fourth—15 to 20 minutes. Taste gravy for salt and pepper, and adjust as needed.

9. To serve, remove strings from beef roll and carve, slightly on the bias, into slices about ½ inch thick. Overlap slices down middle of a heated platter, spoon a little gravy on top but leave colorful filling fully exposed. Pass remaining gravy separately.

MAKES 6 SERVINGS

cho cho

Yet another way to prepare flank steak, this one from Hawaii. Though usually served as part of the pupu or hors d'oeuvre platter, cho cho is delicious, too, as a main dish. Two techniques are used to tenderize the flank steak before it's broiled—first, mechanical (thinly slicing the steak across the grain) and second, chemical (overnight in an acidic marinade). Note: When threading the steak strips on skewers, ruffle them so that three of them will fit end-to-end. Tip: When slicing the steak, hold your knife at a 45-degree angle; this way you'll sever even more of the connective tissue that makes this cut tough.

**A 1½- to 2-pound flank steak,
trimmed of excess fat and sliced across the grain
slightly on the bias into strips ½ inch wide
(see Tip above)**

**1 cup teriyaki sauce blended with
2 tablespoons Japanese soy sauce**

⅓ cup fresh lemon juice

2 large garlic cloves, finely minced

**A 2-inch piece fresh ginger,
peeled and finely grated**

2 tablespoons raw sugar

1. Drop steak strips into a large plastic zipper bag, add remaining ingredients, seal, and massage to coat strips with marinade. Refrigerate overnight, turning bag occasionally.

2. When ready to proceed, preheat broiler. Thread 3 steak strips on each of six 15-inch metal skewers (see Note above), arrange, not touching, on a broiler pan, and brush with marinade.

3. Slide into broiler, setting 5 inches from heat, and broil for 2 minutes. Turn skewers, brush with marinade, and broil until sizzling and brown—2 minutes more.

4. Serve at once with hot boiled rice.

MAKES 6 SERVINGS

grandma's pot roast

I now know why my Illinois grandmother's pot roast was juicier than most—she used a bone-in blade roast cut from the chuck instead of boneless rump. I've changed Grandma's recipe only slightly, substituting whole unpeeled redskin potatoes for quartered all-purpose ones and rubbing the meat with a little thyme as well as salt and pepper.

A 4-pound bone-in chuck blade roast about 3½ inches thick

1 teaspoon salt, or to taste

½ teaspoon crumbled dried leaf thyme

¼ teaspoon freshly ground black pepper, or to taste

1 cup water (about)

6 golf-ball-size redskin potatoes, scrubbed but not peeled

6 medium carrots, peeled and cut in 2-inch chunks

3 large yellow onions, quartered

1. Preheat oven to 325°F.

2. Rub pot roast well on both sides with salt, thyme, and pepper, center in a large heavy Dutch oven, and add water. Slide onto middle oven shelf, cover, and braise 2 hours.

3. Cluster potatoes, carrots, and onions around pot roast and if Dutch oven seems dry, add a little more water—but only what's needed to keep things from sticking. Cover and braise until meat and vegetables are tender—2 to 2½ hours longer.

4. Lift pot roast to a cutting board and slice across the grain about ¼ inch thick, removing bones.

5. To serve, overlap slices down middle of a heated large deep platter and wreathe with vegetables. Taste pan juices for salt and pepper, adjust as needed, and spoon evenly over all.

MAKES 6 SERVINGS

pot roast of beef with olives, onions, and potatoes

This unusual recipe, a Christmas (*Natal*) specialty, comes from the Portuguese island of Madeira, which I've visited many times over the years and written about for *Bon Appétit, Food & Wine, Gourmet,* and *Travel & Leisure.* To honor this special day, Madeiran cooks cut a cross in the top of a large red-ripe tomato (grown there year round) and another in a large peeled onion. Both go into the pot but are fished out and discarded according to the sketchy recipe I picked up years ago in the capital city of Funchal. I've taken the liberty of slicing the onion, substituting a bit of tomato paste for the fished-out tomato, and letting the two braise right along with the meat. Note: The grated potatoes do double duty in this recipe—they add flavor and thicken the pan gravy.

3 pounds boned and rolled beef rump

¼ cup red wine vinegar

1 teaspoon salt, or to taste

½ teaspoon freshly ground black pepper, or to taste

6 whole allspice

½ cup Madeira wine (preferably a semi-sweet Verdelho)

2 large bay leaves, finely crumbled

1 tablespoon extra-virgin olive oil

1 tablespoon lard (not vegetable shortening) or bacon drippings

1 large yellow onion, halved lengthwise and each half thinly sliced

1¾ cups beef broth blended with 1 tablespoon tomato paste

3 large all-purpose potatoes, peeled and coarsely grated

6 ounces pitted oil-cured black olives, drained well and halved lengthwise

1. Rub beef all over with vinegar, salt, and pepper. Using a sharp metal skewer, pierce beef in 6 places and insert allspice. Pour half the wine over beef, pat on crumbled bay leaves, cover loosely, and let stand at room temperature 1 hour. Drain meat, reserving marinade, then pat meat dry.

2. Heat oil and lard over high heat in a heavy nonreactive Dutch oven large enough to accommodate beef comfortably until ripples appear on pan bottom—about 1½ minutes. Add beef and brown well on all sides—12 to 15 minutes.

3. Scatter onion slices around beef, add broth mixture, reserved marinade, and bring to a boil. Adjust heat so liquid barely bubbles, cover, and cook until beef is fork-tender—about 2½ hours.

4. Wreathe potatoes around beef, cover, and cook until potatoes are done—10 to 12 minutes. Add olives and remaining wine and bring to serving temperature. Taste for salt and pepper and adjust, as needed.

5. To serve, lift beef to a cutting board, remove strings, and carve—slightly on the bias—into slices ¼ to ½ inch thick. Overlap slices in center of a heated large platter and smother with pan gravy.

MAKES 6 SERVINGS

olla podrida (spanish one-dish dinner)

Made the old-fashioned way, this is what we'd call a catchall—an earthenware pot of beef, pork, sausages, even chicken simmered with everything from leeks to chickpeas to carrots to potatoes. I've simplified the recipe; still, I suggest waiting till the weekend to "fire up the stove." Notes: Once large unbrowned cuts begin to simmer, they exude froth and scum that float to the top. These should be skimmed off so the broth isn't cloudy. After the first half hour or so, that job's done. You can peel and smash the garlic in a single operation— one good whack with a cutlet bat or meat pounder does it. Tip: For directions on cleaning leeks, see Leeks in How to Use This Book (page xiii).

2 pounds boneless beef rump in one piece

1 pound boneless pork butt in one piece

2 quarts (8 cups) beef broth

1 quart (4 cups) water

2 whole large yellow onions,
each peeled and stuck with 2 cloves

6 large garlic cloves, smashed and skins removed
(see Notes above)

6 large fresh Italian parsley sprigs, bound with twine

3 large whole bay leaves (preferably fresh)

2 teaspoons salt, or to taste

20 black peppercorns

6 large carrots, peeled, sliced 1 inch thick, and
chunky pieces halved lengthwise

½ pound kielbasa or other garlicky sausage,
sliced ¼ inch thick

6 medium leeks, trimmed, washed,
and sliced 1 inch thick (see Tip above)

1 small Savoy cabbage (about 1½ pounds),
trimmed, quartered, cored, and each quarter
sliced crosswise at 2-inch intervals

1 can (15½ ounces) chickpeas, rinsed and drained

½ cup coarsely chopped fresh Italian parsley

1. Bring first ten ingredients (beef through pep-percorns) to a boil in a large heavy soup pot over high heat. Skim froth from surface as it accumulates, adjust heat so liquid bubbles gently, cover, and simmer until meat is almost tender—2 to 2½ hours. Discard bound parsley sprigs.

2. Add carrots and sausage, cover, and simmer 35 minutes. Add leeks, cabbage, and chickpeas, pushing down into broth. Cover and simmer until all meats and vegetables are tender—30 to 40 minutes more, stirring occasionally. Discard bay leaves, taste for salt and pepper, and adjust as needed.

3. Lift beef and pork to a cutting board and carve across the grain into slices ¼ to ½ inch thick. Return to pot, add chopped parsley, and sim-mer uncovered 10 to 15 minutes more.

4. To serve, ladle into heated over-size soup plates making sure everyone gets some of each meat and vegetable as well as plenty of broth. Noth-ing more needed for this hearty meal except crusty chunks of country bread.

MAKES 6 TO 8 SERVINGS

yankee boiled dinner

Someone once called New England Boiled Dinner "jazzed-up corned beef and cabbage," the Irish classic traditionally served on St. Patrick's Day. It does contain cabbage but a garden of root vegetables as well—potatoes, carrots, and onions plus any or all of these options: parsnips, turnips, rutabaga, and beets. Ask six New England cooks how they make boiled dinner and you'll get six different recipes. Most make it with corned beef but sometimes smoked pork shoulder goes into the pot instead, and those of Portuguese heritage are known to use only linguiça, a pork sausage so spicy their boiled dinners need no additional seasoning. This version is fairly classic with one exception: I've substituted golden beets for red, which had to be boiled separately lest they stain everything in the pot. Note: Because of the saltiness of the corned beef, this recipe is not likely to need salt. Tip: If you blanch silverskin onions 20 to 30 seconds in boiling water, their skins will slip right off.

3 pounds boneless corned beef brisket, trimmed of excess fat and wiped with a damp cloth

3 quarts (12 cups) cold water (about)

6 golf-ball-size golden beets, peeled

3 medium carrots, peeled and cut in 2-inch chunks

3 medium parsnips, peeled and cut in 2-inch chunks

2 large whole bay leaves (preferably fresh)

10 black peppercorns

4 whole cloves

6 golf-ball-size redskin potatoes, peeled

12 whole silverskin (small white) onions, peeled (see Tip above)

½ small cabbage, halved lengthwise, cored, and each half sliced crosswise at ½-inch intervals

1. Place corned beef and 6 cups water in a large heavy Dutch oven and bring to a boil over high heat. Adjust heat so water barely ripples, cover, and simmer 1 hour. Drain corned beef and rinse both it and the pot, removing every trace of scum.

2. Return corned beef to pot, add remaining 6 cups water, cover, and simmer 2 hours.

3. Add beets, carrots, parsnips, bay leaves, peppercorns, and cloves, cover and simmer 1 hour. Add potatoes, cover, and simmer 30 minutes. Add onions and cabbage, and if necessary, a little more water so ingredients are submerged—but only just. Cover and simmer until meat and vegetables are tender—about 45 minutes more. Discard bay leaves.

4. Lift corned beef to a cutting board and carve across the grain into slices about ¼ inch thick. Overlap down middle of a heated large platter, then using a slotted spoon, cluster vegetables around corned beef, grouping by type and color.

MAKES 6 TO 8 SERVINGS

cozido

Every country, it seems, has its owned boiled dinner and this one—quintessential comfort food—belongs to Brazil. Because ingredients are added in stages, cozido is best cooked in a heavy Dutch oven on top of the stove. Note: To save time, I use the bagged-in-plastic peeled baby carrots now sold at most supermarkets instead of trimming, peeling, and chunking "grown-up" carrots. I also take advantage of another supermarket staple—frozen corn-on-the-cob chunks.

2 pounds boneless beef chuck,
trimmed of excess fat and cut in 1½-inch cubes

1 medium yellow onion, coarsely chopped

2 large garlic cloves, finely chopped

1 tablespoon cider vinegar

1½ teaspoons salt, or to taste

½ teaspoon freshly ground black pepper,
or to taste

¼ cup bacon drippings or vegetable oil

1 quart (4 cups) cold water (about)

1½ cups peeled baby carrots (see Note above)

2 medium all-purpose potatoes,
peeled and cut in 1-inch cubes

2 medium sweet potatoes,
peeled and cut in 1-inch cubes

2 medium turnips,
peeled and cut in 1-inch cubes

¼ medium cabbage, cored and
sliced crosswise at ½-inch intervals

6 frozen mini sweet corn on the cob,
partially thawed (see Note above)

1. Place beef, onion, garlic, vinegar, salt, and pepper in a large nonreactive bowl, toss well, and let stand at room temperature 30 minutes.

2. Heat drippings in a large heavy nonreactive Dutch oven over high heat until ripples appear on pan bottom—about 1½ minutes.

3. Add beef mixture and cook, stirring often, until nicely browned—8 to 10 minutes. Add enough water to barely cover ingredients and bring to a boil, skimming off froth from surface if it accumulates. Adjust heat so mixture bubbles gently, cover, and simmer until beef is tender—1½ to 2 hours.

4. Add carrots, potatoes, sweet potatoes, turnips, cabbage, and if needed, about 1 cup additional water, and bring to a boil. Adjust heat so mixture simmers lazily, cover, and cook until meat and vegetables are tender—about 30 minutes.

5. Add corn, cover, and cook just until corn is hot—about 10 minutes. Taste for salt and pepper and adjust as needed.

6. To serve, ladle into heated large soup plates, making sure each person gets meat as well as some of each vegetable.

MAKES 6 SERVINGS

puchero (argentine hot pot)

Argentina is beef country so it's not surprising that its one-dish dinner begins with beef. But there's sausage as well, even chicken. The secret—once the short ribs have been brought to a fast initial boil—is to keep the liquid well below the boil at all times, which explains longer than usual cooking times for the various ingredients. For this dish, the meat should literally drop from the bones.

4 pounds beef short ribs, trimmed of
excess fat and cut in 2- to 3-inch pieces

A 2-ounce piece salt pork,
scored in a crisscross fashion

1 quart (4 cups) beef broth

1 quart (4 cups) chicken broth

3 whole large yellow onions,
each peeled and stuck with 2 cloves

6 large garlic cloves, smashed and skins removed

3 large whole bay leaves (preferably fresh)
tied in cheesecloth with 3 large sprigs each
fresh thyme and fresh Italian parsley and
20 black peppercorns (bouquet garni)

1 teaspoon salt, or to taste

Freshly ground black pepper, to taste

6 chicken drumsticks (about 2 pounds)

½ pound kielbasa or other garlicky sausage,
sliced ¼ inch thick

½ pound peeled baby carrots

½ small cabbage, halved lengthwise, cored, and
each half sliced crosswise at ½-inch intervals

2 large sweet potatoes, peeled and
cut in 1-inch cubes

8 frozen mini sweet corn on the cob, thawed

½ cup coarsely chopped fresh Italian parsley

1. Bring first eight ingredients (beef through salt) to a boil in a very large heavy Dutch oven over high heat. Skim froth and scum from surface as it accumulates, adjust heat so liquid barely bubbles, cover, and simmer until meat is becoming tender—about 2 hours. Note: Continue removing froth and scum for the first 30 minutes or so.

2. Add drumsticks and kielbasa, cover, and simmer 45 minutes. Add carrots and cabbage, pushing down into broth. Cover and simmer 30 minutes. Add sweet potatoes and corn, again pushing into broth. Cover, and simmer until meat falls from bones and vegetables are tender—20 to 30 minutes more.

3. Set pot off heat and with a large slotted spoon, lift short ribs and drumsticks to a large bowl. Remove and discard all bones, then cut beef and chicken in bite-size pieces. Skim fat from broth. Discard bouquet garni, taste for salt and pepper, and adjust as needed.

4. Return beef and chicken to pot. Note: At this point, puchero can be cooled, covered, and refrigerated overnight.

5. Mix in chopped parsley, and simmer puchero uncovered 10 to 15 minutes more.

6. To serve, ladle into your largest soup plates (heated, of course) making sure everyone gets some of each meat and each vegetable as well as plenty of broth. Tip: Put out plenty of paper napkins. There's corn-on-the cob in puchero. The easiest way to eat it is to let it cool in the puchero, then pick it up and eat just as you would an ear of sweet corn.

MAKES 8 SERVINGS

corned beef and cabbage

This recipe, perhaps more than any other, gets a bad rap for "stinking up the house" because the cabbage is often cooked to death in greasy brisket broth. Properly prepared, it is surprisingly delicate and deserves a better reputation. Note: Because of the saltiness of the corned beef, this recipe is not likely to need any salt.

3 pounds boneless corned beef brisket in one piece, trimmed of excess fat and wiped with a damp cloth

4 quarts (16 cups) cold water

1 medium yellow onion, quartered

2 large bay leaves (preferably fresh) tied in cheesecloth with 12 black peppercorns and 6 whole allspice (spice bag)

1 medium cabbage (2 to 2½ pounds), trimmed of coarse outer leaves, cut into 8 wedges, and core removed at point of each

1. If necessary, tie corned beef into a compact shape, then bring to a boil in 2 quarts water in a large nonreactive soup pot over moderately high heat. Skim scum from surface as it accumulates, adjust heat so water bubbles gently, cover, and simmer 1 hour.

2. Drain corned beef and rinse both it and the pot, removing every trace of scum. Return corned beef to pot, add remaining 2 quarts water, onion, and spice bag, wringing it gently to release flavors, and bring to a boil. Adjust heat so water bubbles lazily, cover, and simmer until meat is nearly tender—about 3 hours.

3. Add cabbage, pushing down into liquid, cover, and simmer until as tender as you like—for me, 25 to 30 minutes is about right; the cabbage will be tender with a bit of vestigial crispness. Beyond 30 minutes, the cabbage will soften and begin to smell, so time things carefully.

4. Lift corned beef to a cutting board, remove strings, if used, and cut across the grain into slices ¼ to ½ inch thick.

5. Overlap slices down middle of a heated large deep platter. Drain cabbage well, keeping wedges intact, if possible, and wreathe around edge of platter. Serve with boiled, peeled Irish potatoes and horseradish or spicy brown mustard.

MAKES 6 SERVINGS

moravian sauerbraten

Not quite 300 years ago, the Moravians left Bohemia and Moravia (now the Czech Republic) for America, pausing for a spell in Germany en route and bringing with them their Protestant religion and enviable skills as gardeners, craftsmen, and cooks. Landing in Savannah (1735), they soon moved north to Pennsylvania and founded three towns: Bethlehem, Lititz, and Nazareth. In 1753, a group of Bethlehem Moravians returned south, this time establishing a little way station in central North Carolina. "Bethabara," they called it, or "House of Passage." Their mission was to build a proper town nearby. That 18th-century town—the Salem of Winston-Salem—is today both National Historic Landmark and museum village (http://www.oldsalem.org/). Moravian recipes have evolved over time and merged with local cuisines, still they remain heavily Germanic thanks to that early respite in Bavaria. This particular recipe is my interpretation of sauerbratens I've eaten in and around Winston-Salem. Note: Melt the fat trimmed from the beef roast and brown the roast in it.

3 pounds boneless top round beef in one piece, trimmed of excess fat (see Note above)

1 large yellow onion, halved lengthwise and each halve thinly sliced

2 large garlic cloves, thinly sliced

2 large whole bay leaves (preferably fresh)

2 teaspoons pickling spices

2 teaspoons salt

1 teaspoon black peppercorns

2 cups stale beer

1 cup red wine vinegar or cider vinegar

3 tablespoons all-purpose flour mixed with ½ teaspoon salt and ¼ teaspoon freshly ground black pepper (seasoned flour)

3 tablespoons melted beef fat (from beef roast above) or bacon drippings

¾ cup fine gingersnap crumbs

1. Place beef in a large shallow nonreactive container. Add next eight ingredients (onion through vinegar), cover, and refrigerate two days, turning beef in marinade several times.

2. When ready to proceed, remove beef from marinade and wipe dry; reserve marinade. Rub beef all over with seasoned flour.

3. Heat beef fat in a large heavy nonreactive Dutch oven over moderately high heat until ripples appear on pan bottom—1½ to 2 minutes. Add beef and brown well—6 to 8 minutes on each side.

4. Strain marinade into Dutch oven directly over beef and bring to a boil. Adjust heat so liquid bubbles lazily, cover, and simmer until beef is fork-tender—1½ to 2 hours.

5. Lift beef to a heated large platter, cover loosely with foil and keep warm. Measure cooking liquid, then return 3 cups of it to pot. Whisk in gingersnap crumbs and cook, whisking constantly, until thickened and smooth—2 to 3 minutes.

6. To serve, cut beef slightly on the bias into slices about ¼ inch thick and arrange down center of platter, overlapping slightly. Spoon a little gravy over meat and pass the rest.

NOTE: *Though potato dumplings are traditionally served with sauerbraten, I'm happy with boiled potatoes—unpeeled redskins, fingerlings, or Yukon golds.*

MAKES 6 SERVINGS

bifes enrolados brasileira

These little stuffed and rolled beef scallops popular throughout Brazil are tenderized three ways: pounded flat to rupture the sinew, marinated in wine to soften it, then braised long and slow in a tomato-y broth.

6 thin beef scallops (about 2½ pounds top round), pounded thin as for scaloppini

⅔ cup Madeira wine (preferably a Sercial or Verdelho) blended with 1 crushed large garlic clove, 1 teaspoon salt, and ½ teaspoon freshly ground black pepper

6 thin slices prosciutto cut to fit beef scallops

3 tablespoons unsalted butter

1½ cups beef broth blended with 3 tablespoons tomato paste

3 tablespoons all-purpose flour blended with ½ cup cold water (thickener)

STUFFING

4 large hard-cooked eggs, peeled and finely chopped

⅓ cup finely chopped pitted green or black olives

⅓ cup finely chopped blanched almonds or fine dry breadcrumbs

2 medium scallions, trimmed and finely chopped (white part only)

2½ tablespoons unsalted butter, at room temperature

1½ tablespoons finely snipped fresh chives

1½ tablespoons finely chopped fresh Italian parsley

2 teaspoons Dijon mustard

1. Marinate beef scallops in wine mixture in a shallow nonreactive baking dish at room temperature 1 hour.

2. Meanwhile, prepare Stuffing: Fork all ingredients together until paste-like and set aside.

3. When ready to proceed, lay beef scallops flat on a wax-paper-covered counter; reserve marinade. Top each scallop with a prosciutto slice, then spread with stuffing, dividing amount evenly and leaving ¾-inch margins on three sides and a 2-inch margin at one end. Starting at end with ¾-inch margin, roll each scallop up tight—jelly-roll style—and fasten with toothpicks.

4. Melt butter in a large heavy deep skillet over moderately high heat and as soon as it froths and subsides, add beef rolls and brown well on all sides—10 to 12 minutes in all.

5. Add broth mixture and reserved marinade, and bring to a boil. Adjust heat so mixture barely bubbles, cover, and simmer very slowly until a fork will pierce beef rolls easily—1½ to 2 hours. Note: If skillet seems to be boiling dry, add a little water, turn heat to lowest point, and if necessary, slide a diffuser underneath skillet.

6. Lift beef rolls from skillet and remove tooth-picks. Boil skillet liquid uncovered to reduce slightly—about 10 minutes. Blend a little hot skillet liquid into thickener, stir back into skillet, and cook, stirring constantly, until thickened, smooth, and no raw floury taste lingers—about 5 minutes.

7. Return beef rolls to skillet, turn in sauce, and bring to serving temperature—2 to 3 minutes.

8. Serve with mashed potatoes or fluffy boiled rice, spooning plenty of pan gravy over all and passing any extra gravy separately.

MAKES 6 SERVINGS

bavarian rouladen

I've eaten rouladen (stuffed meat rolls) all over Germany but never any as good as these, which I tasted years ago while on Christmas assignment in Munich. In Bavaria, rouladen are so popular butchers sell "rouladen meat"—thin slices of top round pounded as thin as scaloppini. Here, unless your butcher's willing, you'll have to pound the scallops yourself. After pounding, each scallop should be about 7 inches long, 3¾ inches wide, and ⅛ inch thick.

18 small thin beef scallops (about 3 pounds top round), pounded thin as for scaloppini

¾ teaspoon salt

¼ teaspoon freshly ground black pepper

⅓ cup Dijon mustard (measure firmly packed)

FILLING

4 medium yellow onions, finely chopped

½ pound double-smoked slab bacon, finely diced

¾ cup moderately coarsely chopped fresh Italian parsley

¾ cup finely chopped dill pickles

FOR COOKING

3 tablespoons unsalted butter

1½ tablespoons corn oil or vegetable oil

2 medium yellow onions, finely chopped

2 small carrots, peeled and finely chopped

2 small celery ribs, trimmed and finely chopped (include a few leaves)

½ cup coarsely chopped fresh Italian parsley

3 cups beef broth (about)

¼ cup tomato paste (measure firmly packed)

½ cup heavy cream

¾ teaspoon salt, or to taste

¼ teaspoon freshly ground black pepper, or to taste

1. Lay beef scallops flat on a wax-paper-covered counter, season both sides with salt and pepper, then spread one side of each with mustard and set aside.

2. For Filling: Sauté onions and bacon in a large heavy nonreactive skillet over moderately high heat, stirring often, until lightly browned—10 to 12 minutes. Set skillet off heat, cool 15 minutes, and mix in parsley and pickles.

3. Allowing 1 rounded tablespoon filling per scallop, spread over meat leaving a 1-inch margin at one end and ½-inch margins at opposite end and on both sides. Starting at end with ½-inch margin, roll each scallop up tight—jelly-roll style—and fasten with toothpicks. Also close both ends of each roll with toothpicks so filling doesn't ooze out as rouladen cook.

4. To cook, heat butter and oil in a large heavy deep skillet over moderately high heat until ripples appear on pan bottom—1½ to 2 minutes. Brown beef rolls in butter mixture in two batches, allowing 10 to 12 minutes per batch and lifting each to a bowl as it browns.

5. Return beef rolls to skillet along with accumulated juices and push to one side. Add onions, carrots, celery, and parsley and sauté, stirring often, until limp and golden—6 to 8 minutes.

6. Add broth, bring to a boil, then adjust heat so mixture barely bubbles, cover, and simmer until

a fork will pierce rouladen easily—about 1½ hours. Note: Check skillet now and then and if broth is boiling away, add a little more broth, turn heat to lowest point, and slide a diffuser underneath skillet.

7. Using a slotted spoon, lift rouladen to a rimmed baking pan, cover loosely with foil, and set in a keep-warm oven. Strain broth mixture, reserving both liquid and solids.

8. Purée solids with 1 cup strained liquid in a food processor, return to Dutch oven along with remaining strained liquid. Mix in tomato paste,

cream, salt, and pepper and boil uncovered over high heat until reduced by about one-fourth—12 to 15 minutes.

9. Return rouladen to skillet, reduce heat to low, and bring slowly to room temperature, basting often with gravy—10 to 12 minutes. Taste for salt and pepper and adjust as needed.

10. Remove toothpicks from each meat roll, mound rouladen on a heated large platter, and top with some of the gravy. Pass the rest separately. The ideal accompaniment? Boiled potatoes.

MAKES 6 SERVINGS

deviled short ribs

A long-time favorite of mine that's surprisingly easy. I like to precede with a tartly dressed salad of bitter greens (arugula, endive, radicchio, etc.) and accompany with chewy chunks of country bread. Note: Because of the saltiness of the mustard and consommé, this recipe isn't likely to need salt. But taste before serving.

6 pounds beef short ribs,
trimmed of excess fat and cut in 3-inch pieces

⅓ cup Dijon mustard

¼ cup prepared mild yellow mustard

1⅓ cups dry white wine such as
Riesling, Gewürztraminer, or Pinot Grigio

1 can (10½ ounces) condensed beef consommé

1 small yellow onion, finely chopped

4 large garlic cloves,
smashed and skins removed

2 large whole bay leaves (preferably fresh)

3 tablespoons Worcestershire sauce

½ teaspoon freshly ground black pepper,
or to taste

⅛ teaspoon ground hot red pepper (cayenne),
or to taste

1. Place ribs in a large deep nonreactive bowl and set aside. Bring remaining ingredients to a simmer in a medium-size nonreactive saucepan over moderate heat, stirring often.

2. Pour simmering marinade over ribs, cover, and refrigerate overnight, turning ribs occasionally.

3. When ready to proceed, preheat oven to 425°F. Lift ribs from marinade, reserving marinade, and arrange in a single layer on a rack in a foil-lined large shallow roasting pan.

4. Slide onto middle oven rack and brown 15 to 20 minutes. Turn and brown 15 minutes more. Reduce oven temperature to 325°F.

5. Lift rack and ribs from pan, then return ribs to pan without rack, arranging in a single layer on fresh foil. Pour 1 cup reserved marinade evenly over ribs, cover and refrigerate remaining marinade. Cover ribs snugly with foil and braise on middle oven rack until meat nearly falls from bones—2 to 2½ hours.

6. Toward end of cooking, strain refrigerated marinade into a small nonreactive saucepan, quickly bring to a simmer, then cover and keep warm over lowest heat.

7. To serve, mound ribs in a heated large platter. Taste hot marinade for salt, black pepper, and cayenne and adjust as needed. Pour into a heated sauceboat and pass separately.

MAKES 6 SERVINGS

barbecued short ribs

There's nothing like frozen assets to cope with unexpected guests, so I often barbecue these ribs —they're beef, not pork—weeks in advance and store in the freezer. To round out the meal, I make a tart coleslaw and bake a batch of biscuits, adding a teaspoon of chili powder and ½ teaspoon crumbled dried leaf thyme to the dry ingredients.

3 pounds beef short ribs,
trimmed of excess fat and cut in 2-inch pieces

3 tablespoons corn oil or vegetable oil

1 large Spanish or Vidalia onion,
coarsely chopped

4 large garlic cloves, finely minced

2 cans (14½ ounces each) diced tomatoes,
with their liquid

2 cups beef broth

⅓ cup cider vinegar

⅓ cup raw sugar

¼ cup tomato ketchup

3 strips lemon zest,
each about 2 inches long and ½ inch wide

1½ teaspoons salt, or to taste

½ to 1 teaspoon ground hot red pepper
(cayenne; depending on how "hot" you like things)

½ teaspoon freshly ground black pepper,
or to taste

1. Preheat broiler. Arrange ribs in a single layer on a rack in a foil-lined large shallow roasting pan. Slide into broiler, setting 4 inches from heat, and broil, turning frequently so ribs brown evenly—about 10 minutes. Remove from broiler and set aside. Preheat oven to 350°F.

2. Heat oil in a large heavy nonreactive Dutch oven over moderately high heat until ripples appear on pan bottom—1½ to 2 minutes. Add onion and garlic and cook, stirring often, until limp and lightly browned—about 10 minutes.

3. Add ribs to pot along with their drippings and all remaining ingredients, and bring to a boil. Slide onto middle oven shelf, cover, and braise until short ribs are tender—about 2 hours.

4. Discard strips of lemon zest, taste for salt and pepper, and adjust as needed. Serve at once, ladling plenty of sauce over each portion. Or cool to room temperature, cover, and refrigerate until ready to serve—but no longer than two days.

TO FREEZE: Cool short ribs in sauce to room temperature and ladle into 1-quart freezer containers, filling each to within ½ inch of the top. Snap on lids, label, date, and set in a 0°F freezer. When ready to serve, thaw overnight in the refrigerator, then slowly reheat ribs in their sauce in a covered large heavy Dutch oven over moderately low heat, stirring now and then. Freezer shelf life: 3 months.

MAKES 6 SERVINGS

braised oxtails with orange gremolata

Of all the tough cuts of meat, oxtails are one of the least appreciated and for that reason, no longer widely available. A pity, because properly prepared, they are not only more succulent than prime ribs but also deeply flavorful. This recipe is a simpler version of one I developed years ago for a *Bon Appétit* article. Serve with buttered egg noodles (either the green [spinach] or the plain). Note: Do please use fresh herbs for this recipe—every supermarket sells them. Tip: To trim prep time, chunk and processor-chop the onions and carrots. And grate the orange zest on a Microplane.

3 pounds oxtails cut in 2-inch lengths

1½ cups dry white wine
such as Riesling or Pinot Grigio

1 cup dry red wine
such as Chianti or Pinot Noir

3 large yellow onions,
coarsely chopped (see Tip above)

3 large carrots, peeled and coarsely chopped

4 tablespoons extra-virgin olive oil (about)

3 small sprigs fresh rosemary, lightly bruised

3 cups beef broth

2 large sprigs each fresh Italian parsley and lemon thyme tied in cheesecloth with 1 large bay leaf (bouquet garni)

1 teaspoon salt, or to taste

½ teaspoon freshly ground black pepper,
or to taste

2 tablespoons all-purpose flour
blended with 2 tablespoons unsalted butter
(thickener)

¼ cup coarsely chopped fresh Italian parsley
mixed with 3 finely minced garlic cloves
and ¾ teaspoon finely grated orange zest
(gremolata)

1. Place oxtails, both wines, half each of the onions, carrots, and olive oil in a large nonreactive container and drop in rosemary sprigs. Stir oxtails in marinade, cover, and refrigerate overnight, turning occasionally.

2. When ready to proceed, drain oxtails and pat dry; reserve 1½ cups marinade but discard rosemary.

3. Heat remaining olive oil in a large heavy nonreactive Dutch oven over high heat until ripples appear on pan bottom—about 1½ minutes. Brown oxtails in several batches in oil, adding a little more oil, if needed, allowing about 10 minutes per batch, and lifting each to a large bowl as it browns.

4. Return oxtails to pot along with accumulated juices, broth, reserved marinade, remaining onions and carrots, bouquet garni, salt, and pepper, and bring to a boil. Adjust heat so mixture barely bubbles, cover, and simmer slowly until oxtails are fall-off-the-bone tender—3 to 3½ hours. Note: Check pot from time to time and if liquid seems skimpy, add a little water and, if necessary to keep things just below a simmer, slide a diffuser underneath pot.

5. Using a slotted spoon, lift oxtails and vegetables to a large bowl and reserve. Discard bouquet garni. Skim excess fat from cooking

liquid, then boil over high heat until reduced to 2 cups—about 15 minutes.

6. Blend about 1 cup hot cooking liquid into thickener, stir back into pot, reduce heat, and cook, stirring constantly, until thickened, smooth, and no raw floury taste lingers—about 5 minutes. Taste for salt and pepper and adjust as needed.

7. Return oxtails, vegetables, and accumulated juices to pot and heat slowly until mixture steams—about 5 minutes.

8. To serve, transfer all to a heated large deep platter and sprinkle with gremolata.

MAKES 6 SERVINGS

chip smith's braised beef shank with horseradish crust

Chip Smith, one of this country's gifted young chefs, created this unusual recipe to serve—not at his memorable little Chapel Hill restaurant, Bonne Soirée—but at one of the monthly luncheons at Celebrity Dairy, home of fine artisanal chèvres. Dozens of Chip's fans showed up and I, for one, was so wowed by his beef shanks, I asked him how he'd made them. The trick, Chip explained, is to roll the shank meat as tight as possible when shaping it into a "sausage" in plastic wrap, then to refrigerate overnight until good and firm.

4½ pounds beef shanks, cut in 2-inch chunks

1½ teaspoons salt

½ teaspoon freshly ground black pepper

½ cup unsifted all-purpose flour

4 tablespoons extra-virgin olive oil

1 large yellow onion, coarsely chopped

2 medium celery ribs,
trimmed and coarsely chopped

2 medium carrots,
peeled and coarsely chopped

1 tablespoon tomato paste

1 quart (4 cups) beef broth

6 sprigs fresh thyme
or 1 teaspoon crumbled dried leaf thyme

1 large whole bay leaf (preferably fresh)

HORSERADISH CRUST

1 cup soft white breadcrumbs
(2 slices firm-textured white bread)

2 tablespoons prepared horseradish,
well drained

2 tablespoons unsalted butter, softened

2 teaspoons cider vinegar

1 teaspoon powdered mustard

1. Sprinkle beef shanks all over with salt and pepper, then dredge in flour, shaking off excess.

2. Heat 3 tablespoons oil in a large heavy nonreactive Dutch oven over high heat until ripples appear on pan bottom—about 1½ minutes. Add shanks and sauté until richly browned—about 5 minutes on each side, then lift to a large plate.

3. Add remaining oil to pot and when hot, add onion, celery, and carrots and sauté, stirring now and then, until lightly browned—6 to 8 minutes. Blend in tomato paste, and cook and stir 1 minute.

4. Return shanks to pot along with accumulated juices, add broth, thyme, and bay leaf, and bring to a boil. Adjust heat so liquid bubbles gently, cover, and simmer until meat falls from bones—2½ to 3 hours. With slotted spoon, lift meat and bones to a cutting board.

5. Put cooking liquid (broth) through a fine sieve, discarding solids. Pour 4 cups strained broth into Dutch oven and boil uncovered over high heat until reduced to 2 cups—about 5 minutes.

6. Meanwhile, remove meat from bones and finely shred. Also, scoop marrow from bones, then combine with meat and ¼ cup reduced broth. Transfer remaining reduced broth to a small container, cover, and refrigerate.

7. Working on a double thickness of plastic wrap, shape meat mixture into a "sausage" about 10 inches long and 2½ to 3 inches in diameter. Roll up jelly-roll style, twisting ends of plastic wrap as you go to compact meat as tightly as possible. Refrigerate overnight until firm enough to slice neatly.

8. When ready to proceed, prepare Horseradish Crust: Combine all ingredients and set aside. Also preheat oven to 400°F.

9. Cut beef "sausage" into six slices about 1½ inches thick and arrange cut side up on a lightly oiled baking sheet. Slide onto middle oven shelf and bake uncovered until heated through—12 to 15 minutes.

10. Spoon horseradish mixture on top of each slice, smoothing into a crust about ¼ inch thick. Broil about 5 inches from the heat until golden—3 to 4 minutes.

11. Meanwhile, bring reserved reduced broth to serving temperature in a small saucepan over moderate heat.

12. To serve, arrange meat on heated dinner plates and spoon reduced broth over and around each portion. Accompany with boiled redskin potatoes and a green vegetable—asparagus, perhaps, broccoli, or Brussels sprouts.

MAKES 6 SERVINGS

VEAL

VEAL

BREAST, RIBLETS, ROUND, RUMP, SHANKS, AND SHOULDER

Would it surprise you to learn that veal is a byproduct of the dairy industry? That it comes not from beef cattle like Angus, Herefords, or the increasingly popular Charolais? That Holsteins, those black and white "milk machines" whose milk is sold in thousands of supermarkets from Maine to Monterey are the source of this pale, delicate meat? That our best veal comes from four Midwestern states (Indiana, Ohio, Michigan, and Wisconsin) plus Pennsylvania and New York? Not from Texas, Colorado, or Big-Sky Montana?

To be honest, I was astonished. Before my intensive meat-cutting course at Cornell, I assumed that veal came from beef cattle—newborns. Not so. When dairy cows freshen or calve (on average once a year), the females usually grow into the herd, but the males, fed milk-based diets for several months, become veal. "Milk-fed" is key, for once calves begin grazing or nibbling grain, their flesh reddens.

True milk-fed veal is four to five months old, weighs about 400 pounds, and its flesh is the palest and pearliest of pinks. About 15 percent of the veal sold in the U.S. today is even younger. Called "Bob" veal, it is milk-fed and marketed at the tender age of three weeks. Adolescents (eight to 12 months old) are often sold as "baby beef" but in truth, they are not yet "beef" and too-over-the-hill to be called veal. Frankly, I don't find them as good as either.

Premium European-style milk-fed veal is available at good butcher shops across the country as well as at boutique or upscale groceries (Delft Blue, Plume de Veau, and Provimi are brands to look for; for details about each, search online).

Young and tender as veal is, however, certain well-exercised cuts (breast, shanks, shoulder, to name three) are *not* so tender and must be cooked in liquid or with a modicum of it if they're to be succulent. The recipes that follow prove the point. But first, see chart of the most readily available "tough" cuts and best ways to prepare them (pages 86 and 87).

VEAL NUTRITIONAL PROFILE

A low-fat, top-quality protein as well as an excellent source of niacin (an important B vitamin) and a moderate one of riboflavin (B_2), phosphorous, and potassium. No fiber. Fat, calories, and cholesterol vary from grade to grade, cut to cut, and according to how much fat is removed. For comparison, here are approximate counts:

- Braised Boneless Veal Rump (4 ounces) = 200 calories, 5 grams fat, 108 milligrams cholesterol
- Braised Boneless Shoulder (4 ounces) = 226 calories, 7 grams fat, 175 milligrams cholesterol

USDA GRADES OF VEAL

To be honest, the only ones I buy, the only ones I find that will be succulent when cooked are the two top grades—Prime and Choice (those two grades account for 93 percent of all the veal sold in this country). The three lesser grades (Good, Standard, and Utility) are used mainly in processed meats.

SHOPPING TIPS

The flesh of top-quality veal looks much like top-quality chicken—moist (but not wet), and pale, pale pink with little or no visible marbling. Exterior fat should be white and the bones, when cut, should be red at the center—proof that the animal is young.

STORAGE TIPS

Unusually perishable, veal not cooked on the day of purchase should be removed from its store wrapper at once, spread one layer deep on a large plate, loosely covered with foil or plastic wrap, and stored in the coldest part of the refrigerator. Cook and serve within 24 hours.

FREEZER TIPS

Rule No. I: Freeze without delay. Rule No. II: Discard store wrapping, then wrap the different cuts in foil or plastic freezer wrap as follows:

- **Large Steaks and Pot Roasts:** Package each individually.
- **Smaller Steaks, Chops, and Shanks:** Do not stack. Instead, arrange side-by-side, allowing no more than two or three per package.
- **Stew Meat:** Spread in a single layer—easier if you first line a shallow pan with foil—then fold ends in securely over meat. Once veal freezes, remove pan and if necessary, over-wrap the package with foil or plastic freezer wrap

so that it's air-tight. This prevents "freezer burn"—rough white splotches on the surface of the meat. They're especially damaging to tender young veal.
- **Ground Veal:** Flatten into a round no more than two inches thick and wrap as snugly as possible. Or shape into patties and wrap one by one.

In each case, press all air from package, label, date, and set directly on the freezing surface of a 0°F freezer. Maximum storage time: Three months for ground veal and stew meat; six months for larger cuts.

RECYCLING LEFTOVERS

An easy way to plump up small amounts of soup or stew is to reheat with canned beans (I particularly like cannellini and garbanzos or chickpeas along with a can of diced tomatoes, a clove or two of finely minced garlic, and a crumbled dried herb to taste (rosemary, perhaps, oregano, or basil). Leftover pot roast can be diced, creamed with sliced mushrooms, and spooned over toast or waffles, even turned into salad à la chicken salad (veal tastes for all the world like chicken). Another possibility: Slice the veal and top with Tuna Mayonnaise (half the amount given in the Vitello Tonnato recipe, page 111, should be plenty).

VEAL CUTS

(WHERE THE TOUGH CUTS ARE)

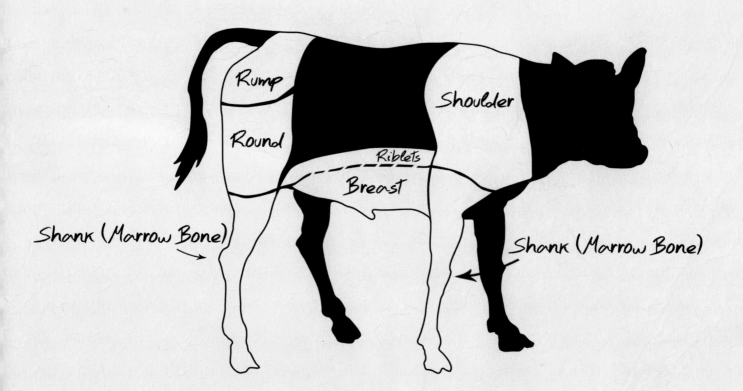

BREAST

Flat, lean cut with a thin covering of fat that's easily removed

BEST USES
- BONED, STUFFED, ROLLED, AND BRAISED

RIBLETS

The veal equivalent of beef short ribs; bony, moderately lean cuts with varying amounts of fat

BEST USES
- SOUPS
- STEWS
- BRAISED

ROUND

Leanest cut of veal. Source of cutlets, round steaks, and roasts

BEST USES
- PAN-BRAISED CUTLETS
- SWISS STEAKS
- POT ROASTS

RUMP

Second leanest veal cut. Source of cube steaks, boned and standing rump roasts, ground veal; may be sold as top round.

BEST USES
- PAN-BRAISED CUBE STEAKS
- POT ROASTS
- MEATLOAVES AND MEATBALLS

SHANKS

Lean, sinewy foreshank (front leg) with marrow-rich bone. Source of ossobuco, Italian for "hole in a bone" or "bone with a hole." Hind shanks best for soup and stock.

BEST USES
- SOUPS (ESPECIALLY SMALL, BONY CROSS-CUTS) AND STOCKS
- BRAISE MEATIER ONES AS OSSOBUCO OR OTHER GRAVY- OR SAUCE-RICH DISHES.

SHOULDER

Like beef chuck, veal shoulder is the single most versatile cut. Source of arm roasts and steaks (single round bone), blade roasts and steaks (long knife-like bone), stew meat, and ground veal

BEST USES
- POT ROAST
- BONED, STUFFED, ROLLED ROASTS
- SWISS STEAK
- STEWS
- MEATLOAVES AND MEATBALLS

veal stew with mushrooms and cauliflower

Cauliflower doesn't often show up in stews, mostly I think, because we underestimate its versatility just as we do that of veal. This slow simmering recipe pairs the two nicely. Tip: To speed-slice mushrooms, use an egg slicer. Or, even easier, use two (8-ounce) packages presliced mushrooms—cremini (baby bellas) or white—but only if they look absolutely fresh.

2½ pounds boneless veal shoulder, cut in 1-inch cubes

1 cup unsifted all-purpose flour mixed with 1 teaspoon salt and ½ teaspoon freshly ground black pepper (seasoned flour)

¼ cup vegetable oil

2 tablespoons unsalted butter

2 large yellow onions, coarsely chopped

1 pound cremini or white mushrooms, stemmed, wiped clean, and thinly sliced (see Tip above)

2 large garlic cloves, finely minced

1 teaspoon crumbled dried leaf marjoram

½ teaspoon crumbled dried leaf thyme

3 cups chicken or vegetable broth

1 small head cauliflower (about 2 pounds), trimmed and divided into 1- to 1½-inch florets

1 cup sour cream (use "light," if you like) blended with 1½ teaspoons anchovy paste or 2 teaspoons Dijon mustard

1½ teaspoons freshly chopped thyme (preferably lemon thyme) or dill, or to taste

1. Dredge veal, a few pieces at a time, by shaking in seasoned flour in a large plastic zipper bag and set aside.

2. Heat oil in a large heavy nonreactive Dutch oven over moderately high heat until ripples appear on pan bottom—1½ to 2 minutes. Brown veal in two batches in oil, lifting each to a bowl as it browns.

3. Add butter to pot and as soon as it froths and subsides, add onions, mushrooms, garlic, marjoram, and thyme and sauté, stirring often, until lightly browned—10 to 12 minutes.

4. Return veal to pot along with accumulated juices, add broth, and bring to a boil.

5. Adjust heat so liquid bubbles gently, cover, and simmer until veal is nearly fork-tender—about 1 hour. Add cauliflower, pushing down into liquid, cover, and cook until both it and veal are tender—about 30 minutes.

6. Smooth in sour cream mixture and chopped thyme and bring just to serving temperature—do not boil or sauce will curdle.

7. Taste for salt and pepper, adjusting each as needed, then dish up and serve with buttered egg noodles or small redskin potatoes boiled in their skins.

MAKES 6 SERVINGS

stufatino

Such an easy stew—a Florentine classic that's a nifty make-ahead for a small dinner party. Because there's plenty of good sauce, fusilli or fettuccine make a fine accompaniment. Ditto boiled rice, risotto, even boiled potatoes.

1 tablespoon extra-virgin olive oil

1 tablespoon unsalted butter

3 thick slices smoked bacon,
snipped crosswise at ¼-inch intervals

3 pounds boneless veal shoulder,
cut in 1-inch cubes

1 large yellow onion,
halved lengthwise and each half thinly sliced

3 large garlic cloves, smashed and skins removed

1 large whole bay leaf (preferably fresh)

1½ teaspoons finely chopped fresh rosemary
or ½ teaspoon crumbled dried leaf rosemary

1½ cups cup dry white wine such as Pinot Grigio
blended with 3 tablespoons tomato paste

2 cups chicken or vegetable broth

1 teaspoon salt, or to taste

½ teaspoon freshly ground black pepper,
or to taste

⅓ cup coarsely chopped fresh Italian parsley

1. Heat oil and butter in a large heavy nonreactive Dutch oven over moderately high heat until ripples appear on pan bottom—1½ to 2 minutes.

2. Add bacon and sauté, stirring often, until crisp and brown—about 5 minutes. Using a slotted spoon, lift brown bits to paper toweling to drain and reserve.

3. Brown veal in three batches in drippings, allowing 8 to 10 minutes per batch and lifting each to a bowl as it browns.

4. Add onion, garlic, bay leaf, and rosemary to drippings and cook, stirring often, until limp and lightly browned—about 8 minutes.

5. Return veal to pot along with accumulated juices, add wine mixture, broth, salt, and pepper. Turn heat to lowest point and simmer uncovered—very slowly—until veal is tender and pan liquid reduced by about half—about 1 hour. Stir occasionally and if liquid seems skimpy, add a little water and slide a diffuser underneath pot. Veal should be succulently tender and liquid the consistency of thin gravy.

6. Discard bay leaf, taste for salt and pepper, and adjust as needed.

7. Ladle into a heated large deep platter, sprinkle with parsley and reserved bacon bits, and serve.

MAKES 6 SERVINGS

veal paprikash

Although my mother made a Viennese Goulash blushed with paprika, I never tasted true paprikash until I lived for a spell in a Hungarian neighborhood on New York's Upper East Side. Little mom-and-pop restaurants could be found then on most any side street and it was there, in the East 80s, that I fell in love with Veal Paprikash. While there, I also learned that Hungarian paprika may be sweet or hot. The sweet predominates here though some people like to use a 50/50 mix of sweet and hot. Fortunately my southern supermarket now sells those glorious Hungarian paprikas so there's no need to order online. Note: What I love about this recipe is that veal doesn't have to be browned separately—a major time-saver. Tip: If you're unable to find canned crushed tomatoes (they're vanishing from my supermarket), buy canned diced tomatoes, drain, and quickly pulse in a food processor or blender. Easy does it—you don't want tomato purée.

2 tablespoons unsalted butter

2 tablespoons vegetable oil

1 medium yellow onion, finely chopped

¾ cup water (about)

3 pounds boneless veal shoulder, cut in 1-inch cubes

1 medium green bell pepper, cored, seeded, and finely chopped

1 can (14½ ounces) crushed tomatoes (see Tip above)

1 tablespoon sweet Hungarian paprika or 1½ teaspoons each sweet paprika and hot paprika

1½ teaspoons salt, or to taste

¼ teaspoon freshly ground black pepper, or to taste

1 cup sour cream, at room temperature

1. Heat butter and oil in a very large deep heavy nonreactive skillet over moderately high heat until ripples appear on pan bottom—1½ to 2 minutes.

2. Add onion and sauté, stirring often, until limp and golden—3 to 5 minutes. Add water, cover skillet, and turn heat as low as it will go. Steam onion until as soft as mush—6 to 8 minutes, checking skillet occasionally, and if liquid seems skimpy, add a little more water and slide a diffuser underneath skillet.

3. Stir in all but final ingredient (sour cream), cover, and simmer slowly, adding water, if needed, to keep mixture sauce-y, until veal is fork-tender—about 1 hour. Smooth in sour cream, taste for salt and pepper, and adjust as needed.

4. Serve with buttered broad noodles tossed with 1 teaspoon poppy seeds, or if you prefer, ladle over boiled brown or white rice.

MAKES 6 SERVINGS

veal and vegetable risotto

A lesson I learned early on is that tomatoes toughen carbohydrates when cooked with them—in this case rice. The solution is to cook the risotto separately, then combine with the veal/tomato mixture just before serving. This recipe is a dandy way to use tag ends of carrots and other root vegetables.

¼ cup (½ stick) unsalted butter

1 large yellow onion, coarsely chopped

2 cups coarsely grated root vegetables (carrots, parsnips, celery root, turnip, rutabaga—preferably a mixture of carrots and one or two others)

1 teaspoon crumbled dried leaf marjoram

½ teaspoon crumbled dried leaf thyme

2 pounds boneless veal shoulder, cut in 1-inch cubes

1 can (14½ ounces) diced tomatoes, with their liquid

¾ teaspoon salt, or to taste

¼ teaspoon freshly ground black pepper, or to taste

2¼ cups chicken broth

1 cup converted rice

½ cup freshly grated Parmigiano Reggiano

1. Melt butter in a heavy medium-size nonreactive Dutch oven over moderately high heat and as soon as it froths and subsides, add onion, root vegetables, marjoram, and thyme and sauté, stirring often, until nicely browned—8 to 10 minutes.

2. Add veal, turn in mixture, then add tomatoes, ½ teaspoon salt, and the pepper, and bring to a boil. Adjust heat so mixture bubbles gently, cover, and simmer until veal is nearly tender—1 to 1¼ hours.

3. About 20 minutes before veal is done, combine 1 cup broth, the rice, and ¼ teaspoon salt in a large, deep heavy skillet and bring to a boil over high heat. Reduce heat to low and cook, stirring occasionally, until almost all broth is absorbed—about 5 minutes. Meanwhile, bring remaining broth to a simmer in a small saucepan over high heat and set aside.

4. Add half the hot broth to risotto and cook, stirring occasionally, until absorbed—about 5 minutes. Add remaining broth and cook, again stirring now and then, until rice is tender and all broth absorbed—about 5 minutes more.

5. Stir veal mixture into risotto, taste for salt and pepper, and adjust as needed.

6. To serve, ladle onto heated plates and top each portion with a generous sprinkling of Parmigiano Reggiano.

MAKES 6 SERVINGS

slow cooker blanquette de veau

The French prefer veal to beef or pork and this creamy white stew, a cherished classic, simmers slowly so why not use a slow cooker, which eliminates the risk of scorching? Note: For directions on cleaning leeks, see Leeks, How to Use This Book (page xiii).

3 pounds boneless veal breast or shoulder, cut in 1½-inch cubes

⅓ cup melted unsalted butter

1 pound button mushrooms, stems discarded, caps wiped clean and quartered

2 small leeks, trimmed, washed, and thinly sliced (see Note above)

1 small yellow onion, finely chopped

1 small garlic clove, finely chopped

1 tablespoon fresh lemon juice

½ cup unsifted all-purpose flour

1 teaspoon salt, or to taste

¼ teaspoon freshly ground black pepper, or to taste

¼ teaspoon freshly grated nutmeg

1¾ cups chicken broth plus enough dry white wine to total 2 cups

⅔ cup heavy cream

1. Turn veal cubes in melted butter until nicely coated and arrange in a single layer around walls of a large (4- to 6-quart) slow cooker. Pour remaining butter into middle of cooker, add mushrooms, leeks, onion, and garlic, and turn in butter to coat. Sprinkle vegetables with lemon juice. Cover and cook on HIGH 1 hour.

2. Sprinkle flour, salt, pepper, and nutmeg evenly over all. Add broth mixture and cream, cover, and cook on LOW 4 hours or until veal is tender. Taste for salt and pepper and adjust as needed.

3. Serve with boiled redskin potatoes or rice. Egg noodles, though far from traditional, are also delicious with this delicate stew.

MAKES 6 SERVINGS

slow 'n' easy veal zingara

Also sometimes called "Gypsy's Stew," this lusty dish is blessed (cursed?) with countless variations. Many call for slivers of boiled ham and/or tongue in addition to veal and a few for truffles, which the gypsies must have dug up themselves. Is Zingara French or Italian? It's popular in both countries. Thumbing through *The New Larousse Gastronomique,* I find this description of Zingara under Compound Brown Sauces: "Add a julienne composed of a tablespoon each of lean cooked ham, pickled tongue, and mushrooms, and 1 heaped teaspoon truffles to a scant cup of demi-glace sauce cooked with a few tablespoons tomato sauce and a few tablespoons mushroom stock. Season with a little paprika." This last suggests that the recipe may be Hungarian. Whatever its origin, this recipe—and my slow cooker variation, in particular—is an excellent way to cook a tough cut of veal. Don't be put off by the long list of ingredients—many are merely seasonings. Note: To save time, I use presliced mushrooms and peeled baby carrots, both now supermarket staples.

3 pounds boneless veal shoulder,
cut in 1½-inch cubes

¼ cup plus 1 tablespoon bacon drippings
or vegetable oil

1 package (8 ounces) sliced cremini
or white mushrooms (see Note above)

1½ cups peeled baby carrots

1 large yellow onion, coarsely chopped

2 large garlic cloves, finely chopped

1 tablespoon sweet paprika

1 teaspoon crumbled dried leaf tarragon

1 teaspoon salt, or to taste

½ teaspoon freshly ground black pepper,
or to taste

½ teaspoon crumbled dried leaf thyme

1 can (14½ ounces) diced tomatoes, drained

½ cup Madeira, sherry, or red table wine
blended with 3 tablespoons all-purpose flour
and 2 tablespoons tomato paste

2 large whole bay leaves (preferably fresh)

½ cup julienne slivers boiled ham,
at room temperature

½ cup julienne slivers pickled tongue,
at room temperature (optional)

¼ cup coarsely chopped fresh Italian parsley

1. Turn veal cubes in drippings until nicely coated and arrange in a single layer around walls of a large (4- to 6-quart) slow cooker. Pour remaining drippings into middle of cooker, add mushrooms, carrots, onion, and garlic, and turn in drippings to coat. Sprinkle paprika, tarragon, salt, pepper, and thyme evenly over all. Cover and cook on HIGH 1 hour.

2. Add tomatoes, Madeira mixture, and bay leaves, cover, and cook on LOW until veal is tender and flavors marry—about 4 hours. Mix in ham, and if desired, tongue. Discard bay leaves, taste for salt and pepper, and adjust as needed.

3. To serve, mound stew on a heated large deep platter and sprinkle with parsley. Accompany with boiled rice or broad egg noodles. Note: For a prettier presentation, wreathe rice or noodles around stew on platter.

MAKES 6 SERVINGS

slow cooker russian goulash

Veal is more popular in cold climes than in warm where pork, mutton, and lamb are mainstays. Europe's "veal belt," sweeping westward from Russia to the Atlantic, includes the Baltic states, Alpine countries, and nearly everything in between. Strangely, Scandinavians dote less on veal and Britons almost not at all. In Russia, this goulash is a ruble-saver both rib-sticking and delicious.

3 pounds boneless veal shoulder,
cut in 1¼-inch cubes

2 tablespoons vegetable oil

2 tablespoons melted unsalted butter

2 large yellow onions, finely chopped

1½ tablespoons sweet paprika

1 teaspoon salt, or to taste

½ teaspoon freshly ground black pepper,
or to taste

1½ cups sour cream, at room temperature,
blended with 3 tablespoons all-purpose flour

1. Turn veal cubes in oil until glistening and arrange in a single layer around walls of a large (4- to 6-quart) slow cooker. Spoon melted butter into middle of cooker, add onions, and turn to coat. Sprinkle paprika, salt, and pepper evenly over all. Cover and cook on HIGH 1 hour.

2. Stir well, reduce heat to LOW, cover, and cook until veal is tender and flavors marry—about 3½ hours.

3. Smooth in sour cream mixture, taste for salt and pepper, and adjust as needed. Cover and cook on HIGH just until goulash reaches serving temperature—about 20 minutes.

4. Serve with buttered broad egg noodles or poppy-seed noodles. Note: For a prettier presentation, wreathe noodles around goulash on a heated large deep platter.

MAKES 6 SERVINGS

veal marengo

The original Marengo was an odds-and-ends dish created in 1800 after Napoleon defeated the Austrians at the battle of Marengo in Italy. To celebrate the victory, Napoleon's chef foraged a local village, turning up some tomatoes, garlic, oil, and a puny hen. There were a few crayfish, too, plus leftover bread. Napoleon liked the dish so much he had his chef prepare it after every victory. And when the chef substituted mushrooms for crayfish, Napoleon objected. His good-luck dish must be made exactly as it was after the battle of Marengo. Today's cooks improvise on the original and one of the better innovations is to skip the crayfish and substitute veal for chicken. The ideal accompaniment? Boiled rice or egg noodles.

3 pounds boneless veal shoulder, cut in 1-inch cubes

1 cup unsifted all-purpose flour combined with 1 teaspoon salt and ½ teaspoon freshly ground black pepper (seasoned flour)

⅓ cup extra-virgin olive oil

1 large yellow onion, coarsely chopped

1 package (8 ounces) sliced cremini or white mushrooms

2 large garlic cloves, finely minced

1 strip orange zest, 3 to 4 inches long and ½ inch wide

1 teaspoon crumbled dried leaf tarragon

½ teaspoon crumbled dried leaf thyme

1 cup dry white wine such as Chardonnay or Riesling

1 can (14½ ounces) diced tomatoes, drained

1¾ cups chicken broth

3 tablespoons coarsely chopped fresh tarragon or Italian parsley

1. Preheat oven to 325°F.

2. Dredge veal, a few pieces at a time, by shaking in seasoned flour in a large plastic zipper bag and set aside.

3. Heat oil in a large heavy nonreactive Dutch oven over moderately high heat until ripples appear on pan bottom—1½ to 2 minutes. Brown dredged veal in three batches in oil, allowing 8 to 10 minutes per batch and lifting each to a bowl as it browns.

4. Add onion, mushrooms, garlic, orange zest, tarragon, and thyme to pot and sauté, stirring often, until limp and lightly browned—10 to 12 minutes. Return veal to pot along with accumulated juices, add wine, tomatoes, and broth, and bring to a boil.

5. Slide pot onto middle oven shelf, cover, and braise until veal is tender—1½ to 2 hours. Taste for salt and pepper and adjust as needed. Discard orange zest.

6. To serve, ladle into a heated large deep platter and sprinkle with chopped tarragon. Or for a showier presentation, bed boiled rice or egg noodles on the platter, ladle stew on top, and sprinkle with tarragon.

MAKES 6 SERVINGS

hassle-free braised rump of veal

You can look long and hard, but you won't find an easier way to cook a boned and rolled veal rump. Serve with tiny boiled turnips and/or baby carrots and Frenched green beans, each seasoned with butter, salt, and freshly ground black pepper.

3 pounds boned and rolled veal rump

½ teaspoon salt, or to taste

½ teaspoon freshly ground black pepper, or to taste

6 thick slices hickory-smoked bacon

1 can (10½ ounces) condensed beef consommé

1 cup water

¼ cup cold water blended with 2 tablespoons all-purpose flour (thickener)

1. Preheat oven to 500°F.

2. Rub veal all over with salt and pepper, place in a Dutch oven just large enough to accommodate it, and drape bacon slices over veal. Slide onto middle oven shelf and brown 15 minutes.

3. Reduce oven temperature to 325°F, add consommé and water, cover, and braise, basting occasionally with pan drippings, until fork-tender—1½ to 2 hours.

4. Lift veal to a heated large platter, drape loosely with foil, and let rest 20 minutes.

5. Meanwhile, set Dutch oven over low heat. Blend about ½ cup hot pan liquid into thickener, stir back into Dutch oven, and heat, stirring constantly, until thickened, smooth, and no raw floury taste remains—about 5 minutes. Taste for salt and pepper and adjust as needed.

6. To serve, slice veal thin and top each portion with gravy.

MAKES 6 SERVINGS

orange-and-mustard-glazed pot roast of veal

One of the problems with veal is that it's unusually lean but draping bacon over a pot roast bastes it as it cooks and helps keep it moist. What I've done here is adapt a centuries-old French recipe for today's cooks and tastes. Note: It's best to use thickly sliced bacon, preferably an artisanal one that hasn't been injected with water—routine, these days, for many big commercial brands. Tip: Ask your butcher to bone the veal carefully, then "butterfly" it (cut through—or rather, *almost* through—the center so the two halves can be opened like a book). This allows you to spread the mustard mixture inside the roast as well as outside and that's essential for flavor.

3 pounds boned veal rump or shoulder,
butterflied (see Tip above)

¼ cup Dijon mustard mixed with
1 teaspoon finely grated orange zest and
½ teaspoon freshly ground black pepper

5 slices hickory-smoked bacon (see Note above)

½ cup chicken broth

⅓ cup heavy cream blended with
2 tablespoons all-purpose flour (thickener)

1. Preheat oven to 400°F.

2. Spread veal on flat surface, cut side up, and spread with half of mustard mixture. Roll veal up jelly-roll style, spread remaining mustard mixture over surface, then drape with bacon, overlapping slices. Finally, tie round with string at 3-inch intervals.

3. Place veal in a heavy Dutch oven just large enough to accommodate it and pour broth on top. Slide onto middle oven shelf and roast uncovered, basting well with pan drippings—30 minutes.

4. Reduce oven temperature to 350°F, cover pot, and braise until veal is fork-tender—about 45 to 55 minutes. Lift veal to cutting board, cover loosely with foil, and keep warm.

5. Skim excess fat from pan drippings, set Dutch oven over moderate heat, and cook, scraping up browned bits on bottom of pot—1 to 2 minutes. Blend in thickener and cook, stirring constantly, until thickened, smooth, and no raw floury taste lingers—about 5 minutes. Taste for salt and pepper and adjust as needed.

6. Remove strings from veal, and with sharpest knife, slice—slightly on the bias—¼ to ½ inch thick, trying to keep bacon intact. If any bits should fall off, simply pat back into place.

7. To serve, overlap veal slices on a heated large platter and smother with pan gravy. Accompany with roasted redskin potatoes or, if you prefer, mashed potatoes.

MAKES 6 SERVINGS

veal rump pot-roasted with carrots, celery, and potatoes

Veal rump, like veal shoulder, is well exercised almost from birth and that makes it too tough to roast. Being lean, it profits from a lazy simmer—the last half hour in the company of vegetables—that keeps it moist, also from a trifle less time in the pot. The pan juices (actually cooked-down onion and celery blended with meat drippings) could be thickened like gravy, but I prefer them *au naturel.*

2 tablespoons all-purpose flour

1 tablespoon light brown sugar

2 teaspoons dry mustard

1 teaspoon poultry seasoning

1 teaspoon salt, or to taste

½ teaspoon freshly ground black pepper, or to taste

3 pounds boned and rolled veal rump

2 tablespoons unsalted butter

1 tablespoon vegetable oil

1 large yellow onion, coarsely chopped

2 large celery ribs, thinly sliced (include leaves)

½ cup dry vermouth or dry white wine such as Riesling or Pinot Grigio

½ to 1 cup chicken or vegetable broth (if needed to keep veal moist)

6 medium carrots, peeled and cut in 1½-inch chunks

6 small whole redskin potatoes, scrubbed but not peeled

1 tablespoon coarsely chopped fresh Italian parsley

1. Combine first six ingredients (flour through pepper) and rub over veal rump; let stand 30 minutes at room temperature.

2. Heat butter and oil in a large heavy nonreactive Dutch oven over moderately high heat until ripples appear on pan bottom—1½ to 2 minutes. Add veal and brown well on all sides—about 10 minutes. Add onion and celery, distributing evenly around veal, and pour vermouth over veal.

3. Turn heat to low, cover, and braise until veal is nearly tender—about 1½ hours. Note: Check pot from time to time, and if pan juices are evaporating too fast, add ½ to 1 cup chicken broth, turn heat to lowest point, and if necessary, slide a diffuser underneath pot.

4. Add carrots and potatoes, again distributing evenly around veal, cover, and cook until meat and vegetables are tender—about 30 minutes more.

5. Lift veal to a cutting board, cover loosely with foil, and let rest 15 to 20 minutes. Meanwhile, taste pan juices for salt and pepper and adjust as needed.

6. To serve, slice veal about ¼ inch thick, overlap slices on a heated large platter, and cluster carrots and potatoes around edge. Spoon pan juices over all, sprinkle with parsley, and serve.

MAKES 6 SERVINGS

tuscan veal pot roast in lemon sauce

This recipe was inspired by one that caught my fancy in *Flavors of Tuscany,* a favorite cookbook written by my friend Nancy Harmon Jenkins, who divides her time between a house in Maine and another in that storied Italian province. I've substituted veal rump for beef round and adapted the seasonings accordingly. I also oven-braise the pot roast to reduce the risk of sticking and scorching. This is an unusually accommodating recipe—no tending needed once the roast's in the pot and the pot's in the oven. Tip: Using a fine-toothed Microplane, grate the lemon zest before you juice the lemon—it's easier this way. Scoop the zest into a small ramekin, cover with plastic wrap, and set aside until needed.

3 pounds boned and rolled veal rump

¾ teaspoon salt, or to taste

½ teaspoon freshly ground black pepper, or to taste

¼ cup extra-virgin olive oil

Juice of 1 large lemon

1 small sprig fresh rosemary or ½ teaspoon crumbled dried leaf rosemary

1 large whole bay leaf (preferably fresh)

1½ cups chicken broth

2 teaspoons finely grated lemon zest (see Tip above)

¼ cup cold water blended with 2 tablespoons all-purpose flour (thickener)

1. Preheat oven to 300°F. Rub veal all over with salt and pepper and set aside.

2. Heat oil over high heat in a nonreactive Dutch oven just large enough to hold veal until ripples appear on pan bottom—about 1½ minutes. Add veal and brown richly on all sides—about 15 minutes.

3. Add lemon juice, rosemary, bay leaf, and broth, and bring to a boil. Slide onto middle oven shelf, cover, and braise slowly until veal is tender—2½ to 3 hours.

4. Lift roast to a cutting board, cover loosely with foil, and let rest 20 minutes.

5. Remove bay leaf and rosemary sprig from pot and discard. Stir lemon zest into pan juices, then add thickener slowly, whisking all the while. Cook over moderate heat, whisking constantly, until thickened, smooth, and no raw floury taste lingers—about 5 minutes. Taste for salt and pepper and adjust as needed.

6. To serve, overlap thin slices of veal on a heated large platter and ladle lemon sauce evenly over all. Accompany with boiled rice.

MAKES 6 SERVINGS

braised veal rump with broccoli and lemon sauce

Purists make this old Flemish recipe with cauliflower, but I decided to substitute broccoli—a more colorful, more nutritious member of the cabbage family. The traditional accompaniment? Boiled, parslied potatoes. Note: You'll need a big bunch of broccoli that can be divided into florets no more than 1½ inches across the top (save stems for another day). Timing is key. I cook the broccoli while I make the sauce. Both are ready in 8 to 10 minutes.

3 pounds boned and rolled veal rump

1 veal soup bone (about 1 pound and not too meaty), cut in 4 pieces

2 small celery ribs, trimmed and thickly sliced (include some leaves)

2 small carrots, peeled and thickly sliced

1 whole small yellow onion, peeled and stuck with 4 cloves

2 large whole bay leaves (preferably fresh)

1½ teaspoons salt

½ teaspoon black peppercorns

½ teaspoon freshly grated nutmeg

Cold water, enough to not quite cover veal

1 large bunch broccoli (about 1½ pounds), trimmed of coarse stems, divided into small florets, boiled until crisp-tender, and drained well (see Note above)

LEMON SAUCE

1½ cups strained veal broth (from rump above)

2 large egg yolks blended with 1 cup heavy cream and 2 tablespoons cornstarch

1 to 1½ tablespoons fresh lemon juice, or to taste

1. Place first ten ingredients (veal through water) in a large heavy Dutch oven and bring to a boil over moderately high heat. Skim froth from the surface as it accumulates and discard. Adjust heat so water bubbles gently, cover, and cook until veal is tender—1¼ to 1½ hours.

2. Lift veal to a cutting board, cover loosely with foil, and keep warm. Strain cooking liquid (veal broth), discarding all solids. Measure out 1½ cups broth (for sauce) and freeze or refrigerate remaining broth to use another day for soup, sauce, or gravy.

3. Cook broccoli and begin Sauce: Bring strained veal broth to a boil in a small nonreactive saucepan over moderately high heat. Blend about 1 cup hot broth into egg yolk mixture, stir back into pan, and cook over moderate heat, stirring constantly, until thickened, smooth, and no raw egg or cornstarch taste lingers—2 to 3 minutes. Do not boil or sauce may curdle.

4. Set saucepan off heat and add lemon juice. Remove strings from veal and slice thin—slightly on the bias.

5. To serve, overlap veal slices on a heated large platter and cluster broccoli florets around edge. Spoon some sauce over veal and broccoli and pass the rest.

MAKES 6 SERVINGS

braised veal rump with anchovies, garlic, and lemon

I find this one of the easiest and most delicious ways to cook veal rump—IF your butcher, like mine—will bone the rump for you, then butterfly it so it can be laid flat and skim-coated with a mixture of anchovy paste, crushed garlic, lemon juice and zest. Once in the oven, the rolled rump cooks unattended. The accumulated juices make amazing gravy. Serve with boiled rice—the perfect sop for that gravy.

3 pounds boned and butterflied veal rump (see headnote)

3 large garlic cloves, crushed

2 tablespoons anchovy paste

1 tablespoon fresh lemon juice

2 teaspoons finely grated lemon zest

½ teaspoon freshly ground black pepper

¼ teaspoon dry mustard

8 slices hickory-smoked bacon

GRAVY

Pan drippings, skimmed of excess fat (from rump above)

2 cups chicken broth (about)

¼ cup unsifted all-purpose flour mixed with ¼ cup cold water (thickener)

1 tablespoon coarsely chopped fresh Italian parsley

1½ teaspoons anchovy paste or 2 teaspoons Dijon mustard

Salt to taste

Freshly ground black pepper to taste

1. Place veal, fat side down, on a large cutting board. Combine garlic, anchovy paste, lemon juice and zest, pepper, and mustard and spread half over face-up side of veal. Roll up jelly-roll style, rub with remaining anchovy mixture, tie with string in four or five places, and let stand at room temperature 1 hour. Twenty minutes before hour is up, preheat oven to 350°F.

2. Place veal in a large shallow nonreactive roasting pan and drape with bacon slices. Slide onto middle oven shelf and braise uncovered, basting occasionally with pan drippings, until fork-tender—2 to 2½ hours. Remove veal from oven and let stand while you prepare the gravy.

3. For Gravy: Combine drippings, broth, and thickener in a medium-size saucepan, set over moderate heat, and cook, stirring constantly, until thickened, smooth, and no raw floury taste lingers—about 5 minutes. If gravy seems thick, thin with a little more broth or water. Mix in parsley, anchovy paste, salt and pepper to taste.

4. To serve, remove strings from veal, then slice about ½ inch thick. Overlap slices on a heated large platter, spoon a little gravy down center, and pass the rest.

MAKES 6 SERVINGS

swiss-style rump of veal with vegetable cream gravy

In Switzerland where cows graze Alpine meadows, veal is the preferred meat. Rump roasts, Swiss cooks know, will toughen and dry unless cooked with a little liquid and/or vegetables, in this case a mirepoix—diced carrot, onion, and celery. Puréed with pan drippings and enriched with cream, that mirepoix makes wondrous gravy. Serve with mashed potatoes. Note: Choose a fruity dry white wine for braising the veal, Pinot Grigio, for example, Vouvray, or Riesling.

3 pounds boned and rolled veal rump

¾ teaspoon salt, or to taste

½ teaspoon freshly ground black pepper, or to taste

¼ cup (½ stick) unsalted butter

1 small yellow onion, diced

1 medium carrot, peeled and diced

1 medium celery rib, trimmed and diced

2 ounces hickory-smoked slab bacon, diced

1 small garlic clove, finely chopped

1 large whole bay leaf (preferably fresh)

2 small sprigs fresh thyme (preferably lemon thyme) or ½ teaspoon crumbled dried leaf thyme

1½ cups dry white wine (about; see Note above)

½ cup heavy cream (about)

½ cup chicken or vegetable broth

¼ cup coarsely chopped fresh Italian parsley

1. Preheat oven to 325°F. Rub veal all over with salt and pepper and set aside.

2. Melt butter in a large heavy nonreactive Dutch oven just large enough to accommodate veal over moderately high heat, and when it foams up and subsides, add veal and brown well on all sides—about 15 minutes.

3. Lift veal to a large bowl, add next seven ingredients (onion through thyme) to pot, and sauté, stirring often, until nicely browned—8 to 10 minutes.

4. Return veal to pot along with accumulated juices, add wine, and bring to a boil. Slide onto middle oven shelf, cover, and braise until veal is tender—about 2½ hours. Note: Check pot from time to time and if liquid is skimpy, add a little more water or wine. There should be about 1 inch liquid in pot at all times.

5. When veal is done, transfer to a heated large platter, drape loosely with foil, and let rest 20 minutes.

6. Meanwhile, lift bay leaf and thyme sprigs from pot and discard. Purée Dutch oven mixture using an immersion blender or cool 10 minutes, then purée in two batches in a food processor. Add cream and broth and blend or pulse until smooth.

7. Bring just to serving temperature over low heat. If gravy seems thick, add a little more cream. Taste for salt and pepper and adjust as needed.

8. To serve, slice veal thin, overlap slices down middle of platter, and top with some of the gravy. Sprinkle with parsley and pass extra gravy separately.

MAKES 6 SERVINGS

sauerkraut-stuffed rolled veal shoulder

Even in young animals, shoulders are well exercised and too tough to roast. Gentle braising renders them succulent and this easy sauerkraut stuffing adds worlds of flavor.

3½ pounds boned and butterflied veal shoulder

1 tablespoon sweet paprika

2 cans (10½ ounces each) condensed beef consommé
mixed with ¾ cup sauerkraut juice
(from sauerkraut below)

STUFFING

2 tablespoons bacon drippings or unsalted butter

½ cup moderately coarsely chopped shallots

1 cup moderately coarsely chopped shiitake
or cremini mushrooms

½ teaspoon crumbled dried leaf rosemary

½ pound fresh sauerkraut,
drained and juice reserved

1 cup moderately fine dry breadcrumbs

1 tablespoon coarsely chopped fresh Italian parsley

¼ teaspoon freshly ground black pepper

1 large egg, lightly beaten

GRAVY

⅓ cup unsifted all-purpose flour

2 cups pan liquid (from veal above)

1 cup water, or as needed to thin gravy

¼ teaspoon freshly ground black pepper

1. Preheat oven to 325°F. Place a rack in a large nonreactive roasting pan and set aside.

2. Spread veal fat side down on a large cutting board and rub with half the paprika. Set aside.

3. For Stuffing: Heat drippings in a large heavy nonreactive skillet over moderately high heat until ripples appear on pan bottom—1½ to 2 minutes. Add shallots, mushrooms, and rosemary and stir-fry until limp and golden—3 to 5 minutes. Set skillet off heat.

4. Fork sauerkraut until fluffy and add to skillet mixture along with remaining stuffing ingredients. Mix well. Pat stuffing over veal shoulder leaving ½ inch margins all round. Roll up jelly-roll style and tie with string in five or six places.

5. Rub veal roll with remaining paprika, then place on rack in roasting pan. Quickly pour consommé mixture over veal.

6. Slide onto middle oven shelf and braise uncovered, basting occasionally with pan drippings, until fork-tender—2 to 2½ hours. Remove veal from oven, lift from pan to a cutting board, drape loosely with foil, and let stand.

7. For Gravy: Blend flour into 2 cups pan liquid, and add 1 cup water and pepper, whisking until smooth. Set over moderate heat, using two burners if necessary, and cook, stirring constantly, until thickened, smooth, and no raw floury taste lingers—about 5 minutes. If gravy seems thick, thin with a little more water.

8. To serve, remove strings from veal and slice—slightly on the bias—about ½ inch thick. Overlap slices on a heated large platter. Spoon a little gravy down center and pass any extra gravy separately.

MAKES 6 SERVINGS

veal braised with carrots, celery root, and port-plumped prunes

Braising can be done on the stove top or in the oven. I prefer the latter because there's less chance of things scorching on the bottom of the pot. Reserve this recipe for a small but elegant dinner party. The recipe can be made a day or two in advance and reheated just before serving. It's never failed to impress. Note: Plump the prunes in port overnight, then begin the recipe.

2 cups pitted prunes

1 cup ruby port or late bottled vintage

3 tablespoons unsalted butter

3 medium carrots, peeled and diced

1½ cups peeled, diced celery root
(about ½ pound)

1 bunch scallions, trimmed and thinly sliced
(white part only)

2 tablespoons vegetable oil

3 pounds boneless veal shoulder,
trimmed of sinew and cut in 2 x 2 x ½-inch slices

1 teaspoon salt, or to taste

¼ teaspoon freshly ground black pepper,
or to taste

½ cup heavy cream

½ cup chicken broth

1. Soak prunes in port in a covered small nonreactive bowl overnight (no need to refrigerate).

2. Next day, melt butter in a large heavy Dutch oven over moderately high heat and as soon as it froths and subsides add carrots, celery root, and scallions and sauté, stirring often, until limp and golden—6 to 8 minutes. Lift to a bowl and reserve.

3. Add oil to pot and heat until ripples appear on pan bottom—1½ to 2 minutes. Sauté veal in two batches in oil, only until lightly golden—about 4 to 5 minutes per batch, and lifting each to a large bowl as it is sautéed.

4. Preheat oven to 350°F. Drain port wine from prunes directly into Dutch oven and cook over moderate heat, scraping up browned bits—2 to 3 minutes. Pour into a measuring cup and reserve. Prunes will be added later.

5. Spread sautéed vegetables evenly over bottom of Dutch oven, add veal along with accumulated juices, again distributing evenly, sprinkle with salt and pepper, pour in reserved port, and bring to a boil over moderate heat.

6. Slide onto middle oven shelf, cover, and braise until veal is almost tender—about 45 minutes. Add prunes, distributing evenly over veal. Cover and braise until veal and vegetables are tender—about 20 minutes more.

7. Lift veal to a heated platter, wreathe with prunes, cover loosely with foil, and keep warm. Purée vegetables and Dutch oven juices using an immersion blender or cool 10 minutes, then purée in two batches in a food processor.

8. With processor or immersion blender running, add cream and chicken broth to give mixture a nice gravy consistency. Bring sauce quickly to serving temperature over moderate heat, taste for salt and pepper, and adjust as needed.

9. Ladle some of the sauce over veal and pass extra gravy in a small gravy boat.

MAKES 6 SERVINGS

braised breast of veal stuffed with artichokes and toasted pignoli

A strut-your-stuff recipe that's perfect for a small dinner party and easier than it looks. To save time, use frozen artichoke hearts—the canned are too soft and the marinated too strong.

5 to 6 pounds bone-in breast of veal
(have butcher make a pocket for stuffing)

2 tablespoons extra-virgin olive oil

1 teaspoon salt

½ teaspoon freshly ground black pepper

12 whole silverskins (small white onions), peeled

1 package (9 ounces) frozen artichoke hearts

12 whole large garlic cloves, peeled

1 cup chicken broth mixed with
½ cup dry vermouth or white wine

STUFFING

1 package (9 ounces) frozen artichoke hearts,
cooked by package directions but not seasoned

2 cups soft white breadcrumbs

½ cup coarsely chopped, lightly toasted pignoli

¼ cup extra-virgin olive oil

¼ cup coarsely chopped fresh Italian parsley

¼ cup freshly grated Parmigiano Reggiano

2 garlic cloves, finely chopped

1 large egg, lightly beaten

½ teaspoon ground fennel

½ teaspoon salt

¼ teaspoon freshly ground black pepper

1. Preheat oven to 450°F. Rub veal inside and out with oil, salt, and pepper; set aside.

2. For Stuffing: Drain artichokes well, coarsely chop, and fork with remaining ingredients.

3. Upend veal and spoon stuffing into pocket, packing lightly and filling to within 1 inch of the top. Spoon remaining stuffing into a buttered small casserole, cover, and refrigerate. Close pocket with poultry pins, then lace crisscross fashion with twine.

4. Stand veal on rib ends in a large shallow roasting pan, slide onto middle oven shelf, and brown 30 minutes. Reduce temperature to 325°F, surround veal with onions, frozen artichokes, and garlic. Pour broth mixture over veal, tent with foil, and braise 1½ hours.

5. Remove foil and braise uncovered until fork-tender—45 to 60 minutes more. Meanwhile, set refrigerated stuffing on counter.

6. When meat tests done, remove from oven and let stand 30 minutes. At same time, raise oven temperature to 375°F, slide covered casserole of stuffing onto middle oven shelf, and bake until hot—about 20 minutes.

7. Remove poultry pins and twine from veal, set on a heated large deep platter and surround with roasted vegetables and pan juices. To carve, slice down between ribs. Pass extra stuffing separately.

MAKES 6 SERVINGS

bavarian veal shanks in wine vinegar broth

The Germans, perhaps more than any other people, dote upon shanks and tails and other cuts we Americans tend to dismiss as hopelessly bony. To stroll Munich's *Viktualienmarkt* or the meat department of tony delicatessens like Dallmayr is to see them in abundance—exquisitely fresh and beautifully displayed. To taste them expertly prepared, you've only to drop by any good restaurant—humble or haute, city-center or village square. This is one of the more unusual ways to prepare veal shanks. Certainly it's one of the easiest. Note: In my upscale grocery, veal shanks are sold as ossobuco. Tip: Halve chunky top parts of carrots and parsnips before slicing.

3 medium yellow onions,
halved lengthwise and each half thickly sliced

3 medium carrots, peeled and thickly sliced
(see Tip above)

1 medium parsnip, peeled and thickly sliced

½ small celery root (about 2 ounces),
peeled and cut in ¼-inch dice

½ small lemon, thinly sliced and seeded

1 cup white wine vinegar combined with
7 cups cold water

1 tablespoon sugar

1½ teaspoons salt, or to taste

4 large whole bay leaves (preferably fresh),
tied in cheesecloth with 4 whole cloves
and ½ teaspoon each juniper berries and
black peppercorns (spice bag)

6 slices (each 1½-inch-thick center-cut) veal shanks
(see Note above)

6 medium all-purpose potatoes, peeled, quartered,
and boiled just until tender (about 20 minutes)

1. Bring all but last two ingredients (veal shanks and potatoes) to a boil in a large, heavy nonreactive Dutch oven over moderate heat.

2. Add veal shanks, adjust heat so mixture barely bubbles, cover, and simmer until veal is fall-off-the-bone tender—about 2 hours. Discard spice bag, taste for salt, and adjust as needed.

3. To serve, center a veal shank in each of six heated large soup plates, bracket with potato quarters, and spoon in about ⅓ cup broth along with some vegetables. Put out a little bowl of mustard (sweet Bavarian mustard, if possible, or Dijon) and another of prepared horseradish so everyone can help themselves. Note: Leftover broth can be strained and frozen to use later in soups and stews. It would be a good start for borsch.

MAKES 6 SERVINGS

vitello tonnato
(cold sliced veal with tuna mayonnaise)

The first few times I made vitello tonnato, I simmered the veal in chicken broth with some flaked tuna and went through all kinds of shenanigans to create the sauce. Then my good friend Alan Tardi showed me the light. Now living in Italy but for years the chef/proprietor of my favorite Italian restaurant (the late, lamented Follonico in New York's Flatiron district), Alan taught me that the veal can simply be roasted or pot-roasted. I choose the latter because veal tends to dry as it cooks and this method preserves its moisture. Note: The beauty of this recipe is that it can be made a day or two in advance. Before serving, you've only to slice the veal and spoon on the sauce.

3 pounds boned and rolled veal rump, round, or shoulder

3 tablespoons extra-virgin olive oil

4 large fresh bay leaves, lightly bruised to release flavors

1 teaspoon salt

¼ teaspoon freshly ground black pepper

1 cup chicken broth or a 50/50 mix of broth and dry white wine

⅓ cup coarsely chopped fresh Italian parsley

TUNA MAYONNAISE

2⅓ cups mayonnaise

⅓ cup extra-virgin olive oil

¼ cup fresh lemon juice

3 cans (3 ounces each) chunk-light tuna (packed in oil), drained and liquid reserved

2 tablespoons pan drippings (from veal above; optional)

⅓ cup well-drained small capers (the tiniest you can find)

¼ teaspoon freshly ground black pepper

1. Preheat oven to 425°F. Place veal fat side up in a small roasting pan, rub well with oil, then with bay leaves, and sprinkle with salt and pepper. Drop bay leaves into pan, slide onto middle oven shelf, and roast uncovered until veal begins to brown—about 30 minutes.

2. Reduce oven temperature to 350°F, pour broth over veal, cover with foil, and braise until tender and an instant-read thermometer, thrust into center of veal, registers 150°F—1½ to 1¾ hours. Remove veal from oven, cool, then cover and refrigerate overnight.

3. Meanwhile, prepare Tuna Mayonnaise: Whiz mayonnaise, oil, lemon juice, reserved tuna liquid, and if desired, pan drippings in a food processor or electric blender until smooth. Scoop into a nonreactive bowl and set aside. Finely mince tuna and mix into mayonnaise along with capers and pepper. Cover and refrigerate overnight.

4. When ready to proceed, remove veal and tuna mayonnaise from refrigerator. Remove strings from veal, set on cutting board, and slice as thin as possible. Discard bay leaves.

5. To serve, overlap slices of veal on a large platter, spoon tuna mayonnaise generously down middle, and sprinkle with parsley. Pass remaining tuna mayonnaise separately.

MAKES 6 SERVINGS

ossobuco

I'd never heard of ossobuco, let alone tasted it, until I spent time in Italy years ago. As soon as I returned to New York, where I then lived, I began making ossobuco for small dinner parties—ideal because it was even better if made the day before and reheated just before serving. My New York butchers carried veal shanks (first Walter's in the West Village, then Tom's near Gramercy Park—my last and favorite New York neighborhood). When I moved south, I feared that the veal so routine in fine New York butcher shops would no longer be available. To my great delight it is. Note: To add a note of mystery, I sometimes vary the gremolata, using 2½ teaspoons finely grated lemon zest and ½ teaspoon finely grated orange or lime zest or even ¼ teaspoon each orange and lime. But I'm careful not to overdo it—a lemony flavor should predominate.

6 slices (each 2-inch-thick center-cut) veal shanks

⅓ cup unsifted all-purpose flour mixed with 1½ teaspoons salt and ½ teaspoon each crumbled dried leaf thyme and freshly ground black pepper (seasoned flour)

3 tablespoons extra-virgin olive oil

3 tablespoons unsalted butter

2 large yellow onions, coarsely chopped

2 large red onions, coarsely chopped

4 large garlic cloves, smashed and skins removed

2 small carrots, peeled and coarsely chopped

2 small celery ribs, peeled and coarsely chopped

2 large whole bay leaves (preferably fresh)

1 tablespoon coarsely chopped fresh basil or 1 teaspoon crumbled dried leaf basil

1 tablespoon coarsely chopped fresh marjoram or 1 teaspoon crumbled dried leaf marjoram

1 teaspoon coarsely chopped fresh thyme (preferably lemon thyme) or ¼ teaspoon crumbled dried leaf thyme

2 strips (each about 2 inches long and ½ inch wide) lemon zest

1 can (14½ ounces) diced tomatoes, with their liquid

1¾ cups chicken or beef broth

1½ cups dry white wine such as Pinot Grigio, Soave, or Verdicchio

¼ cup moderately coarsely chopped fresh Italian parsley

GREMOLATA

2 tablespoons finely chopped fresh Italian parsley mixed with 1 tablespoon each finely minced garlic and finely grated lemon zest (see Note above)

1. Rub veal shanks well all over with seasoned flour, then shake off excess.

2. In a heavy nonreactive Dutch oven large enough to accommodate all shanks in a single layer heat 2 tablespoons each oil and butter over moderately high heat until ripples appear on pan bottom—1½ to 2 minutes.

3. Add all shanks and brown well, allowing 5 to 7 minutes per side and lifting each to a large bowl as it browns.

4. Add remaining oil and butter to pot and as soon as butter melts, add next ten ingredients (yellow onions through lemon zest) and sauté stirring often, until limp and golden—about 10 minutes.

5. Return shanks to pot along with accumulated juices, add tomatoes, broth, and wine, and bring to a boil over moderate heat. Adjust heat so

mixture barely bubbles, cover, and simmer slowly until veal nearly falls from bones—about 3½ to 4 hours. Stir mixture occasionally and if at any time liquid seems skimpy, add a little water, turn heat to lowest point, and if necessary, slide a diffuser underneath pot. Cool to room temperature, cover, and refrigerate overnight.

6. When ready to proceed, let Dutch oven stand 30 minutes at room temperature, set over moderate heat, and bring ossobuco slowly to serving temperature—about 20 minutes; stir occasionally and carefully so shanks remain intact. Discard bay leaves and lemon zest. Taste for salt and pepper, and adjust. Mix in chopped parsley.

7. To serve, arrange ossobuco on a heated large deep platter, smother with pan gravy, then top each shank with a sprinkling of gremolata. Accompany with boiled rice or a favorite risotto.

MAKES 6 SERVINGS

swiss skillet veal in cream

Zurich is where I first tasted this splendid recipe, also where I saw ready-to-cook strips of veal round in local butcher shops. Would that they were available here. As I've said elsewhere, one of the most effective ways to tenderize tougher pieces of meat is to cut them across the grain in slices or strips. And the thinner, the better. Once that's done, this is a fast skillet dish best prepared in amounts for two persons or four. In Switzerland, *roesti* (a big, crisp butter-browned shredded potato pancake) is the traditional accompaniment, but hash browns are perfectly acceptable. Ditto baked potatoes, even tiny redskins or fingerlings roasted in their skins. Tip: If you partially freeze the veal—45 minutes in the freezer should do it—you'll find it easier to cut into strips. Better yet, try to coax your butcher into slicing and trimming the veal for you.

1½ pounds veal round, sliced ⅜ inch thick and trimmed of sinew and fat, if any (see Tip above)

¼ cup (½ stick) unsalted butter

3 large shallots, finely chopped

¼ teaspoon crumbled dried leaf thyme

¼ teaspoon freshly grated nutmeg

3 tablespoons brandy

½ cup dry white wine such as Riesling or, even better, spicy Gewürztraminer

1½ cups heavy cream

1 teaspoon salt, or to taste

¼ teaspoon freshly ground black pepper, or to taste

3 tablespoons finely snipped fresh chives or minced fresh Italian parsley

1. Cut veal across the grain into strips 2½ to 3 inches long and ⅜ inch wide.

2. Melt 2 tablespoons butter in a large (12-inch) heavy nonreactive skillet over high heat and as soon as it froths and subsides, add half the veal and stir-fry until milky white—1 to 2 minutes is all it takes. Using a slotted spoon, transfer veal to a large bowl. In remaining 2 tablespoons butter, cook remaining veal the same way and transfer to bowl.

3. Add shallots, thyme, and nutmeg to skillet, turn heat down low, and sauté, stirring often, until limp and golden—about 2 minutes.

4. Slide skillet off heat and mix in brandy. Set over lowest heat, and cook, stirring often, until brandy evaporates—about 3 minutes.

5. Add wine, raise heat to moderately high, and boil uncovered until wine is reduced to a glaze—3 to 5 minutes. Blend in cream and boil uncovered until almost as thick as sour cream—about 5 minutes.

6. Return veal to skillet along with accumulated juices, reduce heat to low, and bring slowly to serving temperature—3 to 5 minutes, uncovered.

7. Add salt and pepper, mix in chives, dish up, and enjoy.

MAKES 4 SERVINGS

belgian veal loaf in wine sauce

Like the Swiss Skillet Veal that precedes, this recipe uses mechanical means to tenderize a tough cut of veal. And because veal is lean, this Brussels specialty is a 50/50 mix of ground veal and pork. It's shaped into a log, dusted with flour, dotted with butter, and baked at a fairly high temperature. Just before serving, wine poured over all mingles with the drippings to form the basis of the sauce. I like this veal loaf with scalloped or baked potatoes, but boiled brown or white rice is equally good. So, too, wild rice. Note: This meatloaf is delicious served cold or at room temperature and makes a dandy sandwich. I like it on whole-wheat bread spread with horseradish mayo, but choose your own favorite condiments.

1½ pounds ground veal shoulder

1½ pounds ground pork shoulder (not too lean)

½ cup fine, soft white breadcrumbs
(1 slice firm-textured white bread)

⅓ cup finely chopped yellow onion (about 1 small)

2 tablespoons finely chopped fresh Italian parsley

1 tablespoon prepared horseradish

2 large eggs, lightly beaten with 1 tablespoon
sour cream, heavy cream, or evaporated milk

1 teaspoon salt

½ teaspoon freshly ground black pepper

½ teaspoon freshly grated nutmeg

2 tablespoons all-purpose flour

¼ cup (½ stick) unsalted butter, diced

½ cup dry white wine such as
Chardonnay or Riesling

Pan drippings plus enough chicken broth
to total 1½ cups

1. Preheat oven to 425°F. Spritz a large oval baking dish (one with a tight-fitting lid) with nonstick cooking spray and set aside.

2. Using your hands, mix first ten ingredients (veal through nutmeg) thoroughly and shape into a firm, compact log that will fit in casserole. Sift flour over loaf, then dot with butter.

3. Cover and bake on middle oven shelf 45 minutes. Uncover and bake until an instant-read thermometer, thrust into center of loaf, registers 160°F—about 30 minutes longer.

4. Pour wine over loaf, mix with pan drippings, and bake uncovered 10 minutes more.

5. Remove loaf from oven and cool in upright pan on a wire rack 15 minutes. Carefully lift loaf to a cutting board, placing right side up, and slice about ½ inch thick.

6. Quickly bring pan drippings mixture to a simmer in a small saucepan over moderate heat.

7. To serve, overlap meatloaf slices on a heated large platter and spoon hot drippings mixture (called *jus* in French-speaking Belgium) over and around slices.

MAKES 6 TO 8 SERVINGS

russian crumb-crusted veal and beef loaf with sour cream gravy

I've always been fond of crumbed Russian cutlets but had never considered crumbing a meatloaf—a nice touch that adds crispness conventional meatloaves lack. What also distinguish this meatloaf are its seasonings (dill pickles and nutmeg) and sour cream gravy.

5 tablespoons (½ stick plus 1 tablespoon) unsalted butter

10 slices firm-textured white bread

1 large yellow onion, coarsely chopped

½ teaspoon freshly grated nutmeg

½ cup half-and-half

1½ pounds ground veal shoulder or rump (not too lean)

1 pound ground lean beef chuck

½ cup finely chopped dill pickle

¼ cup coarsely chopped fresh Italian parsley

1 extra-large egg

1½ teaspoons salt

½ teaspoon coarsely ground black pepper

GRAVY

1 cup water or chicken broth

3 tablespoons all-purpose flour

1 cup sour cream, at room temperature

Salt to taste

Freshly ground black pepper to taste

1. Spritz a 13 x 9 x 3-inch baking pan with non-stick cooking spray and set aside.

2. Melt 3 tablespoons butter, then using about 1 tablespoon, lightly brush 6 slices bread on both sides. Arrange in single layer on ungreased baking sheet, slide onto middle oven shelf, and preheat oven to 350°F. Reserve remaining melted butter.

3. Toast bread 5 to 6 minutes as oven preheats, turn, and toast 5 to 6 minutes more. Cool toast, then whiz to coarse crumbs in food processor; just tear slices directly into work bowl and alternately pulse and churn. Toss crumbs with reserved 2 tablespoons melted butter and set aside.

4. Melt remaining 2 tablespoons butter in a medium-size heavy skillet over moderately high heat and as soon as it froths and subsides, add onion and nutmeg and sauté, stirring often, until nicely browned—7 to 8 minutes.

5. Cut remaining 4 bread slices into ½-inch pieces and combine with half-and-half in a large bowl. Add skillet mixture along with remaining meatloaf ingredients, and mix well with your hands.

6. Scoop into baking pan and shape into a loaf about 10 inches long, 6½ inches wide and 2½ to 3 inches high. Pat reserved buttered toast crumbs firmly over loaf, reapplying any that drop to bottom of pan.

7. Slide pan onto middle oven shelf and bake meatloaf uncovered until an instant-read thermometer, thrust into center, registers 160°F—about 1 hour. Note: If loaf is browning too fast after 35 to 40 minutes, cover loosely with foil. Lift meatloaf to a cutting board, tent loosely with foil, and keep warm.

8. For Gravy: Using a slotted spoon, remove broth-soaked crumbs in pan that have fallen from meatloaf and reserve, then skim fat from pan drippings—there aren't many. Add water to pan, and cook and stir 2 to 3 minutes over moderate heat, scraping up browned bits. Blend in reserved broth-soaked crumbs, then flour, and cook, stirring constantly, until thickened and no floury taste remains—about 5 minutes. Set off heat, smooth in sour cream, and add salt and pepper to taste.

9. To serve, slice ends off meatloaf, then cut center portion into large squares. Arrange crumb side up on a heated large platter and smother with gravy. Accompany with boiled potatoes or, if you prefer, fluffy boiled rice or buttered noodles.

MAKES 6 TO 8 SERVINGS

lithuanian veal, cabbage, and mushroom pie

During World War II, Nazi-threatened Europeans—Austrians, Lithuanians, Czechs, Hungarians, Poles, and yes, Germans—fled to the U.S. A dozen or more families settled in my home town of Raleigh, and many of the men, like my father, taught at NC State College. My mother made a point of befriending the newcomers—perhaps because she'd lived in Vienna as a bride. Soon she and the expats were swapping recipes and my mother's card file filled up so fast she began a second one. Usually meticulous about noting recipe source in the upper right-hand corner, she slipped up on this one so I don't know whence it originally came. This is my updated version.

3 tablespoons unsalted butter

1 medium yellow onion, coarsely chopped

1 package (8 ounces) sliced white
or cremini mushrooms

1 pound ground veal shoulder (not too lean)

8 cups very coarsely shredded green
or Savoy cabbage (about 2 pounds)

1 teaspoon salt, or to taste

¼ teaspoon freshly ground black pepper,
or to taste

¼ teaspoon freshly grated nutmeg

3 tablespoons all-purpose flour

2 hard-cooked large eggs, shelled and coarsely
chopped (see How to Use This Book, page xiii)

Two 9-inch unroll-and-bake pie crusts
(from a 15-ounce package)

1. Set a heavy baking sheet on middle oven shelf and preheat oven to 425°F.

2. Melt butter in a large heavy skillet over moderately high heat and as soon as it froths and subsides, add onion and sauté, stirring often, until nicely browned—5 to 7 minutes.

3. Add mushrooms and cook, stirring frequently, until they release their juices and these evaporate—about 10 minutes.

4. Add ground veal, breaking up clumps, and cook and stir until no longer pink—about 5 minutes.

5. Add cabbage, salt, pepper, and nutmeg, cover, and steam until cabbage wilts slightly—8 to 10 minutes. Sprinkle flour over surface and cook, stirring constantly, until lightly thickened—about 3 minutes.

6. Mix in hard-cooked eggs, taste for salt and pepper, adjust as needed, and set aside.

7. Line a 9-inch pie pan with one pie crust, pressing over bottom and up sides. Spoon in cabbage mixture, center remaining pie crust on top, and trim overhang until 1 inch larger than pie pan all around. Roll overhang underneath onto rim and crimp making a high fluted edge. With a sharp knife, cut several decorative steam vents near center of crust.

8. Center pie on preheated baking sheet and bake until bubbly and nicely browned—about 30 minutes.

9. Cool 15 minutes, then cut into wedges and serve.

MAKES 6 SERVINGS

norwegian skipper's stew

Yet another recipe that puts ground veal to good use. You'll find this rib-sticking soup an easy, frugal, delicious way to make one pound of meat serve six. I can't think of a better way to warm a wintry day. Note: Norwegians do not add garlic to this soup—I do but make it optional.

¼ cup (½ stick) unsalted butter

½ pound ground veal shoulder

½ pound ground beef chuck or pork shoulder (not too lean)

2 large yellow onions, quartered lengthwise and each quarter thinly sliced

1 large garlic clove, finely chopped (optional; see Note above)

3½ cups beef or chicken broth plus enough cold water to total 1 quart (4 cups)

2 large whole bay leaves (preferably fresh)

1½ teaspoons salt, or to taste

½ teaspoon freshly ground black pepper, or to taste

½ teaspoon crumbled dried leaf thyme

¼ teaspoon freshly grated nutmeg

4 medium-large all-purpose potatoes (about 2 pounds), peeled and cut in 1-inch dice

2 tablespoons finely snipped fresh dill

4 tablespoons coarsely chopped fresh Italian parsley

1. Melt butter in a large heavy Dutch oven over moderately high heat and as soon as it froths and subsides, add veal, beef, onions, and if desired, garlic, and sauté, stirring often, until onions are limp and meat no longer pink—10 to 12 minutes. Do not brown meat.

2. Add broth, bay leaves, salt, pepper, thyme, and nutmeg and bring to a boil. Adjust heat so mixture bubbles gently, cover, and simmer 30 minutes.

3. Add potatoes, cover, reduce heat to its lowest point, and simmer until potatoes disintegrate and thicken soup—2½ to 3 hours. Note: Check pot from time to time and if liquid is evaporating too fast, add ½ to 1 cup water, and if necessary, slide a diffuser underneath pot.

4. Stir in dill and 2 tablespoons parsley and simmer uncovered over low heat just until flavors mellow—about 10 minutes. Discard bay leaves, taste for salt and pepper, and adjust as needed.

5. Ladle into heated large soup plates, sprinkle with remaining parsley, and serve.

MAKES 6 SERVINGS

LAMB

LAMB

BREAST, NECK, RIBLETS, SHANKS, AND SHOULDER

Historians believe that lamb may have been the first red meat eaten by man—and from domesticated sheep at that judging from the cache of 9,000-year-old lamb bones found in Iraq. They further believe that sheep are indigenous to the Middle East, certainly the Bible is strewn with references to them.

Sturdy creatures, sheep can graze hardscrabble heights and endure burning desert sand. They are docile, easily raised in flocks, and to primitive man indispensable for the milk, meat, and wool they provided. As early as 4000 B.C., there was a lucrative wool trade in Babylon (indeed, its name means "Land of Wool"). To this day, lamb is the meat of choice throughout the Eastern Mediterranean, Middle East, and India and figures prominently in Muslim, Christian, and Jewish religious ceremonies.

Sometime between 800 and 500 B.C., sheep were exported to England from the Phoenician ports of Sidon and Tyre and we have the English to thank for developing meatier stock from these rangy imports and introducing them to their overseas colonies of Australia, New Zealand, and South Africa. But not to America.

Columbus brought sheep to Cuba and Santo Domingo on his second voyage. And later Cortés, then Coronado, traveled throughout the American Southwest with flocks of sheep, meaty Spanish *churras* that became the foundation of America's lamb industry. Exploring northern New Mexico not so many years ago, I watched—fascinated—as shepherds, most of them Basques, guided flocks down to the Rio Grande to drink. Rivers of fleece eddying across barren slopes.

The bulk of America's lamb is now raised in the West, but those who relish it live in Eastern metropolises like Boston, New York, and Philadelphia. In central North Carolina where I grew up, lamb didn't land on many dinner tables. My mother turned lamb shoulder into stew or pot roast to the horror of school chums whose mothers only cooked pork or beef. Times change, old prejudices die, and the cuts of lamb my mother special-ordered have come to the supermarket.

So what exactly is lamb? Sheep less than a year old though most lamb coming to market is between five and eight months. One- to two-year-olds are yearlings—well on their way to becoming mutton. Anything older *is* mutton—gamier than lamb and tougher, too.

Baby lamb is six- to eight-weeks old, milk-fed, with flesh more pink than red. Spring lamb, a term coined decades ago to push sales of lambs born in winter is all but obsolete. Back then, raising lambs was low-tech and with newborns often too fragile to weather Arctic temperatures, lambs were rushed to market. Today lamb knows no season thanks to modern farming methods not to mention New Zealand lamb arriving by the jumbo-jet load.

LAMB NUTRITIONAL PROFILE

Like other red meat, lamb is an excellent source of protein and B vitamins (particularly B_{12}). It's rich, too, in iron and zinc but low in sodium. Moreover, approximately half of its fat is unsaturated. Fat, calories, and cholesterol vary from grade to grade, cut to cut, and according to how much fat is removed. Here are approximate counts:

- Braised, Trimmed Lamb Shank (4 ounces) = 204 calories, 7.6 grams fat, 97 milligrams cholesterol Note: This is a bony cut with little meat.
- Braised Boned Shoulder (4 ounces) = 312 calories, 16 grams fat, 137 milligrams cholesterol

USDA GRADES OF LAMB:

The top supermarket grade is Choice (with Prime being reserved for chefs and fancy butchers). Second supermarket best: Good. Lower grades (Utility and Cull) are destined for processed meats although they are sometimes ground, packaged, and sold.

SHOPPING TIPS

The older the lamb, the redder the lean, more yellow the fat (tallow), and stronger the flavor. I suspect that those claiming to "hate" lamb have only eaten mutton. True lamb, top-quality lamb is delicate, its flesh rosy, lightly marbled, and its bones red at the center. NOTE: *The fat blanketing most cuts is covered with fell, a thin, papery membrane that should be removed before lamb is cooked. It peels right off.*

STORAGE TIPS

Like other meat from young animals, lamb is highly perishable. Before refrigerating, remove lamb from its store wrapper, spread in a single layer on a large plate, and cover loosely with foil or plastic wrap. Set in the lower part of the refrigerator and cook within 48 hours.

FREEZER TIPS

Freeze the meat as soon as you get it home from the store and never freeze in the store wrapper. Instead, wrap snugly in foil or plastic freezer wrap as follows:

- **Breast and Pot Roasts:** Package each individually.
- **Shoulder Chops and Shanks:** Do not bundle or stack. Instead, arrange side by side, allowing no more than two per package.
- **Stew Meat:** Spread in a single layer—easier if you first line a shallow pan with foil—then fold ends in securely over meat. Once lamb freezes, remove pan and if necessary, overwrap with foil or plastic freezer wrap to seal out all air.
- **Ground Lamb:** Flatten into a disk no more than two inches thick and wrap as snugly as possible. Or if you prefer, shape into patties and wrap individually.

In each case, press all air from package, label, date, and set directly on the freezing surface of a 0°F freezer. Maximum storage time: Three months for ground lamb and stew meat, six months for pot roasts, shanks, and shoulder chops.

RECYCLING LEFTOVERS

Curry! No meat makes better curry than lamb and this includes leftovers. Simply dice and add to a favorite curry sauce. I also like to grind lamb leftovers and use when making Greek classics like moussaka and pastitsio. Or Turkish boreks. I sometimes slip a little diced or ground leftover lamb into vegetable soup or tomato-y pasta sauce. Even into mac 'n' cheese.

LAMB CUTS

(WHERE THE TOUGH CUTS ARE)

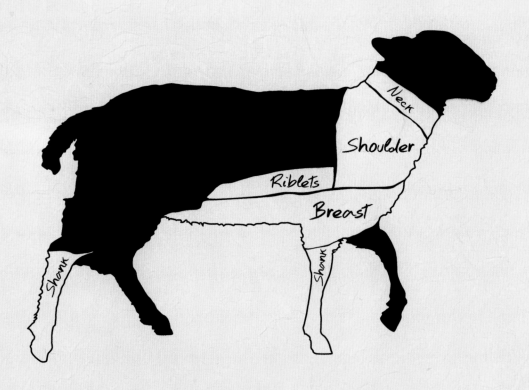

BREAST

Flat, lean, bony cut with
a thin outer layer of fat
that's easily trimmed off

BEST USES
- BONED, STUFFED,
  ROLLED, AND BRAISED
- DIVIDED INTO RIBS AND
  BRAISED

NECK

Lean, gristly round slices
with single round bone
and thin outer layer of fat;
not widely available but
riblets can be used in recipes calling for neck slices.

BEST USES
- SOUPS AND STEWS

RIBLETS

Rib ends with varying
amount of fat and lean.
Mostly bone. Can be used
in place of neck slices

BEST USES
- SOUPS
- STEWS
- BRAISES

SHANKS

Lean, sinewy with marrow-
rich bone; foreshank
preferable

BEST USES
- SOUPS (WITH SMALL,
  BONY CROSS-CUTS)
- BRAISES FOR MEATIER
  PORTIONS

SHOULDER

Single most versatile cut
of lamb; source of blade
chops (one slim bone),
also larger arm chop
(single round bone), stew
meat and ground lamb

BEST USES
- POT ROAST
- BONED, STUFFED,
  ROLLED
- STEWS
- BRAISES FOR CHOPS
- MEATLOAVES AND
  MEATBALLS

umbrian mushroom, lamb, and cannellini soup

Use a variety of mushrooms for this provincial Italian soup—baby bellas (also called cremini), shiitakes, white—and slip in dried porcini for deeper flavor. Most supermarkets now sell little packets of them. They also sell ready-to-use presliced mushrooms and if they look good and fresh (no discoloring, softening, or shriveling), I use them to save prep time. On a recent trip to my high-end grocery, I saw four-ounce packages of sliced "gourmet mushroom blends"—baby bellas, shiitakes, and oyster mushrooms and used some of them here. This soup, by the way, is equally good made with beef, but I prefer lamb—usually cheaper than beef because there's less demand for it. Don't be daunted by this long list of ingredients—many require nothing more than opening a package of this or can of that.

1 package (½ ounce) dried porcini mushrooms

1 cup dry red wine such as Valpolicella or Cabernet

¼ cup extra-virgin olive oil

1 pound boneless lamb neck slices or lamb shoulder, trimmed of excess fat and cut in 1-inch cubes

2 pounds mushrooms of various types, stemmed, wiped clean, and thinly sliced (see headnote)

1 large red onion, halved lengthwise and each half thinly sliced

1 bunch scallions, trimmed and thinly sliced (include some green tops)

1 medium carrot, peeled and cut in ¼-inch dice

4 large garlic cloves, smashed and skins removed

2 teaspoons finely chopped fresh rosemary or ¾ teaspoon crumbled dried leaf rosemary

2 teaspoons finely chopped fresh sage or ¾ teaspoon rubbed sage

1 quart (4 cups) beef or chicken broth

1 can (14½ ounces) diced tomatoes, with their liquid

1 teaspoon salt, or to taste

½ teaspoon freshly ground black pepper, or to taste

1 can (19 ounces) cannellini (white kidney beans), drained and rinsed

½ cup coarsely chopped fresh Italian parsley

1. Place dried porcini in a small nonreactive bowl, add wine, and set aside to soak.

2. Heat oil in a large heavy nonreactive Dutch oven over moderately high heat until ripples appear on pan bottom—1½ to 2 minutes.

3. Add next eight ingredients (lamb through sage) and cook, stirring occasionally, until onion and mushrooms are very soft—about 15 minutes.

4. Add wine-soaked porcini, unabsorbed wine, broth, tomatoes, salt, and pepper and bring to a boil. Adjust heat so liquid bubbles gently, cover, and simmer until lamb is tender—about 2 hours.

5. Mix in cannellini and parsley and simmer uncovered 10 minutes. Taste for salt and pepper and adjust as needed.

6. Ladle into heated large soup plates, put out a bowl of freshly grated Parmigiano Reggiano so everyone can sprinkle a tablespoon or two into their soup, and accompany with thick slices of Italian bread. Tip: I brush the slices with olive oil, arrange on a baking sheet, and toast 8 to 10 minutes in a 350°F oven.

MAKES 6 TO 8 SERVINGS

barley, lamb, and lima soup

Few soups are more welcome on a blustery day than this one and few are more nourishing. Like most soups, this one requires considerable slicing, dicing, and chopping—no problem if you have a food processor to do the work for you. Note: The dried limas must be soaked overnight, so put them on to soak the day before you begin the soup.

3 tablespoons bacon drippings or extra-virgin olive oil

2 large yellow onions,
halved lengthwise and each half thinly sliced

1 small celery root (about 1 pound),
trimmed, peeled, and cut in ½-inch dice
or 3 large celery ribs,
thinly sliced (include a few leaves)

4 large garlic cloves, smashed and skins removed

2 lamb shanks, cracked

1 quart (4 cups) beef or chicken broth

2 cups water (about)

3 medium carrots, peeled and thickly sliced

3 medium parsnips, peeled and thickly sliced

½ cup medium pearl barley, washed

3 large whole bay leaves (preferably fresh)

1½ teaspoons salt, or to taste

½ teaspoon freshly ground black pepper,
or to taste

2 cups dried baby lima beans,
soaked overnight in cold water, rinsed, and drained

1 cup coarsely chopped fresh Italian parsley

1. Heat drippings in a large heavy soup pot over moderately high heat until ripples appear on pan bottom—1½ to 2 minutes.

2. Add onions, celery root, and garlic and sauté, stirring often, until limp and golden—about 10 minutes.

3. Add lamb shanks and all but last two ingredients (limas and parsley) and bring to a boil over high heat. Adjust heat so soup bubbles gently, cover, and simmer 1 hour, stirring occasionally.

4. Add limas, cover, and simmer, stirring now and then, until vegetables are tender and meat falls from bones—about 1 hour longer.

5. Lift lamb shanks from pot, strip meat from bones, add to pot along with parsley, and if soup seems thick, a little more water. Cover and simmer 10 minutes. Discard bay leaves, taste for salt and pepper, and adjust as needed.

6. Ladle soup into heated large soup plates and serve with chunks of country bread lightly brushed with olive oil.

MAKES 6 TO 8 SERVINGS

baltic lamb and kale soup

Except along the Baltic where sheep graze salt marshes, lamb and mutton are not popular in Germany, Poland, Denmark, and other countries washed by these icy waters. Even here in the U.S., I've found few recipes for lamb, and most are for leg of lamb (my focus here—soups that make the most of bony or sinewy cuts). I think this one of the best. Note: Choose flat-leafed kale if you can find it—the curly is difficult to clean and cut. To remove stem and coarse central rib of each leaf, cut alongside each rib with a sharp knife and pull away from leaf, bringing the stem with it. At this point, I stack leaves in groups of four or five, then cut in pieces with my fiercest chef's knife and dump into a large mesh colander. Once all the kale is cut, I wash well under cool running water, then leave the kale to drain while I proceed with the recipe. When it's time to add the kale to the soup, I simply upend the colander over the pot and push the kale into the soup. The water droplets clinging to the leaves increase the amount of soup liquid slightly and that's good.

4 ounces double-smoked slab bacon, cut in ¼-inch dice, or 4 ounces thickly sliced bacon, cut crosswise in ¼-inch strips

1 pound boneless lamb shoulder or neck slices, trimmed of excess fat and cut in ¾-inch cubes

½ pound kielbasa, halved lengthwise and each half thinly sliced

2 large yellow onions, coarsely chopped

1 cup finely diced celery root

2 large whole bay leaves (preferably fresh)

1 quart (4 cups) chicken broth

1 cup water (about)

1 teaspoon salt, or to taste

½ teaspoon freshly ground black pepper, or to taste

1 bunch kale (about 1 pound), stems and central ribs removed and leaves cut in 1- to 2-inch pieces (see Note above)

3 tablespoons Dijon mustard blended with 1½ tablespoons sugar (I prefer raw sugar)

1. Sauté bacon in a large heavy broad-bottomed soup pot over moderately high heat, stirring occasionally, until all fat has rendered out and only crisp brown bits remain—about 10 minutes. Using a slotted, spoon, scoop browned bits to paper toweling to drain and reserve. Pour off all drippings, then spoon 4 tablespoons back into pot. Reserve remaining drippings.

2. Sauté lamb and kielbasa in drippings over moderately high heat, stirring often, until nicely browned—8 to 10 minutes. Using a slotted spoon, lift to a bowl and reserve.

3. Add onions, celery root, and bay leaves to drippings and sauté, stirring often and adding another tablespoon drippings, if necessary, until limp and lightly browned—10 to 12 minutes.

4. Return lamb and kielbasa to pot along with accumulated juices, add broth, water, salt, and pepper, and bring to a boil. Adjust heat so mixture barely bubbles, cover, and simmer slowly for 1½ hours. Check pot occasionally and if liquid seems skimpy, add a little more water.

5. Add kale, pushing down into soup, cover, and simmer until kale and lamb are both tender—about 1 hour longer. Smooth in mustard mixture. Discard bay leaves, taste for salt and pepper, and adjust as needed.

6. To serve, ladle into heated large soup plates, scatter a few reserved bacon bits over each portion, and accompany with crusty chunks of French or Italian bread.

MAKES 4 TO 6 SERVINGS

anglesey cottage caul

Some years back, *Food & Wine* magazine sent me to North Wales to write a food and travel article and while there, I drove over to the Isle of Anglesey—no shortage of lamb here. Or of tourists being photographed in front of a certain village sign—its name is the longest in Britain and, I'm guessing, the world: *Llanfairpwllwyngyllgogerychwyrndrobwllllantysiliogogogoch.* Translation: *The Church of St. Mary in a hollow of white hazel near a rapid whirlpool and near St. Tysilio's church by the red cave.* And here's another translation: In Wales, *caul* means soup and this one, with its abundance of broth and freshly dug root vegetables, explains why the Welsh say "It's as good to drink the broth as it is to eat the meat." In days long gone, farm families would ladle this lamb soup into wooden bowls and eat with wooden spoons to lessen the risk of burning their tongues. Note: If this soup's to have any depth of flavor, use the freshest vegetables you can find—and that means "local." Those harvested weeks earlier and shipped cross country have little flavor. I also like to enrich the soup by using a 50/50 mix of water and beef or chicken broth but the frugal Welsh would no doubt disapprove of such extravagance. Tip: If your butcher has lamb neck slices, use them here. If not—all too often the case—substitute boneless lamb shoulder.

3 pounds bone-in lamb neck slices, trimmed of excess fat and cut in 2-inch chunks or 2 pounds boneless lamb shoulder, trimmed of excess fat and cut in 1-inch chunks

2½ quarts (10 cups) water or for richer soup, 5 cups each water and beef or chicken broth (see Note above)

1 tablespoon salt, or to taste

½ teaspoon freshly ground black pepper, or to taste

½ teaspoon freshly grated nutmeg

2 large yellow onions, halved lengthwise and each half thinly sliced

3 bunches scallions, washed, trimmed, and thinly sliced (include some green tops)

4 medium carrots, peeled and sliced ¼ inch thick (halve chunky top part lengthwise before slicing)

2 large parsnips, peeled and sliced ¼ inch thick (halve chunky top part lengthwise before slicing)

1 small celery root (about 1 pound), trimmed, peeled, and cut in ¼-inch dice

1 small rutabaga (about 1 pound), trimmed, peeled, and cut in ½-inch dice

8 golf-ball-size redskin potatoes, scrubbed and halved (no need to peel)

½ cup coarsely chopped fresh Italian parsley

1. Bring lamb, water, salt, pepper, and nutmeg to a boil in a large soup pot over moderately high heat. Skim froth from surface as it accumulates and discard. Adjust heat so water bubbles gently, cover, and cook 1 hour.

2. Add onions, 2 bunches scallions, carrots, parsnips, and celery root. As soon as mixture boils, adjust heat so it bubbles gently, cover, and simmer 1 hour.

3. Add rutabaga and potatoes, cover, and cook until potatoes are tender—about 40 minutes. Add remaining scallions, cover, and simmer 15 minutes. Mix in parsley, taste for salt and pepper, and adjust as needed.

4. Ladle into heated large soup plates and serve with crusty chunks of country bread—in Wales, that's likely to be *bara,* a quick bread often made with oatmeal. Note: If you made the soup with neck slices, tell people there are bones in their soup.

MAKES 8 SERVINGS

scotch broth

Trust the Scots to stretch puny amounts of meat over many mouths. To "plump up" this water-based soup, they add barley where others might add rice or pasta. And to boost flavor and nutritive value, they stir in plenty of humble root vegetables, most of them home-grown. Note: For directions on cleaning leeks, see Leeks, How to Use This Book (page xiii).

2 pounds lamb riblets or bone-in neck slices, trimmed of excess fat and cut in 2-inch chunks

1 large yellow onion, coarsely chopped

4 medium leeks or 3 bunches scallions, washed, trimmed, and thinly sliced (see Note above)

4 medium carrots, peeled and cut in ¼-inch dice

2 cups diced rutabaga (¼-inch dice)

½ cup medium pearl barley, washed

4 quarts (16 cups) water

2 teaspoons salt, or to taste

½ teaspoon freshly ground black pepper, or to taste

¼ cup coarsely chopped fresh Italian parsley

1. Bring all but last ingredient to a boil in a large soup pot over moderately high heat. Skim froth from surface as it accumulates and discard.

2. Adjust heat so soup bubbles gently, cover, and simmer slowly, skimming off froth and stirring occasionally, until meat almost falls from bones—2 to 2½ hours.

3. Mix in parsley, taste for salt and pepper, and adjust as needed.

4. Ladle into heated large soup plates and accompany with chunks of whole-grain bread. Note: Tell those at the table there are bones in this soup so they'll proceed with caution.

MAKES 6 SERVINGS

mulligatawny (peppery lamb and coconut soup)

There are many versions of Mulligatawny, which, I'm told, means "pepper water." The majority of these curried soups are made with chicken, but I prefer this Indian recipe containing lamb or mutton. Tough and bony lamb neck slices or riblets are perfect for Mulligatawny and the slow cooker makes it almost effortless. To enrich the flavor, I toss the lamb with ghee or clarified butter (for directions on making ghee, see Butter in How to Use This Book, page xii), spread on a large rimmed baking sheet, and broil until brown. Once everything's in the slow cooker, you can forget it for hours. Note: Don't be daunted by the long list of ingredients. Most are quickly measured seasonings that "curry" the soup. No curry powder short-cuts here.

2 medium yellow onions, chunked

6 whole large garlic cloves, peeled

2 (1-inch) cubes fresh ginger, peeled

¼ cup water

1 tablespoon ground coriander

2 teaspoons ground cumin

1 teaspoon ground turmeric

1 teaspoon mustard seeds

½ to 1 teaspoon chili flakes
(crushed dried hot red chili peppers), or to taste

1 teaspoon salt, or to taste

3 pounds lamb neck slices or riblets,
trimmed of excess fat

¼ cup ghee (see headnote)

2 cans (13½ ounces each) coconut milk
(use "light," if you like)

1 quart (4 cups) chicken or vegetable broth

2 large whole bay leaves (preferably fresh)

⅓ cup basmati or converted rice

1 large lemon, thinly sliced

1. Preheat broiler. Meanwhile, purée first 10 ingredients (onions through salt) in a food processor until smooth and set aside.

2. Turn lamb in ghee, spread in one layer on a foil-lined rimmed baking sheet, and broil 5 inches from heat until brown—about 5 minutes.

3. Transfer lamb along with accumulated juices to a large (4- to 6-quart) slow cooker and mix in reserved purée, coconut milk, broth, and bay leaves. Cover and cook on HIGH 1 hour.

4. Add rice, stir well, cover, and cook on LOW 4 hours or until lamb and rice are tender. Discard bay leaves, taste for salt and chili pepper, and adjust as needed.

5. Ladle into heated large soup bowls and float a lemon slice on top of each portion. Note: Tell people there are bones in this soup so they'll proceed with caution.

MAKES 6 SERVINGS

odds and ends lamb soup

Few cooks are more inventive about recycling bits of this and that than the Portuguese. As I've traveled about the country, I've often eaten humble bread-thickened soups like this one, the daily special, it seems, in mom 'n' pop *tascas* (bistros) everywhere. This is a recipe that invites improv, so toss in whatever odds and ends you have—leftover vegetables, meat, chicken, etc.

3 tablespoons bacon drippings
or extra-virgin olive oil

½ pound boneless lamb shoulder or neck slices,
trimmed of excess fat and cut in 1-inch cubes

½ pound pepperoni, diced (the Portuguese would
use chouriço, one of their excellent sausages)

1 large Spanish onion, coarsely chopped

4 large garlic cloves, smashed and skins removed

1½ quarts (6 cups) water (about)

2 large whole bay leaves (preferably fresh)

1½ teaspoons salt, or to taste

½ teaspoon freshly ground black pepper,
or to taste

¼ cup coarsely chopped fresh mint
or Italian parsley or a 50/50 mix of the two

2 to 2½ cups ½-inch cubes
stale French or Italian bread

1. Heat drippings in a medium-size heavy Dutch oven over moderately high heat until ripples appear on pan bottom—1½ to 2 minutes.

2. Add lamb and pepperoni and stir-fry until lightly browned—5 to 8 minutes. Add onion and garlic and stir-fry until limp—about 5 minutes more.

3. Add water, bay leaves, salt, and pepper and bring to a boil. Adjust heat so mixture bubbles gently, cover, and simmer slowly until lamb is fork-tender—about 1½ hours. If at any time liquid seems skimpy, add a little more water, turn heat to lowest point, and if necessary, slide a diffuser underneath pot. Discard bay leaves, taste for salt and pepper, and adjust as needed.

4. Stir in mint, then 2 cups bread cubes—more if needed to give soup a porridge-y consistency.

5. Ladle into heated large soup plates and serve.

MAKES 6 SERVINGS

turkish wedding soup

This festive soup calls for a pound and a half of sinewy mutton and two pounds of beef marrow bones. I've substituted lamb because it's more widely available, also because few Americans like the gamy taste of mutton. Note: This is more stove-top than slow cooker soup because marrow bones throw a scum that must be skimmed off as it collects. Moreover, the double thickening process—first with a roux, then with egg yolks—is more easily done in a stock pot. Begin this soup one day and finish it the next. Tip: Though Turks traditionally make Wedding Soup with water, I like to enrich it by using a mixture of vegetable broth and water.

1½ pounds boneless lamb shoulder, trimmed of excess fat and quartered

¾ cup dry white wine such as Pinot Grigio, Riesling, even a spicy Gewürztraminer

2 pounds beef marrow bones, each cracked in several places

2 quarts (8 cups) vegetable broth plus 4 cups water (see Tip above)

2 large carrots, peeled and diced

1 large yellow onion, coarsely chopped

½ small cinnamon stick

¼ cup (½ stick) unsalted butter

½ cup unsifted all-purpose flour

3 large egg yolks, lightly beaten with ¼ cup fresh lemon juice

1 teaspoon salt, or to taste

3 tablespoons melted unsalted butter blended with 1 tablespoon sweet paprika (garnish)

1. Place lamb in a small nonreactive container, add wine, and toss well. Cover and refrigerate overnight.

2. When ready to proceed, place lamb and wine in a large nonreactive stock pot or heavy Dutch oven, add bones, broth, carrots, onion, and cinnamon, and bring to a boil over moderately high heat.

3. Adjust heat so liquid bubbles gently and simmer uncovered 1 hour, skimming frequently to remove scum as it rises to the top. Continue simmering very slowly, still uncovered, until meat falls from bones—2½ to 3 hours.

4. Pour all into a large sieve set over a large, heatproof, nonreactive bowl. Lift meat and bones to a cutting board, discard solids in sieve, and return strained stock to pot.

5. Cut lamb into julienne strips and return to pot along with marrow scooped from beef bones and any bits of meat stripped from them.

6. Melt butter in a small saucepan over moderate heat, blend in flour, and cook and stir until golden—about 2 minutes. Add 3 cups hot stock and cook, stirring constantly, until thickened and smooth—about 5 minutes. Stir back into pot.

7. Whisking egg-lemon mixture briskly, add salt along with 1½ cups hot soup liquid. Slide pot off heat and when it stops bubbling, blend in egg mixture, stirring all the while. Let stand 5 minutes, stirring often, taste for salt, and adjust as needed.

8. To serve, ladle into heated large soup plates and squiggle a little of the paprika-butter garnish decoratively into each portion.

MAKES 6 SERVINGS

lebanese two-kinds-of-lamb soup

Middle Eastern cooking has always intrigued me not only for the mysterious teaming of ingredients but also for the unusual techniques. A case in point, this soup, which I enjoyed in Beirut—not once but several times. Eager to make it, I scoured local bookstores for a book of Lebanese recipes and picked up a slim volume called *Art of Lebanese Cooking* by George N. Rayess, which—smallest of small worlds—was translated from Arabic into English by Najla Showker, the mother of my New York friend and fellow travel writer Kay Showker. The recipe here, adapted for American tastes and utensils, is a variation of one that appears in that book published nearly 50 years ago in Beirut. Note: Middle Easterners like the golden flavor of ghee or clarified butter (for directions on making ghee, see Butter in How to Use This Book, page xii). Unlike stick butter, it can be heated to fairly high temperatures without smoking. Tips: To quick-chill the broth, solidifying the fat so it's easy to lift off, pour into a shallow pan and set in the freezer for 30 to 45 minutes. For directions on cleaning leeks, see Leeks, How to Use This Book (page xiii).

2 pounds lamb riblets

2 quarts (8 cups) cold water (about)

2 teaspoons salt (about)

½ teaspoon black peppercorns

2 large leeks, washed, trimmed, and thinly sliced (see Tips above)

1 medium carrot, peeled and thickly sliced

1 medium celery rib, peeled and thickly sliced (include some leaves)

2 large whole bay leaves (preferably fresh)

2 tablespoons ghee (see Note above)

¾ pound ground lean lamb shoulder

1 small yellow onion, finely chopped

1 teaspoon sweet paprika

¼ teaspoon ground cinnamon

⅛ teaspoon ground hot red pepper (cayenne)

½ cup converted rice, cooked by package directions

½ cup coarsely chopped fresh Italian parsley

1. Bring first eight ingredients (riblets through bay leaves) to a boil in a large soup pot over high heat. Skim scum and froth from the surface as it accumulates and discard. Adjust heat so liquid bubbles gently, cover, and simmer until lamb is fall-off-the-bone tender—about 2 hours.

2. Lift riblets to a cutting board. Strain soup, reserving broth but discarding solids. Skim fat from broth (see Tips above) and set aside. Strip meat from riblets, cut in 2-inch pieces, and reserve. Discard bones.

3. Meanwhile, heat ghee in soup pot over moderately high heat until ripples appear on pan bottom—1½ to 2 minutes. Add ground lamb and onion and stir-fry until nicely browned—8 to 10 minutes. Blend in paprika, cinnamon, and cayenne and cook and stir 3 to 5 minutes to mellow flavors.

4. Return riblet meat to pot along with strained broth, add cooked rice, and if needed, a little more water for good soup consistency. Bring to serving temperature, mix in parsley, taste for salt, and adjust as needed.

5. Ladle into heated large soup plates and serve with Arabic flat bread or buttered triangles of toast.

MAKES 6 SERVINGS

great plains lamb and snap bean stew

I once drove from North Carolina to Santa Fe and toward the end of that two-and-a-half day trip along I-40, I pulled into a little mom 'n' pop gas station-cum-café. The special that day was a lamb stew chock full of potatoes and carrots (no surprise there) but freshly picked snap beans as well. To be honest, I was surprised that this wasn't a beef stew, lamb never having been very popular in these parts. With such an unusual addition I was soon scribbling notes.

3 pounds boneless lamb shoulder,
trimmed of excess fat and cut in 1-inch cubes

1 cup unsifted all-purpose flour
mixed with 1½ teaspoons salt and
½ teaspoon freshly ground black pepper
(seasoned flour)

¼ cup bacon drippings or vegetable oil
or a 50/50 mix of the two

2 medium yellow onions, coarsely chopped

2 large whole bay leaves (preferably fresh)

1 teaspoon crumbled dried leaf thyme

½ teaspoon crumbled dried leaf rosemary

2½ cups beef broth (about)

6 medium carrots, peeled and cut in 1-inch chunks

6 medium redskin potatoes, halved (no need to peel)

2 large celery ribs, thickly sliced

½ cup water

½ pound green beans,
tipped and snapped in 1-inch lengths

1. Dredge lamb, a few pieces at a time, by shaking in a large plastic zipper bag with seasoned flour and set aside.

2. Heat drippings in a large heavy Dutch oven over moderately high heat until ripples appear on pan bottom—1½ to 2 minutes. Brown dredged lamb in several batches in drippings, allowing about 10 minutes per batch and lifting each to a bowl as it browns.

3. Add onions, bay leaves, thyme, rosemary, and ⅔ cup broth to drippings and cook and stir, scraping up browned bits, until broth reduces to a rich brown glaze—about 5 minutes.

4. Return lamb to pot along with accumulated juices and add remaining broth. Adjust heat so liquid bubbles gently, cover, and simmer until lamb is nearly tender—1 to 1½ hours. Note: Check pot now and then and if liquid seems skimpy, add a little more broth, turn heat to its lowest point, and slide a diffuser underneath pot.

5. Add carrots, potatoes, celery, and water, cover, and simmer slowly until vegetables are nearly tender—35 to 40 minutes.

6. Add beans, pushing down into stew, cover, and cook until crisp-tender—20 to 25 minutes. Discard bay leaves, taste for salt and pepper, and adjust as needed.

7. Ladle into heated large soup plates and serve—nothing more needed to round out the meal except maybe a fruit dessert of some sort.

MAKES 6 SERVINGS

hassle-free oven stew of lamb with peppers and prosciutto

When I was growing up in the "small-town South," my Midwestern mother often served lamb to the horror of southern neighbors who wouldn't touch it. Pork and chicken were their meats of choice with more expensive beef a close third. At long last the South has embraced lamb. Even farmer's markets sell it, pampered organic lamb grazed on pesticide-and herbicide-free meadows. What I've done here is update one of my mother's hearty lamb stews for today's tastes. She'd be appalled by the amount of garlic, and to my knowledge, had never heard of prosciutto.

3 pounds boneless lamb shoulder,
trimmed of excess fat and cut in 1-inch cubes

1 cup unsifted all-purpose flour mixed with
1 tablespoon paprika, 1½ teaspoons salt,
and 1 teaspoon each freshly ground black pepper,
crumbled dried leaf rosemary and thyme
(seasoned flour)

¼ cup extra-virgin olive oil

3 ounces prosciutto, finely diced

2 large yellow onions, halved lengthwise
and each half cut in 2-inch wedges

2 large red bell peppers, halved lengthwise, cored,
seeded, and each half cut in 2-inch wedges

2 large yellow or orange bell peppers,
halved lengthwise, cored, seeded,
and each half cut in 2-inch wedges

8 large garlic cloves, smashed and skins removed

2 large whole bay leaves (preferably fresh)

2 cups dry red wine such as Valpolicella,
Merlot, or Cabernet (about)

1. Preheat oven to 350°F.

2. Dredge lamb, a few pieces at a time, by shaking in a large plastic zipper bag with seasoned flour and set aside.

3. Heat oil in a large heavy nonreactive Dutch oven over moderately high heat until ripples appear on pan bottom—1½ to 2 minutes.

4. Add prosciutto and stir-fry until lightly browned—2 to 3 minutes. Using a slotted spoon, scoop to paper toweling to drain.

5. Brown dredged lamb in several batches in oil, allowing 8 to 10 minutes per batch and lifting each to a bowl as it browns.

6. Add onions, red and yellow bell peppers, garlic, and bay leaves to pot and sauté, stirring often, until limp—about 5 minutes. Return prosciutto and lamb to pot along with accumulated juices, add wine, and bring to a boil.

7. Cover, slide onto middle oven shelf, and braise until lamb is fork-tender—about 2 hours. Check pot now and then and if liquid seems skimpy, add a little more wine. Discard bay leaves, taste for salt and pepper, and adjust as needed.

8. Serve hot with boiled brown or white rice, buttered broad noodles, or boiled or mashed potatoes. I even like this stew ladled over baked sweet potatoes, halved and plumped.

MAKES 6 SERVINGS

wine-and-tomato-braised lamb with fresh basil

Mint and lamb are one of those magical combos, but basil and lamb? Why not? Basil is an important member of the mint family, but until the surge of interest in all things Italian, few of us had ever tasted fresh basil. Twenty, even ten years ago, most of us had to grow our own if we wanted to make pesto or so many other Italian recipes calling for gobs of fresh basil. Today every supermarket carries bouquets of it and farmer's markets sell several varieties to transplant in kitchen gardens. Come May, I fill my backyard planter bed with bush basil, opal basil, and the more popular big green-leafed variety. Fortunately the white-tail deer who devour my hostas have shown little appetite for basil. So far.

3 tablespoons extra-virgin olive oil

3 pounds boneless lamb shoulder, trimmed of excess fat and cut in 1½-inch cubes

2 large yellow onions, coarsely chopped

2 large garlic cloves, finely chopped

1 cup coarsely chopped fresh basil

1 tablespoon finely chopped fresh marjoram or 1 teaspoon crumbled dried leaf marjoram

1 cup canned diced tomatoes, with their liquid

¾ cup dry white wine such as a Pinot Grigio, Sauvignon Blanc, or Chardonnay (about)

1 teaspoon salt, or to taste

½ teaspoon freshly ground black pepper, or to taste

1. Heat oil in a large heavy nonreactive Dutch oven over high heat until ripples appear on pan bottom—about 1½ minutes.

2. Brown lamb nicely in three batches in oil, allowing about 10 minutes per batch and lifting each to a bowl as it browns.

3. Add onions to drippings and cook, stirring often, until limp and lightly browned—8 to 10 minutes. Add garlic, half the basil, and all marjoram and cook and stir 2 minutes.

4. Return lamb to pot along with accumulated juices and add tomatoes, wine, salt, and pepper. Adjust heat so mixture barely bubbles, cover, and braise slowly until lamb is fork-tender—1½ to 2 hours. Stir occasionally and if liquid seems skimpy, add a little water or more wine, turn heat to its lowest point and, if necessary, slide a diffuser underneath pot.

5. Mix in remaining basil, taste for salt and pepper, and adjust as needed.

6. Serve with boiled rice or potatoes, preferably redskins, creamers, or Yukon golds roasted in their skins.

MAKES 6 SERVINGS

spicy lamb hot pot with juniper

Though it's used to make gin, juniper isn't a flavoring most of us know. And yet these resinous berries are especially complementary to lamb and game. You'll find little jars of juniper berries among the spices at most supermarkets and failing that, at boutique groceries or online (see Sources, page 243). I like this stew equally well with boiled potatoes, rice, or hot buttered noodles.

3 tablespoons vegetable oil

3 pounds boneless lamb shoulder,
trimmed of excess fat and cut in 1½-inch cubes

2 large yellow onions, coarsely chopped

4 large garlic cloves, smashed and skins removed

8 juniper berries, bruised and tied in cheesecloth
with 12 black peppercorns, 2 large whole bay leaves
(preferably fresh), a 2-inch strip orange zest,
and 2 whole allspice (spice bag)

4 medium carrots, peeled and thinly sliced

1 can (14½ ounces) diced tomatoes,
with their liquid

1 cup beef or chicken broth (about)

½ cup dry white wine such as Pinot Grigio
or Sauvignon Blanc

1 teaspoon salt, or to taste

1. Heat oil in a large heavy nonreactive Dutch oven over high heat until ripples appear on pan bottom—about 1½ minutes.

2. Brown lamb nicely in three batches in oil, allowing about 10 minutes per batch and lifting each to a bowl as it browns.

3. Add onions to drippings and cook, stirring often, until limp and lightly browned—8 to 10 minutes. Add garlic and spice bag and cook and stir 2 minutes.

4. Return lamb to pot along with accumulated juices and add all remaining ingredients. Adjust heat so mixture barely bubbles, cover, and simmer slowly until lamb is fork-tender—1½ to 2 hours. Stir occasionally and if liquid seems skimpy, add a little water or more broth, turn heat to its lowest point and, if necessary, slide a diffuser underneath pot.

5. Discard spice bag, taste for salt, and adjust as needed.

6. Dish up and serve.

MAKES 6 SERVINGS

old-fashioned irish stew

An easy-on-the-budget, easy-on-the-cook stew made with bargain-priced lamb neck slices. It's a layered affair with plenty of potatoes and onions and once everything's in the pot, you can pretty much go about your business. Fancier Irish stews call for carrots and I've made these optional. Note: An overnight in the refrigerator not only improves the flavor of this stew but also makes it easy to remove the layer of fat on top.

8 medium-small all-purpose potatoes, peeled and halved

4 pounds bone-in lamb neck slices, trimmed of excess fat

4 large yellow onions, halved lengthwise and each half thinly sliced

6 medium carrots, peeled and thinly sliced (optional)

1½ teaspoons salt, or to taste

½ teaspoon freshly ground black pepper, or to taste

1½ quarts (6 cups) water

¼ cup coarsely chopped fresh Italian parsley

1. Beginning and ending with potatoes, layer potatoes, lamb, onions, and if desired, carrots into a large heavy Dutch oven with a snug lid. Sprinkle with salt and pepper as you layer.

2. Add water and bring to a boil. Adjust heat so liquid barely bubbles (or "smiles," the Irish say), cover tightly, and simmer slowly until meat is fall-off-the-bone tender—about 2 hours. Note: If you can't keep stew at a gentle simmer, turn heat to its lowest point and slide a diffuser underneath pot.

3. Cool stew to room temperature in covered pot, then refrigerate overnight.

4. When ready to proceed, skim fat from surface of stew and discard. Set Dutch oven over moderately low heat and bring stew just to serving temperature—15 to 20 minutes. Mix in parsley, taste for salt and pepper, and adjust as needed.

5. Ladle stew into heated large soup plates, making sure that everyone gets plenty of meat, vegetables, and broth. Note: Tell people there are bones in this soup so they'll proceed with caution.

MAKES 6 SERVINGS

navarin of lamb

So brimming with vegetables it needs no "sides," this French stew is a one-dish meal both colorful and nourishing. Though the vegetables may vary from season to season, classic recipes always call for whole small onions and potatoes, baby carrots, and green peas. And here's a surprise: this French stew contains no wine. Note: Baby carrots are in truth misshapen "adults" pared down and reshaped. I don't eat them raw (there have been recalls over the years because of bacterial contamination). But if baby carrots look crisp and fresh, they're fine for long-simmering stews and needless to add, valuable time-savers. Tip: If you blanch silverskin onions 20 to 30 seconds in boiling water, the skins will slip right off.

3 tablespoons unsalted butter

2½ pounds boneless lamb shoulder, trimmed of excess fat and cut in 1-inch cubes

2 large garlic cloves, finely chopped

3 tablespoons all-purpose flour

3 cups chicken broth

1 can (8 ounces) tomato sauce

1 tablespoon sugar or raw sugar

1 teaspoon salt, or to taste

½ teaspoon freshly ground black pepper, or to taste

2 large whole bay leaves (preferably fresh) tied in cheesecloth with 2 medium sprigs each fresh Italian parsley and thyme (bouquet garni)

12 whole silverskins (small white onions), peeled (see Tip above)

12 golf-ball-size redskin potatoes, peeled

½ pound peeled baby carrots (see Note above)

1 package (10 ounces) frozen baby green peas, thawed and drained

1. Preheat oven to 325°F.

2. Melt butter in a large heavy nonreactive Dutch oven over moderately high heat and as soon as it froths and subsides, brown lamb in batches, allowing 8 to 10 minutes per batch and lifting each to a bowl as it browns.

3. Add garlic to drippings and sauté, stirring often, until limp and golden—2 to 3 minutes. Blend in flour, and cook and stir 2 minutes. Whisk in broth, tomato sauce, sugar, salt, and pepper and cook, whisking constantly, until lightly thickened—3 to 5 minutes.

4. Return lamb to pot along with accumulated juices and drop in bouquet garni, wringing to release flavors. Cover, slide onto middle oven shelf, and bake until lamb begins to turn tender—45 minutes to 1 hour.

5. Add onions, pushing down into gravy, cover, and bake 15 minutes. Add potatoes and carrots, push into gravy, cover, and bake until tender—about 30 minutes more.

6. Mix in peas, cover, and bake 5 to 8 minutes more. Remove bouquet garni, taste for salt and pepper, and adjust as needed.

7. Serve at once (I do it at table straight from the Dutch oven) and accompany with a good yeasty country bread to sop up the gravy.

MAKES 6 SERVINGS

crofter's lamb and potato pie

What's a crofter? A Scottish farmer who works the land for a laird (titled gentry) or who may own his own croft (small farm). This humble recipe is popular in the Highlands where lamb is preferred to beef. The trick here is to cook the lamb until tender without burning the pie crust—something practiced cooks know how to do. Note: In Scotland, the crust would be made from scratch and shortened with lard or suet. To short-cut prep time, I've substituted a prepared unroll-and-bake pie crust (you'll find it at your supermarket near the refrigerated biscuits).

1½ pounds boneless lamb shoulder, trimmed of excess fat and cut in ¾-inch cubes

6 tablespoons unsifted all-purpose flour

¼ cup coarsely chopped fresh Italian parsley

1½ teaspoons salt

1 teaspoon crumbled dried leaf thyme

½ teaspoon freshly ground pepper

6 medium redskin potatoes, sliced ½ inch thick (peeled or unpeeled)

2 medium yellow onions, halved lengthwise and each half thinly sliced

1⅔ cups hot beef or chicken broth

One 9-inch unroll-and-bake pie crust (from a 15-ounce package; see Note above)

1. Preheat oven to 425°F.

2. Toss lamb with flour in an ungreased round 3-quart casserole or soufflé dish, then arrange in a single layer. Sprinkle with some of the parsley, salt, thyme, and pepper. Layer potatoes, then onions on top, sprinkling with remaining parsley, salt, thyme, and pepper as you layer. Pour hot broth evenly over all.

3. Ease pie crust into place, centering over ingredients. Roll overhang underneath onto rim that has been moistened with cold water and crimp, making a fluted edge. With a sharp knife, cut several decorative steam vents near center of crust.

4. Set casserole on a rimmed baking sheet, slide into lower third of oven, and bake 15 minutes. Reduce oven temperature to 350°F, place a sheet of foil over the crust, and bake until lamb is fork-tender—1 to 1¼ hours longer. To test, poke metal skewer through a steam vent; it should pierce meat easily.

5. Serve at table, making sure each person gets plenty of meat, potatoes, pie crust, and gravy.

MAKES 6 SERVINGS

andalusian shepherd's stew

This rib-sticking lamb, potato, and artichoke stew, like so many other Spanish recipes, owes its distinctive flavor to pimentón, a dark smoky paprika developed centuries ago, it's said, by monks in the La Vera valley of Extramadura. The best pimentón comes from that same valley where paprika is grown along the Tietar River, harvested in autumn, and smoke-dried over hardwood coals (usually oak). You can buy pimentón here at high-end groceries or order it online (see Sources, page 243).

1 thick slice country bread
(boule, baguette, or ciabatta, etc.),
liberally brushed with olive oil and lightly toasted
(3 to 4 minutes per side in a 350°F oven)

3 cups water (about)

3 whole large garlic cloves, peeled

1½ teaspoons pimentón (see headnote)

1½ teaspoons salt, or to taste

½ teaspoon freshly ground black pepper,
or to taste

½ teaspoon crumbled dried leaf thyme

8 tablespoons extra-virgin olive oil

2½ pounds boneless lamb shoulder,
trimmed of excess fat and cut in 1½-inch cubes

2 medium onions, coarsely chopped

1½ cups dry red wine such as a Spanish Rioja

6 golf-ball-size redskin potatoes,
scrubbed but not peeled

1 package (9 ounces) frozen artichoke hearts,
thawed and drained

3 tablespoons coarsely chopped fresh mint
or Italian parsley

1. Purée toasted bread with 1 cup water, garlic, pimentón, salt, pepper, thyme, and 2 tablespoons olive oil in a food processor or electric blender at high speed and set aside.

2. Heat 2 tablespoons remaining oil in a large heavy nonreactive Dutch oven over high heat until ripples appear on pan bottom—about 1½ minutes.

3. Add half the lamb and sauté, turning frequently, until richly browned—8 to 10 minutes; lift to a plate and reserve. Heat another 2 tablespoons oil in Dutch oven, brown remaining lamb the same way, and add to plate.

4. Add final 2 tablespoons oil and onions to Dutch oven and cook, stirring now and then, until lightly browned—5 to 8 minutes.

5. Return lamb to pot along with accumulated juices, mix in reserved purée, wine, and remaining water, and bring to a boil. Adjust heat so mixture bubbles gently, cover, and cook, stirring occasionally, until lamb is nearly tender—1 to 1½ hours. Note: Check pot occasionally and if liquid seems skimpy, add a little more water, turn heat to lowest point, and if necessary, slide a diffuser underneath pot.

6. Add potatoes, cover, and cook, stirring occasionally, 30 minutes. Add artichoke hearts, cover, and continue cooking until lamb and potatoes are tender—15 to 20 minutes more. Taste for salt and pepper and adjust as needed.

7. To serve, ladle into heated large soup plates and scatter a little mint over each portion.

MAKES 6 SERVINGS

alentejo lamb stew with country bread

Alentejo, that vast "bread basket" east of Lisbon, is for me the most Portuguese of Portuguese provinces, a land of shepherds whittling wooden spoons while their sheep peacefully graze, of wheat fields and Van Gogh-ish sunflowers, of onions and garlic and tomatoes as big as grapefruits. There are miles of olive groves here, too, along with cork orchards sweeping beyond the horizon. If pork is king in Alentejo, lamb is surely queen. This peppery stew (*Ensopado de Borrego*) is an Alentejo specialty that's ladled over *pão* (the yeasty country bread for which Portugal is famous). The best substitute? A rustic round French or Italian loaf with slices big enough to cover (or almost) the bottom of a soup plate—*boule*, for example, or *ciabatta*, both widely available here. Note: I've significantly reduced the amount of lard in the recipe and offer bacon drippings as a substitute.

3 pounds boneless lamb shoulder,
trimmed of excess fat and cut in 1½-inch cubes

½ cup unsifted all-purpose flour

6 tablespoons lard (hog lard) or bacon drippings
(see Note above)

2 large yellow onions,
halved lengthwise and each half thinly sliced

4 large garlic cloves, coarsely chopped

1 tablespoon sweet paprika

½ tablespoon black peppercorns

1 teaspoon salt, or to taste

¼ to ½ teaspoon chili flakes
(crushed dried hot red peppers),
depending on how "hot" you like things

1 large whole bay leaf (preferably fresh)

5 cups (1 quart plus 1 cup) water (about)

6 large slices rustic country bread,
each about ½ inch thick (see headnote)

1. Dredge lamb in three batches in flour by shaking in a large plastic zipper bag and set aside.

2. Melt 4 tablespoons lard in a large heavy Dutch oven over high heat until ripples appear on pan bottom—about 1½ minutes.

3. Brown lamb in two batches in lard, making sure all sides are nicely colored, allowing 8 to 10 minutes per batch and lifting each to a bowl as it browns.

4. Add remaining lard to Dutch oven and when it melts, add next seven ingredients (onions through bay leaf) and sauté over moderately high heat until golden brown—8 to 10 minutes.

5. Return lamb to pot along with accumulated juices, add water, and bring to a boil. Adjust heat so stew bubbles gently, cover, and simmer until lamb is tender—about 2 hours. Discard bay leaf, taste for salt, and adjust as needed. Note: Check pot occasionally as stew simmers, and if liquid seems skimpy, add a little more water, turn heat as low as it will go, and if necessary, slide a diffuser underneath the pot.

6. To serve, place a slice of bread in each of six heated large soup plates and cover generously with stew.

MAKES 6 SERVINGS

serra da estrêla lamb stew

Those who've never visited Portugal are surprised to hear how mountainous this little country is, that there are ski resorts in the Serra da Estrêla or "Mountains of the Star." Dramatic country this, with lichened boulders as big as buses, skinny roads scaling precipitous cliffs, and wild herbs carpeting sky-high meadows. Sheep graze these meadows and their milk goes into Portugal's "Queen of Cheeses"—*Queijo da Serra*, to my mind finer than any Brie or Camembert. Once those ewes go "dry," they're eaten as mutton. A tad gamy for most Americans; moreover, mutton isn't readily available. So I've substituted lamb in this rich brown stew.

3 pounds boneless lamb shoulder, trimmed of excess fat and cut in 1½-inch cubes

1 cup unsifted all-purpose flour mixed with 1 tablespoon sweet paprika, 1½ teaspoons salt, and ½ teaspoon each ground hot red pepper (cayenne) and freshly ground black pepper (seasoned flour)

¼ cup extra-virgin olive oil

3 medium yellow onions, coarsely chopped

1 medium red bell pepper, cored, seeded, and coarsely chopped

1 large carrot, peeled and coarsely chopped

3 large garlic cloves, smashed and skins removed

1 tablespoon sweet paprika

1 tablespoon coarsely chopped fresh thyme or 1 teaspoon crumbled dried leaf thyme

¼ teaspoon ground cumin

2 large whole bay leaves (preferably fresh)

¼ cup diced lean smoked bacon

2 cups beef or chicken broth

1½ cups dry red Portuguese wine (*tinto*), such as a Bairrada, Dão, or Douro

1. Dredge lamb, a few pieces at a time, by shaking in a large plastic zipper bag with seasoned flour and set aside.

2. Heat oil in a large heavy nonreactive Dutch oven over moderately high heat until ripples appear on pan bottom—1½ to 2 minutes. Brown dredged lamb in several batches in oil, allowing 8 to 10 minutes per batch and lifting each to a bowl as it browns.

3. Add next seven ingredients (onions through cumin) to drippings and sauté, stirring often, until limp and touched with brown—10 to 12 minutes.

4. Return lamb to pot along with accumulated juices, add remaining ingredients, and bring to a boil. Adjust heat so stew barely bubbles, cover, and simmer slowly until lamb is very tender—about 2 hours. Discard bay leaves, taste for salt and pepper, and adjust as needed.

5. Serve with boiled rice or potatoes. Portuguese *tascas* (bistros) often serve both plus chunks of country bread. No carb hysteria here.

MAKES 6 SERVINGS

ragout of lamb with roasted cipollini onions

An unusually fragrant stew that cooks virtually unattended in a moderate oven. I like to garnish with clusters of cipollini onions, which can roast alongside the stew in a separate pan. Note: Cipollini are golf-ball-size Italian onions, more flat than round, and exquisitely sweet. Look for them in high-end groceries—where I live they're sold in net bags.

3 pounds boneless lamb shoulder, trimmed of excess fat and cut in 1-inch cubes

1 cup unsifted all-purpose flour mixed with 1 tablespoon sweet paprika, 1½ teaspoons salt, and ½ teaspoon freshly ground black pepper (seasoned flour)

¼ cup extra-virgin olive oil

2 large garlic cloves, finely chopped

1 tablespoon finely minced fresh marjoram or 1 teaspoon crumbled dried leaf marjoram

½ teaspoon crumbled dried leaf savory

1½ cups chicken broth (about)

½ cup dry white wine such as Riesling or Pinot Grigio

8 whole small cipollini onions, peeled and turned in 1 tablespoon extra-virgin olive oil

2 tablespoons coarsely chopped fresh Italian parsley

1 tablespoon fresh lemon juice

½ teaspoon finely grated lemon zest

1. Preheat oven to 350°F.

2. Dredge lamb, a few pieces at a time, by shaking in a large plastic zipper bag with seasoned flour and set aside.

3. Heat oil in a large heavy nonreactive Dutch oven over moderately high heat until ripples appear on pan bottom—1½ to 2 minutes. Brown lamb in several batches in oil, allowing about 10 minutes per batch and lifting each to a bowl as it browns.

4. Return lamb to pot along with accumulated juices and add garlic, marjoram, savory, broth, and wine. Cover, slide onto middle oven shelf, and braise 1 hour. Check pot and if ragout seems dry, mix in a little more chicken broth.

5. Arrange onions in single layer in a small shallow pan, slide into oven alongside Dutch oven, and roast uncovered until nicely browned and crisp-tender—about 20 minutes. Remove from oven, cover loosely with foil, and keep warm.

6. Continue braising lamb until fork-tender and pan liquid is the consistency of gravy—about 20 minutes. Note: If ragout is soupy, set Dutch oven over direct moderate heat and boil uncovered until liquid is as thick as gravy.

7. Mix in parsley, lemon juice and zest. Taste for salt and pepper and adjust as needed.

8. To serve, ladle ragout into a heated large deep platter and cluster onions around edge in groups of two and three. Accompany with buttered broad noodles, or boiled or mashed potatoes.

MAKES 6 SERVINGS

tuscan ragout of lamb with polenta

This robust ragout calls for less lamb than most stews because it's ladled over buttery polenta and sprinkled with freshly grated Parmigiano Reggiano—both rich and filling. Also unlike most stews, this one simmers uncovered so that the juices cook down into a thin but flavorful sauce and that explains the longer cooking time. Note: Canned crushed tomatoes are increasingly hard to find; to approximate their texture, pulse canned diced tomatoes with their liquid in a food processor until uniformly lumpy. Easy does it. You don't want tomato purée.

3 tablespoons extra-virgin olive oil

2 pounds boneless lamb shoulder,
trimmed of excess fat and cut in 1-inch cubes

1 large yellow onion, coarsely chopped

4 large garlic cloves, smashed and skins removed

1 tablespoon finely chopped fresh thyme
(preferably lemon thyme) or 1 teaspoon crumbled
dried leaf thyme

1 tablespoon finely chopped fresh rosemary
or 1 teaspoon crumbled dried leaf rosemary

¼ teaspoon freshly grated nutmeg

3 cups dry red Italian wine such as Valpolicella,
Bardolino, or affordable Barolo (if you can find it)

1 can (14½ ounces) crushed tomatoes,
with their liquid (see Note above)

1 teaspoon salt, or to taste

½ teaspoon freshly ground black pepper, or to taste

1½ cups polenta, cooked by package directions
until creamy, then mixed with
2 tablespoons unsalted butter

⅔ cup freshly grated Parmigiano Reggiano

1. Heat oil in a medium-size heavy nonreactive Dutch oven over moderately high heat until ripples appear on pan bottom—1½ to 2 minutes.

2. Brown lamb in two batches in oil, allowing 8 to 10 minutes per batch and lifting each to a bowl as it browns.

3. Add onion, garlic, thyme, rosemary, and nutmeg to drippings and cook, stirring often, until limp and lightly browned—8 to 10 minutes.

4. Return lamb to pot along with accumulated juices and add wine, tomatoes, salt, and pepper. Turn heat to lowest point and simmer uncovered—very slowly—until lamb is tender and pan liquid has reduced significantly—about 2½ hours. Stir occasionally and if liquid is reducing too fast—it shouldn't if you keep the flame low enough—add a little water and slide a diffuser underneath pot. Lamb should be succulently tender and liquid the consistency of rich broth.

5. Taste for salt and pepper and adjust as needed.

6. To serve, scoop polenta into heated large soup plates, ladle ragout on top, and sprinkle generously with Parmigiano Reggiano.

MAKES 6 SERVINGS

flavors-of-the-east sicilian lamb bake

I once spent two weeks poking about the back roads of Sicily, moving from populous Palermo and Siracusa and Taormina to mountainous vineyards and meadows where sheep grazed among tumbled columns. The Greek and Roman temples were the reason I'd come to Sicily, but I was eager, too, to taste what was cooking. I'd expected tomato-sauced pastas mostly, but was pleased to discover a complex cuisine impacted by Greeks, Romans, Visigoths, Normans, Saracens, and others who'd once occupied this epic island. The Saracen (Arab) influence seemed especially strong—the teaming of sweets (in this case raisins) with meat, fish, and fowl plus a light hand with spices we associate with the East, turmeric and cinnamon to name two. This recipe is one I created shortly after returning home to New York. It's a fix-and-forget oven stew, a good dinner party choice because it frees you to focus on the rest of the meal. Moreover, it can be made a day or two in advance and reheated just before serving.

3 tablespoons extra-virgin olive oil

3 pounds boneless lamb shoulder, trimmed of excess fat and cut in 1-inch cubes

3 medium yellow onions, coarsely chopped

4 large garlic cloves, smashed and skins removed

1 teaspoon crumbled dried leaf oregano

¾ teaspoon crumbled dried leaf thyme

¾ teaspoon chili flakes (crushed dried hot red chili peppers)

½ teaspoon ground turmeric

¼ teaspoon ground cinnamon

1 can (14½ ounces) diced tomatoes, with their liquid

1 cup raisins plumped in ½ cup each chicken broth and sweet marsala or ruby port

1½ teaspoons salt, or to taste

¼ cup coarsely chopped fresh Italian parsley

2 cups converted rice, cooked by package directions

1 cup lightly toasted slivered almonds (about 10 minutes in a 350°F oven)

1. Preheat oven to 350°F.

2. Heat oil in a large heavy nonreactive Dutch oven over high heat until ripples appear on pan bottom—about 1½ minutes.

3. Brown lamb in three batches in oil, allowing 8 to 10 minutes per batch and lifting each to a bowl as it browns.

4. Add next seven ingredients (onions through cinnamon) to drippings and cook, stirring often, until limp and lightly browned—8 to 10 minutes.

5. Return browned lamb to pot along with accumulated juices, add tomatoes, plumped raisins (including soaking liquid), and salt, and bring to boil over moderately high heat.

6. Cover, slide onto middle oven shelf, and braise until lamb is fork-tender—about 2 hours. Mix in parsley, taste for salt, and adjust as needed.

7. To serve, mound rice on a heated large deep platter, ladle stew on top, and scatter with toasted almonds.

MAKES 6 SERVINGS

taverna lamb and kalamata stew

Many, many years ago, after touring the ruins and reconstructed portions of King Minos's palace at Knossos on the north shore of Crete, a friend and I paused at a tiny taverna (café) for lunch. Unable to read Greek, we simply pointed to items chalked on a slate and before long, a steaming bowl of stew was set before me. I savored it slowly, trying to ID the ingredients—lamb or goat (probably shoulder) . . . onions and garlic . . . plump, deeply flavorful Kalamata olives . . . maybe rosemary . . . and definitely wine. Note: I suspect that the wine in that long-ago stew was retsina, the resinated Greek wine that tastes of pine pitch. For those who don't like retsina, here are two excellent alternatives for this lamb stew: Pinot Grigio or the buttery Portuguese Catarina.

3 pounds boneless lamb shoulder, trimmed of excess fat and cut in 1-inch cubes

1 cup unsifted all-purpose flour mixed with 1½ teaspoons salt and ½ teaspoon freshly ground black pepper (seasoned flour)

¼ cup extra-virgin olive oil

2 medium yellow onions, coarsely chopped

2 large garlic cloves, smashed and skins removed

2 large whole bay leaves (preferably fresh)

1 teaspoon finely minced fresh rosemary or ½ teaspoon crumbled dried leaf rosemary

½ teaspoon finely minced fresh thyme or ¼ teaspoon crumbled dried leaf thyme

1 cup coarsely chopped, pitted, oil-cured Kalamata olives, well drained

1 cup Greek retsina or other dry white wine (see Note above)

1 cup beef or chicken broth (about)

1. Dredge lamb, a few pieces at a time, by shaking in a large plastic zipper bag with seasoned flour and set aside.

2. Heat oil in a large heavy nonreactive Dutch oven over moderately high heat until ripples appear on pan bottom—1½ to 2 minutes. Brown dredged lamb in several batches in oil, allowing about 10 minutes per batch and lifting each to a bowl as it browns.

3. Add onions, garlic, bay leaves, rosemary, and thyme to drippings and sauté, stirring often, until limp and lightly browned—8 to 10 minutes.

4. Return lamb to pot along with accumulated juices, add olives, wine, and broth, and bring to a boil. Adjust heat so stew bubbles gently, cover, and simmer until lamb is fork-tender—1½ to 2 hours. Note: Check pot now and then and if liquid is skimpy, add a little more broth, turn heat to its lowest point, and slide a diffuser underneath pot. Discard bay leaves, taste for salt and pepper, and adjust as needed.

5. Serve hot with boiled potatoes or rice (in that tiny Cretan taverna, I got both, and exhausted as I was from clambering over acres of Stone- and Bronze-Age ruins under a down-pouring sun, I welcomed that carb spurt of energy).

MAKES 6 SERVINGS

greek lamb, green bean, and tomato stew

Here's another popular Greek stew, this one reworked for the slow cooker. This recipe, or rather one similar to it, is the specialty of an inexpensive restaurant across the street from the National Archaeological Museum in downtown Athens. But I've eaten variations of it all over Greece.

3 pounds boneless lamb shoulder, trimmed of excess fat and cut in 1½-inch cubes

3 tablespoons extra-virgin olive oil

1½ teaspoons salt, or to taste

¼ teaspoon freshly ground black pepper, or to taste

2 large celery ribs, trimmed and coarsely chopped (include some leaves)

1 large yellow onion, coarsely chopped

2 large garlic cloves, coarsely chopped

¼ cup coarsely chopped fresh Italian parsley

2 tablespoons coarsely chopped fresh mint

1 cup vegetable broth

1 can (8 ounces) tomato sauce

2 packages (9 ounces each) frozen cut (*not French-cut*) green beans, thawed and drained well

1. Drizzle lamb cubes with 1 tablespoon oil, toss well, and arrange around edge of a large (4- to 6-quart) slow cooker, then sprinkle with salt and pepper.

2. Pour remaining oil into middle of cooker, add celery, onion, garlic, parsley, and mint, and toss well without disturbing lamb. Add broth, cover, and cook on HIGH 1 hour.

3. Add tomato sauce and beans, mixing well with other ingredients. Cover and cook on LOW 4 hours or until lamb is tender and flavors marry.

4. Taste for salt and pepper, adjust as needed, and serve with boiled potatoes.

MAKES 6 SERVINGS

lemony lamb stew with mint and artichoke hearts

This stew, more than most, profits from a night in the fridge because the sharp lemony flavor mellows. The big sweet onions help temper the tartness, too. Note: The mint to use here is peppermint—the crisp leafy herb that goes into mint sauce. Do not substitute spearmint.

3 tablespoons extra-virgin olive oil

3 pounds boneless lamb shoulder, trimmed of excess fat and cut in 1½-inch cubes

2 large Spanish onions (about 2 pounds), halved lengthwise and each half thinly sliced

8 large garlic cloves, smashed and skins removed

2 large whole bay leaves (preferably fresh)

2 teaspoons crumbled dried leaf oregano

1½ teaspoons finely grated lemon zest

1 cup beef or chicken broth (about)

2 tablespoons fresh lemon juice

1 teaspoon salt, or to taste

½ teaspoon freshly ground black pepper, or to taste

2 packages (9 ounces each) frozen artichoke hearts, thawed and drained

¼ cup unsifted all-purpose flour blended with ¼ cup cold water (thickener)

⅓ cup coarsely chopped fresh mint (see Note above)

1. Heat oil in a large heavy nonreactive Dutch oven over high heat until ripples appear on pan bottom—about 1½ minutes.

2. Brown lamb lightly in three batches in oil, allowing 6 to 8 minutes per batch and lifting each to a bowl as it browns.

3. Add onions to drippings and cook, stirring often, until limp and lightly browned—8 to 10 minutes. Add garlic, bay leaves, oregano, and lemon zest and cook and stir 2 minutes.

4. Return lamb to pot along with accumulated juices and add broth, lemon juice, salt, and pepper. Adjust heat so mixture barely bubbles, cover, and simmer until lamb is fork-tender—1½ to 2 hours. Stir occasionally and if liquid seems skimpy, add a little more broth, turn heat to its lowest point and, if necessary, slide a diffuser underneath pot.

5. Mix in artichoke hearts, cover, and simmer 15 minutes. Discard bay leaves, taste for salt and pepper, and adjust as needed.

6. Blend a little hot stew liquid into thickener, stir back into pot, and cook, stirring often, until thickened and no raw floury taste lingers—about 5 minutes.

7. Stir in mint and serve with small redskin or Yukon gold potatoes, roasted or boiled in their jackets.

MAKES 6 SERVINGS

aegean lamb and fennel stew

Throughout Greece and the Aegean Islands, lamb is the meat of choice though much of it is tough because sheep scramble up and down ragged slopes to graze. This is my re-creation of a stew I ate at a taverna near Crete's Plains of Lisithi, where a friend and I had searched all morning for Dikti, the mountain cave where the god Zeus is said to have hidden from Chronos, his murderous father. With a frosty bottle of ΦΙΧ (a light Greek beer we took to pronouncing FIX), it was just what I needed. I never found the legendary cave, but more important, I came away with scribbled notes for this unusual lamb stew. The recipe here is adjusted for the slow cooker.

3 pounds boneless lamb shoulder, trimmed of excess fat and cut in 1½-inch cubes

3 tablespoons extra-virgin olive oil

2 to 4 tablespoons fresh lemon juice (depending on how tart you like things)

1½ teaspoons salt, or to taste

¼ teaspoon freshly ground black pepper, or to taste

12 large scallions, trimmed, washed, and coarsely chopped (include some green tops)

2 large garlic cloves, coarsely chopped

¼ cup freshly snipped dill or 1 teaspoon dill weed

¼ cup coarsely chopped fresh Italian parsley

1 cup vegetable broth blended with 1 tablespoon tomato paste

1 large fennel bulb (about 1¼ pounds), trimmed, cored, and sliced ¼ inch thick

1 cup plain whole-milk Greek yogurt, at room temperature

1. Preheat broiler. Place lamb cubes on a foil-lined large, rimmed baking sheet, drizzle with 1 tablespoon oil, toss, then spread in a single layer. Broil 5 inches from heat until nicely browned—about 5 minutes.

2. Arrange lamb and accumulated juices around edge of a large (4- to 6-quart) slow cooker, drizzle with lemon juice, then sprinkle with salt and pepper.

3. Pour remaining oil into middle of cooker, add scallions, garlic, dill, and parsley, and toss well without disturbing lamb. Add broth mixture, cover, and cook on HIGH 1 hour.

4. Add fennel, mixing well with other ingredients. Cover and cook on LOW 4 hours or until lamb is tender and flavors marry.

5. Blend in yogurt, taste for salt and pepper, and adjust as needed.

6. Serve with boiled rice or potatoes.

MAKES 6 SERVINGS

turkish lamb with yogurt and cucumbers on pita bread

I remember ordering a dish much like this while in Izmir working on the *Convention Daily*, a newspaper published during an ASTA (American Society of Travel Agents) International Congress. Based in the Buyuk Efes, a surprisingly luxurious hotel run by the Turkish government, we worked all day in balconied rooms overlooking acres of gardens, then strolled over to dine in little waterfront restaurants with views across the Aegean to the not-so-distant Greek island of Kos. I never had a bad meal, and from that day on, have doted on Turkish food. Our hotel, now the Grand Efes under Swiss management, seems grander than ever.

¾ cup firmly packed plain yogurt, preferably Greek yogurt (not reduced fat)

¼ cup extra-virgin olive oil

3 tablespoons finely grated yellow onion

4 large garlic cloves, crushed

1½ tablespoons fresh lemon juice

1½ tablespoons finely chopped fresh thyme (preferably lemon thyme)

1 teaspoon salt

½ teaspoon freshly ground black pepper

2 pounds boned lamb shoulder, trimmed of excess fat and cut in ½-inch cubes

1 cup chicken broth blended with 2 tablespoons all-purpose flour (thickener)

6 pita breads (each about 7 inches across)

SAUCE

2 medium-large Kirby (pickling) cucumbers, peeled, halved lengthwise, seeded, and thinly sliced

1 teaspoon salt

1½ cups firmly packed plain yogurt, preferably Greek yogurt (not reduced fat)

1 teaspoon finely chopped fresh thyme (preferably lemon thyme)

¼ teaspoon freshly ground black pepper

1. Combine yogurt and next seven ingredients (oil through pepper) in a large nonreactive bowl. Add lamb, toss well, cover, and refrigerate several hours or overnight, turning now and again in marinade. When ready to proceed, let lamb stand in marinade 1 hour at room temperature.

2. Preheat oven to 325°F. Using a slotted spoon, transfer lamb to a medium-size heavy nonreactive Dutch oven, discarding any marinade that does not cling to lamb. Add broth mixture, mix well, and spread over bottom of Dutch oven. Cover and bake until lamb is very tender—about 1½ hours.

3. Meanwhile, begin Sauce: Place cucumbers in a large sieve set over a large bowl, sprinkle with salt, toss well, and let stand while lamb bakes.

4. When lamb is tender, scoop to a large plate. Set Dutch oven over moderately high heat and boil pan juices uncovered, stirring constantly toward end, until reduced to thick gravy—5 to 6 minutes. Return lamb to pot along with accumulated juices, turn in gravy, and set off heat.

5. To finish sauce, drain cucumbers well, pat dry on paper toweling, and place in a small nonreactive bowl. Add remaining ingredients and toss well.

6. To serve, center one pita on each of six small dinner plates, ladle on lamb mixture, dividing total amount evenly, and top with sauce.

MAKES 6 SERVINGS

istanbul casserole of lamb and vegetables

Turkish cooks put everything into a large clay casserole and bake in a moderate oven as long as it takes for the lamb to tenderize. I've updated their recipe for the slow cooker and though I add the tender greens toward the end of cooking, the recipe couldn't be easier. Note: Don't be put off by the long ingredient list—many are seasonings. And once all are in the cooker, job's done! Tip: To trim and slice scallions zip-quick, leave bunched and tackle one bunch at a time.

2½ pounds boneless lamb shoulder,
trimmed of excess fat and cut in 1½-inch cubes

6 small redskin potatoes, peeled and quartered

2 medium yellow onions,
halved lengthwise and each half thickly sliced

12 large scallions (about 2 bunches),
trimmed and thickly sliced (see Tip above;
include some green tops)

2 medium red bell peppers,
cored, seeded, and thickly slivered

6 large whole garlic cloves,
smashed and skins removed

⅓ cup coarsely snipped fresh dill
or 1½ teaspoons dill weed

¼ cup coarsely chopped fresh sorrel,
nasturtium leaves, or mint

2 large whole bay leaves (preferably fresh)

1½ teaspoons salt, or to taste

½ teaspoon freshly ground black pepper,
or to taste

⅓ cup extra-virgin olive oil

1 can (14½ ounces) diced tomatoes,
with their liquid

½ cup dry red wine such as Rioja or Valpolicella

1 medium romaine lettuce,
trimmed and thickly sliced

18 nasturtium flowers (optional garnish)

1. Place first 12 ingredients (lamb through olive oil) in a large (4- to 6-quart) slow cooker and toss well. Mix in tomatoes and wine, cover, and cook on HIGH 1 hour.

2. Stir, cover, and cook on LOW 3½ to 4 hours until lamb is tender and flavors marry.

3. Mix in romaine, cover, and cook on LOW ½ hour longer or until lettuce wilts. Discard bay leaves, taste for salt and pepper, and adjust as needed.

4. To serve, ladle into heated large soup plates and, if you like, garnish each portion with three nasturtium flowers.

MAKES 6 SERVINGS

persian green stew

A most unusual lamb stew "greened" with fresh spinach, cilantro, parsley, and mint. Prunes and lemon juice go into it, too, so it's slightly sweet-sour. Make when you're feeling adventurous and serve over fluffy boiled rice or bulgur (tabbouleh). Note: It's important to use baby spinach for this recipe because it wilts nicely and needn't be chopped. Tip: For directions on making ghee or clarified butter, see Butter in How to Use This Book (page xii).

3 pounds boneless lamb shoulder,
trimmed of excess fat and cut in 1½-inch cubes

1½ teaspoons ground cinnamon

1½ teaspoons salt, or to taste

½ teaspoon freshly ground black pepper,
or to taste

6 tablespoons ghee (see Tip above)

1½ teaspoons ground turmeric

1 quart (4 cups) water (about)

¾ pound pitted prunes

1 pound baby spinach leaves, washed
(see Note above)

1½ cups coarsely chopped fresh cilantro
(measure loosely packed)

1 cup coarsely chopped fresh Italian parsley
(measure loosely packed)

2 large yellow onions,
halved lengthwise and each half thinly sliced

½ cup coarsely chopped fresh mint

¼ to ⅓ cup fresh lemon juice, or to taste

1. Sprinkle lamb with cinnamon, salt, and pepper, toss well, and let stand at room temperature 30 minutes.

2. Heat 4 tablespoons ghee in a large heavy non-reactive Dutch oven over high heat until ripples appear on pan bottom—about 1½ minutes. Brown lamb in two batches in ghee, allowing 8 to 10 minutes per batch and lifting each to a large bowl as it browns.

3. Return lamb and accumulated juices to pot, add turmeric and water, and bring to a boil. Adjust heat so mixture simmers slowly, cover, and cook until lamb is nearly tender—about 1½ hours.

4. Add prunes and if stew seems dry, add a little more water. Cover and simmer until prunes are soft—about 15 minutes. Add spinach, cilantro, and parsley, cover, and simmer until lamb is fork-tender—15 to 20 minutes more.

5. Meanwhile, heat remaining ghee in a large heavy skillet over moderately high heat until ripples appear on pan bottom—1½ to 2 minutes. Add onions and stir-fry until richly browned—8 to 10 minutes. Stir in mint.

6. When lamb is fork-tender, stir in onion mixture and lemon juice. Taste for salt and pepper and adjust as needed.

7. Ladle over boiled rice or bulgur and serve.

MAKES 6 SERVINGS

slow cooker lamb with raisins and toasted almonds

Who among us had heard of tagines until Paula Wolfert introduced them to us in her benchmark *Couscous and Other Good Food from Morocco* published—can it be?—more than 35 years ago? Wolfert defines them this way: "Though they are not among the most elegant of dishes, these hearty stews are absolutely delicious." Quite so. I also find them ideal candidates for the slow cooker. This recipe was inspired by one of many tagines in Wolfert's valuable cookbook. Tip: Plump the raisins while the tagine cooks. Also toast the almonds: Spread in a pie tin, set uncovered in a preheated 350°F oven, and leave until the color of pale caramel—8 to 10 minutes; stir the nuts occasionally as they toast. I call for slivered almonds because supermarkets carry them but rarely carry the whole blanched almonds Wolfert specifies.

3 pounds boneless lamb shoulder,
trimmed of excess fat and cut in 1½-inch cubes

1 large Spanish or other sweet onion,
coarsely chopped

3 large garlic cloves, finely chopped

2 tablespoons vegetable oil

2 tablespoons melted unsalted butter

1½ teaspoons salt, or to taste

1 teaspoon ground turmeric

½ teaspoon freshly ground black pepper,
or to taste

¼ teaspoon ground hot red pepper (cayenne)

¼ teaspoon ground ginger

1 can (14½ ounces) diced tomatoes, drained

1 cup water

½ cup seedless raisins, plumped 1 hour in
1 cup water and drained well (see Tip above)

1 tablespoon finely chopped fresh cilantro

1 tablespoon finely chopped fresh Italian parsley

1 cup slivered almonds tossed with
1 tablespoon vegetable oil and lightly toasted
(see Tip above)

1. Place lamb and next nine ingredients (onion through ginger) in a large (4- to 6-quart) slow cooker and toss well. Arrange around edge of slow cooker, add tomatoes and water, cover, and cook on HIGH 1 hour.

2. Add raisins, cilantro, and parsley, stir well, cover, and cook on LOW 4 hours or until lamb is tender and flavors marry. Taste for salt and pepper and adjust as needed.

3. To serve, ladle into heated large soup plates and scatter almonds on top of each portion.

MAKES 6 SERVINGS

cape malay lamb and cabbage bredee

Brought as slaves to South Africa from the Malay Peninsula (courtesy of the Dutch East India Company), Cape Malays arrived early in the 17th century and their spicy food was soon so popular they opened cookhouses in Cape Town's ethnic enclaves. Bredees, now integral to South African cuisine, are basically "dry" stews, spicy braises of meat (usually lamb or mutton) and two or three vegetables. Of all the bredees I tasted while traveling about South Africa, this lamb and cabbage combo was my favorite. Note: The Cape Malay technique is unusual in that the chunks of lamb are washed and laid wet on richly browned onions. Tip: For directions on making ghee or clarified butter, see Butter in How to Use This Book (page xii).

¼ cup ghee (see Tip above)

2 large yellow onions, halved lengthwise and each half moderately thinly sliced

1 teaspoon raw sugar

½ teaspoon chili flakes (crushed dried hot red chili peppers), more if you like things "hot"

½ teaspoon freshly grated nutmeg

2½ pounds boneless lamb shoulder, trimmed of excess fat, cut in 1½-inch cubes, washed well in cool water but not patted dry (see Note above)

1 small cabbage (2¼ to 2½ pounds), trimmed, quartered, cored, and each quarter thinly sliced

1½ teaspoons salt, or to taste

¼ teaspoon freshly ground black pepper, or to taste

2 cups water (about)

4 medium all-purpose potatoes (about 2 pounds), peeled and sliced about ¼ inch thick

1 large lemon or red-ripe tomato, cut in slim wedges (optional garnish)

1. Heat ghee in a large heavy nonreactive Dutch oven over moderately high heat until ripples appear on pan bottom—1½ to 2 minutes. Add onions, sugar, chili flakes, and nutmeg, then cook and stir until onions are nicely browned—about 10 minutes. Add lamb along with all water clinging to it, and layer on top of onions. Cover lamb with cabbage, sprinkle with salt and black pepper, pour in water, and bring to a boil. Adjust heat so mixture simmers gently, cover, and cook until lamb is nearly tender—1½ to 2 hours.

2. Layer potatoes on top of cabbage and spoon some of cooking juices over potatoes. Cover and simmer until potatoes are done—about 30 minutes longer. Taste for salt and black pepper and adjust as needed.

3. To serve, mound meat and vegetables in a heated large deep platter. For a prettier presentation, garnish with lemon or tomato wedges— far from traditional but an easy way to beautify a brown stew.

MAKES 6 SERVINGS

rogan josh

Wherever I've traveled in India, I've eaten "local" because I'm fond of curry and also know that many of its ingredients are preservatives. Early on I learned that all curries are not yellow and that one curry powder "doesn't fit all." Indian cooks vary the components according to what they're cooking. For vindaloos, they add chilies with a heavy hand but tame the heat for Rogan Josh. This unusually delicate version, adapted from one I enjoyed in India, is unlike those I've eaten in this country, which tend to reek of curry powder. Here garam masala, the most aromatic Indian spice blend, prevails (many supermarkets now carry it). Note: For directions on making ghee or clarified butter, see Butter in How to Use This Book (page xii).

1/3 cup ghee (see Note above)

3 pounds boneless lamb shoulder, trimmed of excess fat and cut in 3/4-inch cubes

2/3 cup firmly packed plain yogurt, preferably Greek yogurt (not reduced fat), at room temperature

2 teaspoons raw sugar

1 1/2 teaspoons chili powder

1 teaspoon garam masala (see headnote)

1 teaspoon ground anise

1 teaspoon salt

1/2 teaspoon curry powder

1/2 teaspoon ground ginger

1/2 teaspoon ground turmeric

1/2 teaspoon ground caraway seeds

6 green cardamom pods, bruised and tied in cheesecloth with 4 whole cloves, 4 small sprigs fresh Italian parsley, and a broken 3-inch cinnamon stick (spice bag)

1. Heat ghee in a medium-size heavy Dutch oven over moderately high heat until ripples appear on pan bottom—1 1/2 to 2 minutes.

2. Add lamb, turn in ghee to coat, then reduce heat to low, cover, and cook 1 hour.

3. Blend in yogurt and cook and stir over moderate heat 2 minutes. Add remaining ingredients, turn heat to low, cover, and simmer very slowly, stirring occasionally, until lamb is tender— about 1 1/2 hours. Check pot after 1/2 hour and if mixture is bubbling actively, slide a diffuser underneath pot.

4. When lamb is tender, scoop to a bowl using a slotted spoon. Boil pan liquid uncovered over high heat, whisking briskly and often, until reduced to rich brown sauce—12 to 15 minutes. Discard spice bag, taste for salt, and adjust as needed.

5. Return lamb and accumulated juices to pot, turn in sauce, and warm 1 to 2 minutes.

6. Serve with boiled basmati rice.

MAKES 6 SERVINGS

goan lamb curry

I didn't make it to Goa while traveling about India, but I've eaten Goan curries in Lisbon and found them less explosive than many other Indian curries. The reason, I learned, is that Goan cooking is a fusion of the spicy cuisines of Brazil, Angola, and the Moluccas (all former Portuguese colonies) mellowed by recipes from the Mother Country. Early in the 16th century the Portuguese planted their flag in Goa on the southwest coast of India and sent Jesuits out to convert its people. With them came a love of meat and in particular, of lamb. Soon Goans, once devoutly vegetarian, began to eat meat. The Portuguese held Goa for more than 450 years—from 1510 to 1961—and with the collapse of empire, Goans began trickling into Lisbon. Vasco da Gama, the first European to sail round the Cape of Good Hope, cross the Indian Ocean, and find the water route to the East's treasury of spices, was Portuguese and he's known to have visited India at the turn of the 15th century. Whenever I'm in Alentejo, the vast province east of Lisbon, I pause in the regional capital of Évora and stroll by the house where the great navigator once lived. How appropriate that it's the color of curry powder. Note: For directions on making ghee or clarified butter, see Butter in How to Use This Book (page xii).

1/3 cup ghee (see Note above)

3 pounds boneless lamb shoulder, trimmed of excess fat and cut in 1-inch cubes

4 medium yellow onions, finely chopped

4 large garlic cloves, finely chopped

1 large bay leaf, finely crumbled

2 tablespoons curry powder

1 tablespoon sweet paprika

1 teaspoon ground cinnamon

1 teaspoon ground coriander

1 teaspoon ground cumin

5 whole cloves

1 teaspoon salt, or to taste

1 teaspoon freshly ground black pepper, or to taste

1 can (14½ ounces) crushed tomatoes, with their liquid

1 cup water (about)

1. Heat ghee in a large heavy nonreactive Dutch oven over high heat until ripples appear on pan bottom—about 1½ minutes.

2. Brown lamb nicely in three batches in ghee, allowing about 10 minutes per batch and lifting each to a bowl as it browns.

3. Add onions and garlic to drippings and cook, stirring often, until limp and golden—5 to 6 minutes. Mix in next seven ingredients (bay leaf through cloves), cover, and cook 5 minutes.

4. Return lamb to pot along with accumulated juices and add all remaining ingredients. Adjust heat so mixture barely bubbles and cook uncovered—very slowly—until lamb is fork-tender and liquids are as thick as gravy—1 to 1½ hours. Stir occasionally and if pot is cooking dry, add a little more water, turn heat to its lowest point, and, if necessary, slide a diffuser underneath pot. Taste for salt and pepper and adjust as needed.

5. Serve with boiled rice, preferably basmati, and good mango chutney.

MAKES 6 SERVINGS

lamb korma

For me, lamb is the perfect "curry meat" and for many Indians as well. Hindus do not eat beef (to them cows are sacred). Muslims do not eat pork, but both dote upon mutton and lamb and curry them many ways. There are explosive vindaloos, which I eat only to clear my sinuses (her majesty, Queen Elizabeth II, is said to do the same). But at other times I prefer more tepid curries like this korma. It's a fairly dry curry, so resist the temptation to water down the gravy. Note: For directions on making ghee or clarified butter, see Butter in How to Use This Book (page xii). Tip: To pulverize the spices, use a little electric coffee grinder or, if you must, mortar and pestle.

¼ cup ghee (see Note above)

2½ pounds boneless lamb shoulder, trimmed of excess fat and cut in 1-inch cubes

4 large yellow onions, coarsely chopped

4 large garlic cloves, finely chopped

1 tablespoon finely chopped fresh ginger

½ teaspoon each cardamom seeds (those inside the pithy pods), coriander seeds, and black peppercorns pulverized with ¼ teaspoon each cumin seeds and chili flakes (crushed dried hot red chili peppers) and 4 whole cloves (see Tip above)

½ teaspoon ground cinnamon

½ teaspoon ground turmeric

¾ cup water (about)

¼ cup coconut milk (not low-fat)

¼ cup fresh lemon juice

½ teaspoon salt, or to taste

⅓ cup heavy cream

1. Heat ghee in a large heavy nonreactive Dutch oven over moderately high heat until ripples appear on pan bottom—1½ to 2 minutes.

2. Brown lamb nicely in three batches in ghee, allowing about 10 minutes per batch and lifting each to a bowl as it browns.

3. Add onions, garlic, and ginger to drippings and cook, stirring often, until limp and lightly browned—8 to 10 minutes. Mix in pulverized spices, cinnamon, and turmeric and cook and stir 5 minutes.

4. Return lamb to pot along with accumulated juices and add water, coconut milk, lemon juice, and salt. Adjust heat so mixture barely bubbles, cover, and simmer slowly until lamb is fork-tender—about 1½ hours. Stir occasionally and if pot is cooking dry, add a little more water, turn heat to its lowest point, and, if necessary, slide a diffuser underneath pot.

5. Mix in cream and simmer uncovered, stirring occasionally, until gravy thickens slightly— about 5 minutes. Taste for salt and pepper and adjust as needed.

6. Serve with boiled rice, preferably basmati, and put out a good chutney.

MAKES 6 SERVINGS

lancashire hot pot

This homely one-dish dinner remains popular all over Lancashire in the northwest of England. Purists add lamb kidneys to the pot, but they're rarely available here beyond big metropolitan areas. If you like lamb kidneys and can find them, buy four, remove excess fat, membranes, and cores, slice ¼ inch thick, and layer into the pot along with the lamb, reducing amount to 3 pounds.

3½ pounds bone-in lamb neck slices, trimmed of excess fat and cut in 2-inch pieces (see headnote)

3 large yellow onions, coarsely chopped

8 medium all-purpose potatoes, peeled and thickly sliced

6 medium carrots, peeled and thickly sliced

4 cups water mixed with 1 tablespoon salt and ½ teaspoon freshly ground black pepper (brine)

Additional water as needed to cover ingredients in pot

2 tablespoons unsalted butter, diced

1. Preheat oven to 325°F. Butter dull side of a large square of heavy-duty foil and set aside.

2. Layer lamb, onions, potatoes, and carrots in a large heavy Dutch oven, ending with potatoes and arranging these as close together as possible. Pour brine evenly over all, then add cold water until it not quite reaches top layer of potatoes.

3. Cover pot with foil, placing buttered side down and sealing around edge. Set Dutch oven lid in place. Slide onto middle oven shelf and bake 1 hour.

4. Remove lid and foil, dot potatoes with butter, and bake uncovered until lamb is tender and potatoes are richly browned—about 1 hour longer.

5. Ladle into heated large soup plates and serve. Note: Warn people that there are bones in this soup.

MAKES 6 SERVINGS

lamb neck slices in dill and lemon sauce

It's everything into the pot for this unusual stew—no initial browning needed for the lamb. The sauce, made shortly before serving, recycles the lamb cooking liquid. Serve with boiled potatoes.

4 pounds bone-in lamb neck slices, trimmed of excess fat and cut in 2-inch pieces

2 medium yellow onions, finely chopped

2 large garlic cloves, smashed and skins removed

4 large sprigs fresh dill, tied in cheesecloth

4½ cups water

1½ teaspoons salt, or to taste

½ teaspoon freshly ground black pepper, or to taste

2 tablespoons finely snipped fresh dill

SAUCE

3 tablespoons unsalted butter

½ teaspoon finely grated lemon zest

¼ cup unsifted all-purpose flour

Cooking liquid (from lamb above)

3 large egg yolks lightly beaten with 1½ tablespoons fresh lemon juice

1. Bring lamb, onions, garlic, dill sprigs, water, salt, and pepper to a boil in a large heavy Dutch oven over high heat, skimming froth and scum from surface as they collect. Adjust heat so liquid bubbles gently, cover, and simmer until lamb is fall-off-the-bone tender—about 2 hours.

2. Pour cooking liquid through a fine sieve into a large heatproof bowl, and discard solids. Cool cooking liquid 15 to 20 minutes, then skim off all fat.

3. For Sauce: Melt butter with lemon zest in a large heavy nonreactive saucepan, blend in flour, and cook and stir 1 to 2 minutes over moderate heat. Add strained cooking liquid and cook, stirring constantly, until sauce thickens slightly and no raw floury taste remains—about 5 minutes.

4. Add lamb to sauce and cook uncovered, stirring occasionally, 10 minutes.

5. Ladle a little hot sauce into egg yolk mixture, stir back into pan, and cook and stir 2 to 3 minutes. Do not boil or sauce may curdle. Taste for salt and pepper and adjust as needed.

6. Mix in snipped dill and serve. Note: Warn people that there are bones in this stew.

MAKES 6 SERVINGS

juniper-scented pueblo lamb and bell peppers

Lying near or along "The Great River of Life" (Rio Grande) as it meanders across New Mexico are nineteen Indian pueblos, some more open or welcoming than others. A long-time favorite of mine is San Ildefonso some 15 to 20 miles northwest of Santa Fe, which not only borders the sacred ground of Black Mesa but also the river (the pueblo's native name—*Po-woh-ge-oweenge*—means "where the water cuts through"). I had friends here, who have since died, and it was they who invited me to the Corn Dance, an all-day affair held each September with everyone—toddlers to tribal elders—participating. To fortify the dancers, women pre-pare great cauldrons of soup and stew, among them one made with breast of lamb (this is my attempt to crack that recipe). Note: Many supermarkets sell juniper berries. Look for them among the herbs and spices. Tip: The fastest way to make the dry rub? Whiz in a small food processor or spice grinder.

6 juniper berries crushed with 2 teaspoons salt, ½ teaspoon coriander seeds, and ¼ teaspoon each chili flakes (crushed dried hot red chili peppers) and black peppercorns (dry rub; see Note and Tip above)

2 pounds breast of lamb, trimmed of excess fat

3 tablespoons all-purpose flour

3 tablespoons bacon drippings or corn oil

2 medium yellow onions, coarsely chopped

2 large garlic cloves, finely chopped

1 quart (4 cups) water

1 can (15 ounces) posole (whole hominy) with its liquid

3 large green bell peppers, cored, seeded, and cut in slim wedges

⅓ cup coarsely chopped fresh cilantro

1. Massage dry rub into both sides of lamb breast and let stand at room temperature 1 hour.

2. With a sharp knife, divide lamb into individual ribs, sprinkle with flour, and toss well.

3. Heat drippings in a large heavy nonreactive Dutch oven over moderately high heat until ripples appear on pan bottom—1½ to 2 minutes.

4. Brown lamb in two batches in drippings, allow-ing 8 to 10 minutes per batch and lifting each to a bowl as it browns.

5. Add onions and garlic to drippings and cook, stirring often, until limp and touched with brown—8 to 10 minutes.

6. Return lamb to pot along with accumulated juices, add water, and bring to a boil. Adjust heat so mixture bubbles gently, cover, and sim-mer 1 hour.

7. Set off heat and cool stew, then refrigerate until fat rises to top. Note: Pueblo cooks refrigerate overnight and finish the stew the next day.

8. Skim fat from surface, set stew over moderate heat, and bring to a boil. Mix in posole, adjust heat so stew barely bubbles, and simmer uncovered 30 minutes.

9. Add bell peppers, pushing into liquid, and continue simmering uncovered until lamb is tender—40 to 45 minutes more. Stir in cilantro, taste for salt and pepper, and adjust as needed.

10. To serve, ladle into heated large soup plates and accompany with freshly baked bread. My San Ildefonso friends baked crusty-chewy loaves in *hornos* (wood-fired outdoor adobe ovens). Note: Warn people that there are bones in this stew.

MAKES 6 SERVINGS

braised blade chops of lamb with coffee and cream gravy

It wasn't until I spent time in Sweden that I discovered this unusual way to cook lamb. In truth, the cut was leg of lamb and the coffee leftover from breakfast. I liked the recipe and decided to rework it using bone-in lamb chops cut from the blade portion of the shoulder, which more and more supermarkets now sell—prepackaged like steak and chicken. For the record, a ½-inch-thick lamb blade chop weighs about ½ pound. Note: Blade chops tend to be fatty, so remove as much of the fat as possible before cooking so there's less of it to skim off later. Tip: A 12-inch nonstick skillet is the pan to use here.

1 tablespoon vegetable oil

1 tablespoon unsalted butter

6 half-inch-thick bone-in blade lamb chops
(about 3 pounds), trimmed of excess fat
(see Note above)

¾ cup hot water blended with 1 tablespoon each
sugar and espresso powder, 1 teaspoon salt,
and ¼ teaspoon freshly ground black pepper

3 tablespoons all-purpose flour blended with
¼ cup cold water (thickener)

½ cup heavy cream

1 tablespoon red currant jelly

1. Heat oil and butter in a very large heavy skillet over high heat until ripples appear on pan bottom—about 1½ minutes.

2. Brown half the lamb chops well in oil and butter, allowing 3 to 4 minutes per side and lifting to a plate when brown. Repeat with remaining chops but leave in skillet.

3. Return reserved browned chops to skillet along with accumulated juices, pour in hot water mixture, and bring to a boil. Adjust heat so liquid bubbles gently, cover, and simmer until lamb is fall-off-the-bone tender—about 1½ hours,

basting occasionally with pan liquid. Note: Check chops after first 20 minutes or so and if liquid is actively boiling, slide a diffuser underneath skillet and turn heat to lowest point. The chops should not boil for any length of time because if they do, they will surely be tough.

4. When lamb is tender, lift to a cutting board. Pull out and discard bones, then tear meat into bite-size pieces. Skim and blot as much fat from cooking liquid as possible.

5. Blend about ½ cup cooking liquid into thickener, stir back into skillet, and cook and stir over moderate heat until thickened, smooth, and no raw floury taste lingers—about 5 minutes.

6. Blend in cream and jelly and boil over moderately high heat, stirring often, until consistency of thin gravy—about 5 minutes. Taste for salt and pepper and adjust as needed.

7. Return lamb to skillet and warm in gravy over low heat—about 5 minutes.

8. Ladle lamb and gravy over roasted redskin potatoes that have been forked open or, if you prefer, over brown or white rice. Good, too, over wild rice but that's an extravagance.

MAKES 4 TO 6 SERVINGS

braised blade chops with roasted garlic and eggplant tahini

Bigger than loin or rib chops and tougher, too, these meaty shoulder slices are best when braised with fragrant herbs like mint and dill. I ate them cooked this way in a little Athens taverna and this is my approximation of that dish. To roast eggplants: Prick with a fork, place on a baking sheet, and roast uncovered about 45 minutes at 400°F or until soft; cool. To roast garlic: Slice ½ inch off top of bulb, exposing cloves, wrap bulb snugly in foil, and roast alongside eggplants, removing after 35 to 40 minutes or when soft; cool until easy to handle. Needless to add, roast eggplants and garlic while lamb braises. Note: Once a special-order item, tahini (sesame seed paste) is now carried by most supermarkets; look for it in the "international foods" aisle.

6 half-inch-thick bone-in blade lamb chops (about 3 pounds), trimmed of excess fat

¾ cup unsifted all-purpose flour combined with 1½ teaspoons salt and ½ teaspoon freshly ground black pepper (seasoned flour)

¼ cup extra-virgin olive oil

½ cup dry white wine such as retsina, Riesling, or (my choice) Gewürztraminer

2½ cups chicken or vegetable broth (about)

6 medium dill sprigs tied in cheesecloth with 2 large mint sprigs and 3 (2-inch) strips lemon zest (cheesecloth bag)

TAHINI SAUCE

2 medium eggplants, roasted (see headnote)

1 medium garlic bulb, roasted (see headnote)

½ cup cooking liquid (from lamb chops above)

¼ cup tahini (see Note above)

¼ cup heavy cream

¼ cup plain yogurt, preferably Greek yogurt (not reduced fat)

1 tablespoon fresh lemon juice, or to taste

1. Dredge lamb chops on both sides in seasoned flour. Heat oil in a very large, deep heavy non-reactive skillet over moderately high heat until ripples appear on pan bottom—1½ to 2 minutes.

2. Brown half the chops well, allowing 6 to 8 minutes per side and lifting to a large plate when brown. Repeat with remaining chops but leave in skillet. Return first batch along with accumulated juices to skillet, add wine and enough broth to not quite cover chops, drop in cheesecloth bag, wringing to release flavors, and bring to a boil.

3. Adjust heat so mixture barely bubbles, cover, and cook until lamb chops are fork-tender—1 to 1¼ hours. Lift chops from skillet, overlap on heated large platter, cover loosely with foil, and keep warm.

4. Skim fat from cooking liquid, measure out ½ cup liquid, and reserve. Simmer remaining cooking liquid uncovered over low heat until reduced to 1½ cups gravy. Taste for salt and pepper and adjust as needed.

5. Meanwhile, prepare Tahini Sauce: Scoop roasted eggplant flesh into food processor, squeeze in roasted garlic flesh, add reserved ½ cup cooking liquid, and purée. Add remaining ingredients and pulse until smooth. Taste for lemon juice, adjust as needed, and transfer to serving bowl.

6. To serve, uncover chops and top with skillet gravy. Pass Tahini Sauce separately.

MAKES 6 SERVINGS

grilled lamb shoulder chops corfu-style

I once spent Easter on the Greek island of Corfu, where bishops in cloth-of-gold paraded through streets filled with the scent of lamb grilling and roasting. Of all the lamb I feasted upon that weekend, this simple recipe was my favorite. Arm chops are best here, but the arm bone must be removed so the chops can be pounded as flat as scaloppini—the first step in tenderizing them. The second? Overnight in a marinade of olive oil, lemon juice, garlic, oregano, salt, and pepper. Lacking a charcoal grill, I broil the chops quickly until nicely browned on both sides but still pink inside. I'm guessing that grill time would be about the same, but experienced hands will know exactly. Tip: To pound the chops cleanly without tearing them, slide each between a double thickness of plastic wrap. A cutlet bat (also called a meat pounder) is the implement of choice, but a rolling pin works almost as well.

½ cup extra-virgin olive oil

⅓ cup fresh lemon juice

1 large garlic clove, crushed

1 teaspoon crumbled dried leaf oregano

½ teaspoon salt

½ teaspoon freshly ground black pepper

6 lamb shoulder arm chops, cut ¾ to 1 inch thick (about 3 pounds), boned, and pounded flat (see Tip above)

1. Prepare a marinade by combining oil, lemon juice, garlic, oregano, salt, and pepper in a large, shallow nonreactive baking pan. Dip lamb chops in marinade, coating well on both sides, then arrange in a single layer in marinade, cover, and refrigerate overnight.

2. When ready to proceed, remove pan of chops from refrigerator and let them stand 1 hour in marinade at room temperature.

3. Place broiler rack about 5 inches from heating element and preheat broiler.

4. Arrange lamb chops, not touching, on broiler pan, slide onto rack, and broil until somewhere between medium-rare and medium—about 5 minutes on each side, brushing, if you like, with a little marinade. Chops will be pink inside.

5. Serve at once with boiled potatoes or rice. Note: If I'm serving rice, I often mix in 1 to 2 tablespoons marinade about 5 minutes before rice is done. Adds welcome flavor.

MAKES 6 SERVINGS

curried lamb shanks with almond pilaf

Few Americans cook lamb shanks these days and that's a pity because properly prepared, they are supremely succulent. Is our "supermarket mentality" to blame? I've seen pig's trotters in meat counters but nary a lamb shank. For anything more exotic than rib or loin chops, breast, leg, or shoulder of lamb, you need a good butcher. If you should spot lamb shanks, by all means try this recipe. It contains no curry powder, only individual components. That's the Indian way. Note: For directions on making ghee or clarified butter, see Butter in How to Use This Book (page xii).

6 lamb shanks, each cut in 3 pieces

1 cup unsifted all-purpose flour mixed with
1½ teaspoons salt and ½ teaspoon freshly ground
black pepper (seasoned flour)

⅓ cup ghee (see Note above)

2 large yellow onions, coarsely chopped

3 large garlic cloves, finely chopped

A 2-inch cube fresh ginger, peeled and finely chopped

1 teaspoon ground coriander

1 teaspoon ground cumin

1 teaspoon ground turmeric

½ teaspoon ground cinnamon

½ teaspoon ground hot red pepper (cayenne)

¼ teaspoon ground cloves

2¾ cups chicken or vegetable broth

2 cans (14½ ounces each) diced tomatoes,
with their liquid

½ cup heavy cream blended with ½ cup plain yogurt
(preferably Greek and not reduced fat)

⅓ cup coarsely chopped fresh cilantro

PILAF

3 tablespoons ghee

1½ cups long-grain rice

½ cup coarsely chopped slivered almonds

⅓ cup dried currants

¼ teaspoon finely grated orange zest

¼ teaspoon salt

3 cups chicken or vegetable broth

1. Dredge lamb, a few pieces at a time, by shaking in a large plastic zipper bag with seasoned flour and set aside

2. Heat ghee in a large heavy nonreactive Dutch oven over moderately high heat until ripples appear on pan bottom—1½ to 2 minutes.

3. Brown dredged lamb in several batches in ghee, allowing 8 to 10 minutes per batch and lifting each to a bowl as it browns.

4. Add onions, garlic, ginger, and all ground spices (coriander through cloves) to drippings and cook and stir 5 minutes.

5. Mix in broth and tomatoes, return lamb to pot along with accumulated juices, and bring to

a boil. Adjust heat so mixture bubbles gently, cover, and simmer until lamb is fall-off-the-bone tender—about 2 hours.

6. Some 30 minutes before lamb is done, make Pilaf: Heat ghee in a medium-size saucepan over moderately high heat until ripples appear on pan bottom—1½ to 2 minutes. Add rice and almonds and cook, stirring often, until rice is translucent—about 5 minutes. Mix in currants, orange zest, salt, and broth. Bring to a boil, adjust heat so liquid simmers gently, and cook uncovered until broth has been absorbed and dimples appear on surface of rice—about 20 minutes. Turn heat down low, cover rice, and steam 5 minutes.

7. Lift lamb shanks to a large bowl and keep warm. Skim fat from pan gravy and blend in cream/yogurt mixture and half the cilantro. Return lamb to Dutch oven and heat 1 to 2 minutes—do not boil or gravy may curdle. Taste for salt and adjust as needed.

8. To serve, mound pilaf on a heated large deep platter, ladle curried lamb shanks on top—no stinting on gravy—and sprinkle with remaining cilantro. Accompany with mango chutney.

MAKES 6 SERVINGS

braised sweet-sour lamb shanks

You can look long and hard but you're not likely to find an easier way to prepare lamb shanks. Note: This recipe calls for no salt or pepper, but taste before serving and adjust as needed.

6 lamb shanks, each cracked in several places

¼ cup unsifted all-purpose flour

¼ cup vegetable oil or a 50/50 mix of vegetable oil and bacon drippings

1 cup tomato ketchup

1 cup water blended with 2 teaspoons dry mustard

½ cup rice or cider vinegar

¼ cup firmly packed light brown sugar

2 tablespoons soy sauce

1 large yellow onion, halved lengthwise and each half moderately thinly sliced

1. Dredge lamb shanks in flour, shaking off excess, and set aside.

2. Heat oil in a large heavy nonreactive Dutch oven over moderately high heat until ripples appear on pan bottom—1½ to 2 minutes.

3. Brown shanks in batches in oil, allowing about 10 minutes per batch and lifting each to a bowl as it browns. Return browned shanks to pot along with accumulated drippings.

4. Combine ketchup, water mixture, vinegar, brown sugar, and soy sauce, pour over shanks, top with sliced onion, and bring to a boil. Adjust heat so liquid barely bubbles, cover, and braise slowly, basting several times with pan liquid, until lamb falls from bones—about 2 hours. Note: If pot is cooking dry, add a little water, turn heat to its lowest point and, if necessary, slide a diffuser underneath pot.

5. If pan juices seem soupy, remove lid and simmer until they thicken slightly—15 to 20 minutes. Taste for salt and pepper and add as needed.

6. To serve, mound lamb shanks in a heated large deep platter and smother with pan juices. Accompany with boiled rice.

MAKES 6 SERVINGS

welsh honied lamb with cider sauce

Before I went to Wales on article assignment for *Food & Wine,* I'd heard that Welsh lamb knew no equal. And indeed, wherever I drove, I saw sheep grazing meadows and mountainsides, most of them with hot pink numbers spray-painted on their fleece (I wondered about those numbers and was told that they identified the owner). Honied lamb was one of the first dishes I tried and I liked it so much I tracked down several recipes for it. This one is an amalgam with the amount of honey reduced. In Wales, as in other Celtic countries, myths and legends are often dished up with food. On Halloween, for example, Welsh girls once "wished upon" the blade bone of lamb shoulder to catch the man of their dreams. Note: Lamb shoulder is often quite fatty, so have your butcher trim away as much fat as possible. If you like, substitute pork shoulder for lamb.

3 pounds boned and rolled lamb shoulder (see Note above)

1 tablespoon finely chopped fresh rosemary or 1 teaspoon crumbled dried leaf rosemary

1 teaspoon salt, or to taste

½ teaspoon ground ginger

¼ teaspoon freshly ground black pepper, or to taste

¼ cup honey (not too dark or thick)

1½ cups apple cider (not apple juice)

1. Preheat oven to 400°F.

2. Place lamb fat side up in a 13 x 9 x 2-inch non-reactive baking pan. Combine half the rosemary with all the salt, ginger, and pepper and rub all over lamb. Pour honey slowly over lamb and let stand at room temperature ½ hour.

3. Pour cider over lamb, slide pan onto middle oven shelf, and roast lamb uncovered 30 minutes. Baste well with pan juices.

4. Reduce oven temperature to 325°F, cover lamb with heavy-duty foil, and braise until tender—about 1½ hours. Baste with pan juices two to three times as lamb braises, re-covering each time with foil.

5. Remove foil, baste lamb well, sprinkle with remaining rosemary, and braise uncovered 15 minutes more. Lift lamb to a carving board, cover loosely with foil, and let rest while you prepare the sauce.

6. Skim fat from pan juices. Note: When cold, lamb fat (tallow) is hard and brittle, so spoon melted fat into a small container—never pour down the sink—and dispose of properly. Pour skimmed pan juices into a medium-size heavy nonreactive skillet and boil uncovered over moderately high heat, stirring often, until reduced by about half—10 to 15 minutes. Taste this cider "sauce" for salt and pepper and adjust as needed.

7. Remove strings from lamb and carve—on the bias—into slices no more than ¼ inch thick.

8. To serve, overlap lamb slices on a heated platter, spoon a little sauce on top, and pass the rest. Accompany with boiled potatoes.

MAKES 6 SERVINGS

highland lamb loaf

I descend from a long line of Scots and it wasn't until I spent time in the Highlands that I realized Scottish cooking doesn't deserve the bum rap it's been given. Although I never took to haggis, I enjoyed many other Scottish dishes, among them this easy meatloaf that turns sinewy lamb shoulder into something savory and succulent. Frugal Scots, I discovered, stretch meatloaves with oatmeal the way we do with breadcrumbs. And to add moisture, they mix in leftover cooked vegetables and/or applesauce made from windfalls. Note: The best applesauce to use is a good lumpy one, preferably homemade, not one of the soupy bottled brands.

2 pounds ground fairly lean lamb shoulder

1 cup quick-cooking oatmeal

1 cup applesauce (see Note above)

1 cup moderately finely chopped leftover cooked carrots or a 50/50 mix of leftover carrots and parsnips, rutabaga, turnips, or beets

1 medium-large yellow onion, moderately finely chopped

2 large eggs

1 can (5 ounces) evaporated milk (use fat-free, if you like)

⅓ cup coarsely chopped fresh Italian parsley

1 tablespoon finely chopped fresh thyme or 1 teaspoon crumbled dried leaf thyme

1½ teaspoons salt

½ teaspoon freshly ground black pepper

¼ teaspoon freshly grated nutmeg

1. Preheat oven to 350°F. Spritz a 9 x 5 x 3-inch loaf pan with nonstick cooking spray and set aside.

2. Using your hands, mix all ingredients together well and pack in pan, mounding slightly in center and making a little trough around edge to catch drippings.

3. Set meatloaf on a baking sheet, slide onto middle oven shelf, and bake uncovered until richly browned and an instant-read meat thermometer, inserted in center of loaf, reads 160°F— 1 to 1¼ hours.

4. Cool loaf in upright pan on a wire rack 20 minutes, drain off drippings, and reserve. Turn loaf out and cut into slices ½ to ¾ inch thick.

5. Serve with mashed or boiled potatoes and, if you like, spoon drippings over meatloaf and potatoes. Or save drippings to use another day in soup, stew, or gravy.

MAKES A 9 X 5 X 3-INCH LOAF

lebanese lamb burgers

Called *kufta* or *kofta* throughout the Middle East, these nicely spiced burgers are the local equivalent of Big Macs—and far more interesting. While on magazine assignment in Beirut, I ordered them every chance I got. As I've said elsewhere, the fastest way to tenderize a gristly cut of meat is to grind it—especially if your butcher does it for you. Note: Mix the burger ingredients really well—I've seen Lebanese women knead them until as smooth as paste. Also, cook the burgers well done. That's how they're served all across the Middle East.

1½ pounds ground lamb shoulder (not too fat)

¾ pound ground lean beef chuck

2 cups fine, soft white breadcrumbs
(4 slices firm-textured white bread)

1 medium yellow onion, finely chopped

1 cup finely chopped fresh Italian parsley

½ cup milk

3 large egg yolks

1¼ teaspoons salt

¼ teaspoon ground allspice

¼ teaspoon ground cinnamon

¼ teaspoon ground cumin

¼ teaspoon ground hot red pepper (cayenne)

1½ cups fine dry breadcrumbs

¼ cup (½ stick) unsalted butter

1. Mix all but last two ingredients (breadcrumbs and butter) thoroughly and shape into six large patties about 5 inches across and ½ inch thick. Dip each in dry breadcrumbs, turn, and dip flip side; burgers should be nicely "crumbed" on both sides.

2. Melt butter in a large heavy skillet over moderately high heat and as soon as it froths and subsides, add burgers and brown well—about 4 to 5 minutes per side.

3. Turn heat to low, cover, and cook slowly until burgers are well done—5 to 10 minutes.

4. Serve hot—on plates, not in buns—and accompany with a tartly dressed green salad.

MAKES 6 SERVINGS

albóndigas with tomato sauce

Mexican meatballs (*albóndigas*) are traditionally made with a mix of ground beef and pork, but being partial to lamb, I've taken the liberty of substituting it for beef. With excellent results, I think.

MEATBALLS

¾ pound ground lean lamb shoulder

¾ pound ground pork shoulder (not too lean)

2 slices firm-textured white bread
soaked in ¼ cup milk and squeezed dry

1 large egg

⅓ cup finely chopped yellow onion
(about 1 small onion)

1 large garlic clove, finely chopped

1 teaspoon salt

¼ teaspoon ground coriander

¼ teaspoon ground cumin

¼ teaspoon ground hot red pepper (cayenne)

¼ teaspoon freshly ground black pepper

SAUCE

2 tablespoons vegetable oil

1 medium yellow onion, moderately finely chopped

1 large garlic clove, finely chopped

1 teaspoon crumbled dried leaf oregano
(preferably Mexican oregano)

2 cans (8 ounces each) tomato sauce

1⅓ cups beef broth

¼ teaspoon salt, or to taste

¼ teaspoon freshly ground black pepper,
or to taste

1. For Meatballs: Mix all ingredients thoroughly, shape into 1-inch balls, and set aside.

2. For Sauce: Heat oil in a large heavy deep non-reactive skillet over moderately high heat until ripples appear on pan bottom—1½ to 2 minutes.

3. Add onion, garlic, and oregano, and cook, stirring often, until limp and golden—about 5 minutes. Add remaining ingredients and bring to a boil. Adjust heat so mixture bubbles gently and simmer uncovered 5 minutes.

4. Add meatballs, arranging in a single layer deep in sauce, cover, and simmer until well done—about 45 minutes. Taste for salt and pepper and adjust as needed.

5. To serve, ladle over boiled rice or alongside boiled potatoes.

MAKES 6 SERVINGS

PORK

PORK

BELLY, FRESH HAM, HOCKS (SHANKS), PIG'S FEET, SPARERIBS, AND SHOULDER (BUTT, PICNIC)

Shaw, some day you'll eat a pork chop and then God help all women.

Back then (1914), pork—indeed meat—was said to fire men's aggressions. So when devoutly vegetarian George Bernard Shaw grew increasingly sexist during rehearsals for *Pygmalion,* the play he'd written for the British actress, she told him off. God forbid that meat would pass the lips of the cantankerous playwright who dined on leaves, roots, and shoots.

Pork, we now know, was eaten by prehistoric man, or at least the flesh of feral swine. Carbon-dated fossils found in Europe and Asia tell us that porcine creatures were there forty million years ago.

As early as 5000 B.C., perhaps earlier, the Chinese listed pork Number One Favorite on their "eight marvels of the table" and ham Number Two. But it was the Russians, culinary historians believe, who first tamed wild boars, then bred and fed them for succulence.

The Etruscans, settling in Italy in the 12th century B.C., not only feasted upon pork but also taught hogs to march when certain tunes were played (presumably not to slaughter). Later Pliny, the first-century Roman scholar, boasted that he could discern more than fifty different flavors in pork.

What accounts for such early and widespread appreciation of pork? Hogs can subsist on almost anything. In Medieval Europe they were loosed in the streets to clean up garbage.

The first hogs to set foot in the New World were the eight Ibericos Queen Isabella ordered Columbus to carry on his second voyage west; they arrived in Cuba in 1493. But Hernando de Soto is called "The Father of America's Pork Industry," for within three years the thirteen pigs he'd offloaded at Tampa Bay in 1539 had multiplied to several hundred.

At roughly the same time, a third Spaniard—Coronado—was galloping across the American Southwest searching for the fabled, gold-rich Seven Cities of Cibola. And he, too, traveled with hogs, some of whom wandered off into Indian pueblos.

Some seventy years later (in 1608), the English shipped hogs to their Virginia Colony at Jamestown, and those pigs, like de Soto's, were soon so numerous and troublesome they were exiled to an island in the James River (now called Hog Island).

Small American farms have always had hogs and when pioneers pushed west into the Great Plains and beyond, crates of piglets went with them. Farmers bred their pigs for succulence and flavor, fattening them to sell at the tender age of six or seven months (now as then the market-ready age).

But by the 1980s, with diet-conscious Americans choosing chicken over pork, sales plummeted. What to do? Give pork a new image. Reposition it as "The Other White Meat." But the new lean pork lacked flavor and with so little juice, even the tender cuts often emerged tough and dry from skillet or oven.

So it's back to well-fleshed heritage breeds—Tamworth, Berkshire, Old Spot, and others. There's even renewed interest in Ossabaws, feral descendants of the Ibericos de Soto brought ashore nearly 500 years ago. With fat so unsaturated it's nearly liquid at room temperature, these supremely succulent hogs have been called "four-legged olive trees."

Though two major religions (Judaism and Islam) forbid the eating of pork, nearly 40 percent of the meat consumed today is pork.

Quicker to cook than the tough cuts, chops and roasts from rib and loin are also trickier. There's a delicate balance: preserving their original tenderness while cooking them to an internal temperature of 160°F (necessary, the U.S. Department of Agriculture says, to eliminate all risk of trichinosis, a parasitic disease caused by eating undercooked pork).

There's no such problem with tougher cuts, all of which cook until fall-off-the-bone tender.

PORK NUTRITIONAL PROFILE
A first class source of protein, pork is also richer in thiamin (an important B vitamin) than any other meat as well as a good source of niacin (another valuable B vitamin), phosphorous, and potassium. It's fatty, but much of its fat is unsaturated. Moreover, the outer layer is easily trimmed or thinned leaving lightly marbled lean. To give some notion of pork's calorie, fat, and cholesterol content, here are approximate figures for two popular cuts:
- Braised Fresh Ham (4 ounces) = 332 calories, 28 grams fat, 105 milligrams cholesterol
- Braised Spareribs (4 ounces meat) = 450 calories, 35 grams fat, 137 milligrams cholesterol

USDA GRADES OF PORK
The U.S. government no longer grades pork for quality because it is more uniformly fat and tender than beef, veal, or lamb.

SHOPPING TIPS
For top quality, look for pork blanketed with a creamy layer of fat and delicately marbled pale rosy-beige lean. TIP: *Because there is some risk of trichinosis, double-bag pork in plastic bags (I use those from the produce counter) to keep raw pork juices from trickling onto other food in your grocery cart.*

Caution: Wash hands thoroughly in hot, soapy water after handling raw pork and also wash counters, cutting boards, and knives, etc. to avoid possible cross-contamination of other food.

STORAGE
The first job, always, is to remove pork from its grocery wrapper unless shrink-wrapped in plastic and cooked within several days. Place or spread pork on a large plate, cover loosely with foil or plastic wrap, and set in the coldest (lowest) part of the refrigerator. Cook roasts or other large cuts within three days, smaller ones within 48 hours, ground pork within 24.

FREEZER TIPS
Fresh pork is highly perishable and should be frozen on the day of purchase. Discard store wrappings, then rewrap—snugly—in foil or plastic freezer wrap as follows:
- **Fresh Ham, Shoulder Roast, Picnic, Shoulder Steaks:** Package each individually.
- **Shoulder Chops, Shanks, Hocks, Pig's Feet:** Do not bundle. Wrap side by side, no more than two per package.
- **Stew Meat:** Spread in a single layer—easier if you first line a shallow pan with foil—then fold ends down securely over meat. Once pork is frozen, lift from pan and return to freezer. If necessary, over-wrap in foil or plastic freezer wrap.
- **Ground Pork:** Flatten into a round 1 to 2 inches thick and wrap as snugly as possible. Or shape into burgers and wrap each separately.

Press all air from each package, label, date, and set directly on the freezing surface of a 0°F freezer. Maximum storage time: Three months for ground pork, stew meat, and pig's feet, six months for roasts, steaks, chops, shanks, cured and/or smoked pork.

RECYCLING LEFTOVERS
Dice and turn into a salad or sandwich spread; mince and add to meatloaf or meatball mixtures, even stuffings; sliver or dice into vegetable soups.

PORK
CUTS
(WHERE THE TOUGH CUTS ARE)

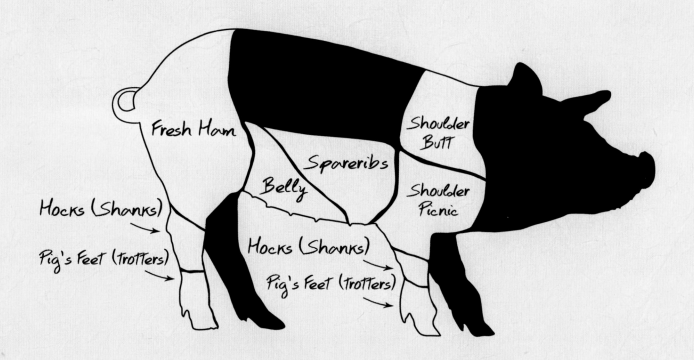

Fresh Ham

Spareribs

Belly

Shoulder Butt

Shoulder Picnic

Hocks (Shanks)

Pig's Feet (Trotters)

Hocks (Shanks)

Pig's Feet (Trotters)

BELLY

Fresh "bacon," unsalted, uncured, unsmoked; cut from the portion of the belly nearest the hind leg, this cut is exceedingly rich.

BEST USES
- BRAISES
- SEASONING FOR VEGETABLES

BUTT
(SHOULDER)

Blocky cut from the upper part of the shoulder. Source of blade (pot) roasts. blade steaks (with a single knife-like bone), stew meat, and ground pork.

BEST USES
- STEWS
- POT ROASTS
- SWISS STEAK
- MEATLOAVES
- MEATBALLS

FRESH HAM

The meaty hind leg of a hog; fresh, not cured, not smoked.

BEST USES
- POT ROAST
- OTHER BRAISES

HOCKS
(SHANKS)

Moderately meaty upper portion of front or hind legs with single round bone. Cured and/or smoked ham hocks are more flavorful and widely available than the fresh.

BEST USES
- SOUPS AND STEWS
- SEASONING FOR DRIED BEANS AND OTHER VEGETABLES
- PORK VERSION OF OSSOBUCO

PICNIC
(SHOULDER)

Chunky cut from the lower part of the shoulder and upper portion of front leg; shaped like ham. It's the source of arm (pot) roasts, arm steaks (with one round bone), stew meat, and ground pork.

BEST USES
- POT ROAST
- STEWS
- SWISS STEAK
- MEATLOAVES
- MEATBALLS

PIG'S FEET

Also called "trotters," the feet of young pigs; front feet more tender and delicate than hind feet

BEST USES
- PICKLED PIG'S FEET
- BRAISES

SPARERIBS

Ribs ends with varying amounts of meat cut from belly; back ribs come from belly or back. Baby back ribs from younger animals are less meaty and less flavorful.

BEST USES
- BARBECUE
- BRAISES
- GLAZED CHINESE-STYLE RIBS

black-eyed pea soup with collards and ham hocks

I call this my "lucky three soup" because it contains black-eyed peas, bitter greens, and pork, the three foods southerners eat on New Year's Day to ensure good luck, good health, and prosperity in the coming year. Some southerners choose turnip or mustard greens over collards for their traditional New Year's feast, but for this soup, I think collards are best. Put them in the pot at the start, or if you prefer crunchier collards, hold half of them back and add about thirty minutes before serving. I use country ham hocks for this soup because of their deep smoky/salty flavor, but "packing house" hocks are perfectly good. Whichever you choose, make sure there's "plenty of meat on them bones." Tip: Collards are easier to wash after they're trimmed and sliced. And here's a trick I learned from the Portuguese who've elevated collards to national dish status. Strip stems and coarse central ribs from each collard leaf (I simply cut down both sides of each rib with a sharp knife). Then working in batches, stack half a dozen leaves, roll into a fat cigar, and slice crosswise at half-inch intervals. For Caldo Verde (Green Soup), Portugal's national dish, women whisk razor-sharp knives back and forth across the collard rolls, freeing shreds as fine as baby's hair. Once all the collards have been sliced, wash by plunging gently up and down in a sink of cold water, then drain well. Note: Because of the saltiness of the ham, this soup may need no salt. But taste before serving and adjust as needed.

1 pound dried black-eyed peas, washed, sorted, and soaked overnight in enough cold water to cover

¼ cup bacon drippings or vegetable oil

3 large yellow onions, coarsely chopped

3 large garlic cloves, finely minced

1 large bunch fresh collards (about 1½ pounds), washed, trimmed, and sliced ½ inch thick (see Tip above)

2½ pounds meaty smoked ham hocks (see headnote)

1 quart (4 cups) beef or chicken broth

1 quart (4 cups) cold water

12 black peppercorns

½ teaspoon hot red pepper sauce, or to taste

Salt, if needed to taste (see Note above)

1. Drain black-eyed peas, rinse well, drain again, and set aside.

2. Heat drippings in a large heavy Dutch oven over moderately high heat until ripples appear on pan bottom—1½ to 2 minutes.

3. Add onions and garlic and sauté, stirring often, until limp and lightly browned—about 10 minutes. Add collards and cook, stirring now and then, until wilted—about 5 minutes. Mix in black-eyed peas.

4. Anchor ham hocks in vegetables, add broth, water, and peppercorns, and bring to a boil over high heat. Adjust so liquid bubbles gently, cover, and simmer, stirring now and then, until black-eyed peas are tender and ham all but falls from bones—1½ to 2 hours. Note: Check pot now and then and if soup threatens to scorch, reduce burner heat to lowest point and slide a diffuser underneath pot.

5. Lift ham hocks to a cutting board and strip meat from bones. Add to soup along with hot pepper sauce to taste, and salt, if needed. Discard bones.

6. Ladle into heated soup plates and accompany with freshly baked corn bread or chunks of good country bread. Better yet, cool soup, cover, and refrigerate overnight. Next day, reheat and serve.

MAKES 6 TO 8 SERVINGS

jade soup with pork-and-veal-dumpling-balls

With buttermilk adding a note of tartness and frozen chopped spinach a vibrant green hue, this soup is both refreshing and nutritious. Prepare the dumpling-balls ahead of time and chill several hours so they're firm when dropped into the soup. Note: For 1 cup breadcrumbs, tear two slices firm-textured white bread directly into a food processor and alternately pulse and churn until fairly fine.

DUMPLING-BALLS

½ pound ground pork shoulder (not too lean)

½ pound ground veal shoulder

1 cup moderately fine soft white breadcrumbs (see Note above)

⅓ cup finely chopped scallions

¼ cup freshly grated Parmigiano Reggiano

1 large egg

¼ teaspoon salt

¼ teaspoon crumbled dried leaf thyme

¼ teaspoon freshly ground black pepper

¼ teaspoon freshly grated nutmeg

SOUP

3 tablespoons extra-virgin olive oil

2 large yellow onions, finely chopped

2 large garlic cloves, finely chopped

2 packages (10 ounces each) solidly frozen chopped spinach

5¼ cups chicken or vegetable broth

½ teaspoon salt, or to taste

½ teaspoon freshly ground black pepper, or to taste

¼ teaspoon freshly grated nutmeg

2½ cups buttermilk, at room temperature

1. For Dumpling-Balls: Mix all ingredients together well, shape into 1-inch balls, arrange in single layer on foil-lined baking sheet, cover loosely, and refrigerate until fairly firm—about 3 hours.

2. For Soup: Heat oil in a large heavy nonreactive Dutch oven over moderately high heat until ripples appear on pan bottom—1½ to 2 minutes.

3. Add onions and garlic and sauté, stirring often, until richly browned—12 to 15 minutes. Add frozen spinach, turn heat to lowest point, cover, and cook until spinach is soft—about 30 minutes.

4. Purée spinach mixture in three or four batches in food processor and return to Dutch oven. Add all but final soup ingredient (buttermilk) and bring to a simmer over moderate heat.

5. Drop well-chilled dumpling-balls into soup, spacing evenly. Adjust heat so liquid barely bubbles, cover, and simmer slowly until dumpling-balls are cooked through—about 45 minutes. Note: Never allow soup to boil or dumpling-balls may fall apart.

6. Mix in buttermilk, taste for salt and pepper, adjust as needed, and bring just to serving temperature—about 5 minutes. Do not boil or soup may curdle.

7. Ladle into heated large soup plates and serve with good yeasty country bread.

MAKES 6 SERVINGS

glazed sweet-sour spareribs

I suppose you might call these barbecued spareribs, but they're a long way from true barbecue cooked long and slow over hickory coals. No matter. These ribs are succulent and full of flavor. The perfect accompaniments? Coleslaw and fresh-baked corn bread.

6 pounds meaty spareribs, divided into 2- or 3-rib widths

Cold water to cover ribs by about 1½ inches

1 teaspoon salt

⅞ cup cider vinegar (1 cup minus 2 tablespoons)

½ cup (1 stick) unsalted butter

⅓ cup firmly packed light brown sugar

2 tablespoons balsamic vinegar

1 tablespoon tomato ketchup

2 tablespoons soy sauce, preferably a dark Asian one

¾ teaspoon freshly ground black pepper

¼ to ½ teaspoon ground hot red pepper (cayenne), or to taste

1. Place ribs, water, and salt in a large heavy Dutch oven, bring to a boil over moderate heat, reduce heat till water barely bubbles, cover, and simmer until ribs are tender—1¾ to 2 hours.

2. Meanwhile, combine remaining ingredients in a small, heavy, nonreactive saucepan, and cook over low heat, stirring constantly, just until butter melts and sugar dissolves—3 to 5 minutes. Taste for cayenne and adjust as needed. Set off heat, cover, and reserve.

3. When ribs are tender, preheat broiler. Lift ribs from Dutch oven and arrange in a single layer in a very large shallow nonreactive roasting pan. Brush well with the reserved sauce. Discard Dutch oven liquid.

4. Slide pan into broiler, setting about 5 inches from heat, and broil until brown—5 to 6 minutes, brushing at half-time with more sauce. Remove ribs from broiler, turn, and brush flip-sides generously with sauce. Broil 5 to 6 minutes longer, again brushing with sauce at half-time. Don't be stingy.

5. When ribs are glistening and brown, arrange on a heated large platter and spoon any remaining sauce over ribs.

MAKES 4 TO 6 SERVINGS

kc ribs

KC means Kansas City and Kansas City means barbecued ribs. I'd been hearing about KC ribs long before I ever made it to Kansas City. But once there, I headed for Arthur Bryant's, whose ribs, it's said, are done in the quintessential KC style—more heavily sauced than the ribs I grew up with in North Carolina. KC sauce is thicker, redder, more complex. I won't say I prefer KC ribs to the Tar Heel. Only that they're different. This recipe is my stab at KC ribs—hardly authentic but altogether tasty.

RIBS

2 tablespoons light brown sugar

2 teaspoons chili powder

2 teaspoons sweet paprika

2 teaspoons salt

1 teaspoon freshly ground black pepper

1 teaspoon crumbled dried leaf oregano

¾ teaspoon crumbled dried leaf thyme

¼ to ½ teaspoon ground hot red pepper (cayenne)

6 pounds meaty spareribs, in one piece

Boiling water (need 1½ to 2 inches in bottom of roasting pan)

BARBECUE SAUCE

¾ cup tomato sauce or purée

⅓ cup tomato ketchup

¼ cup molasses

3 tablespoons cider vinegar

1 tablespoon Worcestershire sauce

1½ teaspoons hot red pepper sauce, or to taste

1. For Ribs: Combine first eight ingredients (brown sugar through cayenne) and rub over both sides of ribs. Place ribs in a large shallow non-reactive baking dish, cover with plastic wrap, and refrigerate overnight.

2. When ready to proceed, preheat oven to 350°F. Remove ribs from refrigerator, lift from baking dish, and arrange in a single layer on a wire rack in a very large shallow nonreactive roasting pan. Slide onto pulled-out middle oven shelf and pour boiling water into pan to a depth of 1½ to 2 inches. Cover pan loosely with foil, and steam ribs 1 hour and 15 minutes.

3. Meanwhile, prepare Barbecue Sauce: Combine all ingredients in a large glass measuring cup and set aside.

4. Remove ribs from oven and discard foil. Lift wire rack of ribs from pan, pour off all liquid, then set rack and ribs back in pan and brush with about one-fourth of barbecue sauce. Return to oven and bake uncovered, brushing every 20 minutes with more sauce, for about 1½ hours or until ribs are fall-off-the-bone tender.

5. Remove from oven, divide into 2-rib widths, pile onto a heated large platter, and serve with plenty of paper napkins. The perfect accompaniments? A good sweet-sour coleslaw and fresh-baked corn bread. In North Carolina cue joints, that corn bread would be hushpuppies right out of the deep-fat fryer.

MAKES 4 TO 6 SERVINGS

ribs lanai-style with pineapple

For years known as "The Pineapple Island," Lanai was the private enclave of the Dole family, whose plantations not so long ago produced 75 percent of the world's supply of pineapples. Tourism has now come to Lanai and with it pampering seaside resorts.

6 pounds meaty spareribs, divided into 2- or 3-rib widths

Boiling water to cover ribs by about ½ inch

1 teaspoon salt

2 cans (8 ounces each) crushed pineapple, with their liquid

⅔ cup firmly packed light brown sugar

⅔ cup cider vinegar

⅓ cup dark Asian soy sauce

A 1-x-2-inch piece fresh ginger, peeled and finely grated

1 teaspoon dry mustard

1. Preheat oven to 375°F. Spread ribs in a single layer in a very large shallow nonreactive roasting pan, set on pulled-out middle oven shelf, add boiling water and salt, and cover with heavy-duty foil. Steam ribs until tender—about 1½ hours.

2. Reduce oven temperature to 350°F. Pour liquid from pan, reserving 2 tablespoons, and combine this with all remaining ingredients in a medium-size nonreactive saucepan. Cook and stir over moderate heat until sugar dissolves— 3 to 5 minutes.

3. Once again spread ribs in pan and pour pineapple mixture over all. Return to oven and bake uncovered, spooning pineapple mixture in bottom of pan over ribs every 15 minutes, until glistening and brown—about 1 hour.

4. Spoon pineapple mixture over ribs and serve at once accompanied by plenty of paper napkins—messy to eat but oh, so good.

MAKES 4 TO 6 SERVINGS

gingery lacquered spareribs

In an attempt to "crack" the recipe for spareribs served at a favorite Chinese restaurant in Lower Manhattan, I developed this one after several false starts. I won't pretend it's the original but will say it's delicious because the ribs marinate overnight in a soy marinade with plenty of fresh ginger. Most Chinese restaurants serve ribs as an appetizer, but they're equally good as a main course. Tip: Grate the ginger on a fine-textured Microplane; it should be the consistency of prepared horseradish.

6 pounds meaty spareribs, divided into 2- to 3-rib widths

Boiling water to cover ribs by about ½ inch

½ teaspoon salt

1½ cups soy sauce, preferably a dark Asian one

1 cup chicken broth

¾ cup firmly packed light brown sugar

½ cup dry sherry, port, or Madeira

4 large garlic cloves, finely chopped

A 2-inch cube fresh ginger, peeled and finely grated (see Tip above)

1 tablespoon Asian toasted sesame oil

1. Preheat oven to 350°F. Spread ribs in a single layer in a very large shallow nonreactive roasting pan, set on pulled-out middle oven shelf, add boiling water and salt, and cover with heavy-duty foil. Steam ribs until nearly tender—about 1½ hours.

2. Meanwhile, combine all remaining ingredients in a very large nonreactive mixing bowl and reserve this marinade.

3. Remove ribs from oven and cool in their liquid 30 minutes or until easy to handle. Pour off all liquid, add ribs to the marinade, and turn to coat well. Cover and refrigerate overnight, turning ribs several times as they marinate.

4. When ready to proceed, preheat oven to 350°F. Spread ribs in a single layer in a very large shallow roasting pan and pour marinade evenly over all. Slide onto middle oven shelf and bake uncovered, turning every 20 to 30 minutes in the marinade, until meat all but falls from the bones—about 1½ to 2 hours. Note: If marinade seems skimpy toward the end, simply blend in a little hot water.

5. Pile ribs on a heated large platter, or plate each portion separately. Serve with fluffy boiled rice and put out plenty of paper napkins. This is "finger food."

MAKES 4 TO 6 SERVINGS

ribs 'n' red beans

Such a simple recipe yet robust enough to satisfy the most ravenous appetite. Better yet, few main dishes are easier on the budget than this one. Serve in soup bowls or ladle over boiled rice. Note: Though some chefs think it silly to soak dried beans, insisting that they hold their color and shape better if cooked straight away, I always soak mine, drain and rinse well, then cook in fresh water. Here's why: dried beans—and red kidney beans in particular—contain a toxic substance that can cause severe gastric distress. Soaking removes some of it, cooking much of the rest.

1 pound dried red kidney beans, washed, sorted, and soaked overnight in cold water

1½ quarts (6 cups) cold water (about)

1 pound meaty spareribs, separated into individual ribs

2 ounces smoked slab bacon, diced

2 large yellow onions, cut in slim wedges

2 large garlic cloves, slivered

2 large whole bay leaves (preferably fresh)

1 teaspoon crumbled dried leaf oregano or marjoram

¼ teaspoon crumbled dried leaf thyme

Salt to taste

Freshly ground black pepper to taste

1. Drain beans, rinse well in cold water, and place in a large heavy kettle. Add enough cold water to cover by about 1 inch, add all remaining ingredients except salt and pepper, and bring to a boil over moderate heat.

2. Adjust heat so water barely ripples, cover, and cook until beans are tender and rib meat falls from the bones—about 1½ hours.

3. Remove ribs from the kettle, strip meat from bones, and cut into bite-size pieces; discard bones. Also, remove and discard bay leaves.

4. Return rib meat to kettle and simmer uncovered over lowest heat about 20 minutes or until flavors meld. Stir often lest beans stick or scorch and if necessary, slide a diffuser underneath pot.

5. Season to taste with salt and pepper, ladle into heated soup bowls, and serve.

MAKES 6 SERVINGS

far east spareribs on sesame sauerkraut

Spareribs and sauerkraut may seem an odd combination. Not really. Chief among the rations for laborers building the Great Wall more than 2,000 years ago were barrels of shredded cabbage, soon fermenting despite salt added to preserve it. The Chinese preferred this fermented cabbage to the fresh. So, too, the Germans—centuries later—who named it "sauerkraut" (sour cabbage). This recipe is adapted from one I developed years ago for a *Bon Appétit* article. "Kindest Cuts," I called it because for me the tough cuts have always been the most economical, versatile, and flavorful. Note: Use fresh sauerkraut here; the canned is too salty. Fresh sauerkraut may be sold by the quart or by the pound. For the record, 1 quart equals 2 pounds.

SAUERKRAUT

1 quart (4 cups) firmly packed fresh sauerkraut, rinsed and squeezed dry (see Note above)

¼ teaspoon red chili flakes

⅓ cup mirin (sweet rice wine)

⅓ cup cider vinegar

¼ cup dark Asian soy sauce

2 tablespoons Asian toasted sesame oil

2 tablespoons firmly packed light brown sugar

A 1 x 2-inch piece fresh ginger, peeled and halved

1 whole medium garlic clove, peeled

RIBS

6 pounds meaty spareribs, divided into 2- to 3-rib widths

Boiling water to cover ribs by about ½ inch

1 teaspoon salt

1½ cups firmly packed light brown sugar

1 cup dark Asian soy sauce

½ cup freshly squeezed orange juice

¼ cup dry sherry, port, or Madeira

¼ cup rice vinegar

2 tablespoons tomato paste

2 tablespoons firmly packed finely grated fresh ginger

6 large garlic cloves, thickly slivered

1. For Sauerkraut: Place sauerkraut and chili flakes in a large nonreactive bowl. Whiz remaining seven ingredients in a food processor 15 to 20 seconds until smooth. Pour over sauerkraut, toss well, cover, and refrigerate.

2. For Ribs: Preheat oven to 375°F. Spread ribs in a single layer in a very large shallow nonreactive roasting pan, set on pulled-out middle oven shelf, add boiling water and salt, and cover with heavy-duty foil. Steam ribs until tender—about 1½ hours.

3. Reduce oven temperature to 350°F. Pour liquid from the pan, reserving 1 cup, and combine this with all remaining ingredients in a medium-size nonreactive saucepan. Cook and stir over moderate heat until the sugar dissolves—3 to 5 minutes.

4. Once again spread ribs in pan in a single layer and pour hot soy mixture over all. Return to oven and bake uncovered, basting every 15 minutes, until glistening and brown—about 1 hour. Meanwhile, set refrigerated sauerkraut on kitchen counter so it warms to room temperature.

5. To serve, bed sauerkraut on a heated large platter and arrange ribs on top. Strain hot soy mixture, drizzle some of it over ribs and sauerkraut, and pass the rest.

MAKES 4 TO 6 SERVINGS

casserole of ribs and white beans

A spin on everyone's favorite—Boston Baked Beans. This is a meatier recipe, slow-simmering, deeply flavorful. And talk about fall-off-the-bone tender!

1 pound dried navy or pea beans, washed, sorted, and soaked overnight in cold water

1½ quarts (6 cups) cold water (about)

4 pounds meaty spareribs, separated into individual ribs

Cold water to cover ribs by about 1½ inches

¼ cup vegetable oil

1 tablespoon salt, or to taste

½ teaspoon freshly ground black pepper, or to taste

1 large yellow onion, coarsely chopped

4 large garlic cloves, finely chopped

1½ teaspoons crumbled dried leaf marjoram

1 teaspoon crumbled dried leaf thyme

⅓ cup molasses

2 tablespoons tomato paste or ketchup

2 tablespoons cider vinegar

1. Drain beans, rinse well in cold water, and place in a large heavy kettle. Add just enough cold water to cover by about 1 inch and bring to a boil over moderate heat. Adjust heat so water barely ripples, cover, and cook until beans are nearly tender—about 1 hour.

2. Meanwhile, place ribs and water in a large heavy Dutch oven and bring to a boil over moderate heat. Adjust heat so water barely bubbles, cover, and simmer until rib meat is nearly tender—about 1 hour. Remove ribs from water and pat dry. Also drain beans, reserving 2½ cups cooking liquid.

3. Preheat oven to 350°F. Spritz a 4-quart casserole with nonstick cooking spray and set aside.

4. Heat oil in a large heavy skillet over moderately high heat until ripples appear on pan bottom—1½ to 2 minutes. Sprinkle ribs with 1 teaspoon salt and ¼ teaspoon pepper, then brown in batches in oil, making sure all sides are richly browned—12 to 15 minutes in all. Drain on paper toweling.

5. Add onion, garlic, marjoram, and thyme to skillet drippings and sauté, stirring often, until limp and touched with brown—8 to 10 minutes. Mix in reserved bean cooking liquid, molasses, tomato paste, vinegar, remaining salt and pepper, and bring to a boil.

6. Place ribs and beans in casserole, tossing lightly to distribute evenly, and pour boiling skillet mixture on top.

7. Cover and bake on middle oven shelf until beans and ribs are both very tender—about 1 hour. Taste for salt and pepper and adjust as needed.

8. Serve in heated large soup plates and accompany with a tartly dressed salad of crisp greens.

MAKES 6 SERVINGS

slow cooker brunswick stew with pork

Created nearly 200 years ago in Brunswick County, Virginia, by a camp cook in service to a group of gentlemen hunters, Brunswick Stew was originally made with squirrels. Today a family reunion staple with over-the-hill hens replacing squirrels, Brunswick Stew is still cooked all day over open fires. "Low 'n' slow" is the secret of good Brunswick Stew and that makes it ideal for slow cookers. Moreover, sinewy pork is as delicious in Brunswick Stew as any tough old bird and that's why I call for it in this scaled-down version. Note: Bacon drippings give the stew better flavor but use vegetable oil, if you must.

3 pounds boneless pork shoulder (not too lean), cut in 1½-inch cubes

3 tablespoons melted bacon drippings or vegetable oil

1 large Vidalia or other sweet onion, coarsely chopped

3 medium all-purpose potatoes, peeled and cut in ½-inch cubes

2 teaspoons salt, or to taste

½ teaspoon freshly ground black pepper, or to taste

1 teaspoon crumbled dried leaf thyme

2 large whole bay leaves (preferably fresh)

1¾ cups chicken broth

2 cups frozen baby lima beans, thawed

2 cups frozen whole-kernel yellow corn, thawed

1 tablespoon sugar or raw sugar

1 can (14½ ounces) diced tomatoes, with their liquid

3 tablespoons coarsely chopped fresh Italian parsley

1. Turn pork cubes in bacon drippings until nicely coated and arrange in a single layer around walls of a large (4- to 6-quart) slow cooker; pour any remaining drippings on top. Add onion and potatoes, sprinkle with salt, pepper, and thyme, and mix lightly without disturbing pork.

2. Drop in bay leaves, cover, and cook on HIGH 1 hour. Mix in broth, limas, corn, and sugar, cover, and cook on LOW 4 hours.

3. Mix in tomatoes, cover, and cook on LOW 2 hours more or until pork is tender and flavors marry. Discard bay leaves, taste for salt and pepper, and adjust as needed. Mix in parsley.

4. Ladle stew into heated large soup plates, making sure that everyone gets several pieces of pork. The traditional accompaniment? Fresh-baked corn bread.

MAKES 6 TO 8 SERVINGS

milwaukee "brew" stew

Nothing showcases Milwaukee's German heritage quite like this lusty beer-simmered pork stew. Served with redskin or fingerling potatoes boiled in their jackets (or, if you prefer, ladled alongside mashed potatoes), it's a wonderful way to warm a wintry day. Note: Like most stews, this one is better if made one day and served the next.

3 pounds boneless pork shoulder (not too lean), cut in 1-inch cubes

1½ cups unsifted all-purpose flour combined with 1 teaspoon salt and ½ teaspoon freshly ground black pepper (seasoned flour)

¼ cup bacon drippings, lard, or vegetable oil

4 large yellow onions, halved lengthwise, and each half thinly sliced

2 large garlic cloves, finely minced

2 large whole bay leaves (preferably fresh)

1 teaspoon caraway seeds

1¾ cups chicken broth

1 can (12 ounces) beer, at room temperature

1 tablespoon red wine vinegar

1 tablespoon raw sugar

⅓ cup coarsely chopped fresh Italian parsley

1. Dredge pork, a few pieces at a time, by shaking in seasoned flour in a large plastic bag.

2. Heat drippings in a large heavy nonreactive Dutch oven over moderately high heat until ripples appear on pan bottom—1½ to 2 minutes. Brown pork in several batches in drippings, allowing 8 to 10 minutes per batch and lifting each to a bowl as it browns.

3. Add onions, garlic, bay leaves, and caraway seeds to drippings and sauté, stirring often, until limp and lightly browned—10 to 12 minutes.

4. Return pork to pot, add broth, beer, vinegar, and sugar, and bring to a boil. Adjust heat so liquid bubbles gently, cover, and simmer until pork is fork-tender—about 2 hours. Discard bay leaves and mix in parsley.

5. If stew gravy seems thin when pork is done, scoop pork from pot and boil gravy uncovered until slightly thinner than pasta sauce.

6. Return pork to pot and heat 2 to 3 minutes. Taste for salt and pepper, adjusting as needed, then dish up and serve.

MAKES 6 SERVINGS

wine-and-garlic pork

On a trip to Madeira, I tasted this unusual dish at an inn shelved halfway up intricately terraced green mountains and vowed to get the recipe. It's easy enough though it does take time—*unattended time*—because the pork must marinate in the refrigerator overnight. Madeiran cooks use pork loin or tenderloin for this island classic and marinate it several days before committing it to a skillet—in my opinion, a good way to toughen such tender cuts. I've substituted pork shoulder, a much cheaper cut as well as one that benefits from marinating and slow cooking in a wine/vinegar mixture. Prepared my way, the pork's equally flavorful and deeply succulent.

3 pounds boneless pork shoulder (not too lean), cut in 1-inch cubes

3 cups dry white wine such as a Portuguese *vinho verde* (about)

1¼ cups white wine vinegar

6 large garlic cloves, smashed and skins removed

2 whole small yellow onions, peeled and each stuck with 2 whole cloves

4 large whole bay leaves (preferably fresh)

4 large sprigs fresh marjoram or 1 teaspoon crumbled dried leaf marjoram

4 small sprigs fresh thyme (preferably lemon thyme) or ½ teaspoon crumbled dried leaf thyme

2 strips (each about ½-inch wide and 2 to 3 inches long) lemon zest

8 black peppercorns

¼ teaspoon salt

6 tablespoons extra-virgin olive oil (about)

1 long slim loaf French or Italian bread, cut into diagonal slices about 1 inch thick

1. Place pork in a large nonreactive bowl. Combine next ten ingredients (wine through salt) and pour over pork. Mixture should cover pork; if not, add a little more wine or water. Cover and refrigerate overnight, turning pork occasionally in marinade.

2. When ready to proceed, lift pork to several thicknesses paper toweling with a slotted spoon and pat dry. Reserve marinade.

3. Heat 2 tablespoons oil in a large, heavy, non-reactive Dutch oven over moderately high heat until ripples appear on pan bottom—1½ to 2 minutes.

4. Brown pork in two to three batches in oil, allowing 8 to 10 minutes per batch, adding another 2 tablespoons oil as needed, and lifting each batch to a bowl as it browns.

5. Add marinade to Dutch oven and bring to a boil over moderate heat, stirring occasionally and skimming froth from surface as it collects.

6. Add pork to pot along with accumulated juices and bring to a simmer. Adjust heat so marinade barely bubbles, cover, and cook until pork is fork-tender—about 1½ hours.

7. About 30 minutes before pork is done, preheat oven to 350°F. Arrange bread slices in one layer on an ungreased baking sheet and brush tops with remaining oil—don't be stingy. Slide onto middle oven shelf and toast until lightly browned—10 to 12 minutes. Remove from oven, arrange in single layer on a heated large platter, and keep warm.

8. Meanwhile, ladle 2½ cups cooking liquid from pot and put through a fine sieve set over a small nonreactive saucepan. Set over high heat and boil uncovered until reduced by about one-third—about 6 to 8 minutes.

9. To serve, with slotted spoon scoop pork (and pork only) from pot to platter, arranging on top of toast, and drizzle with some reduced marinade. Accompany with boiled rice or potatoes, drizzling either with any leftover reduced marinade.

MAKES 6 SERVINGS

oven ragout of pork, mushrooms, and tomatoes

The advantages of oven stews are that they need little attention and rarely scorch on the bottom of the pot. Most supermarkets now sell packaged sliced mushrooms—both baby bellas (cremini) and white mushrooms. They're terrific time-savers and if they look good and fresh—no sign of withering or discoloring—I'm not ashamed to use them. If you prefer to slice your own, speed-slice the stemmed caps in an egg slicer. Tip: The reason for blending a little flour into sour cream is to keep it from curdling when added to a bubbling stew.

2 tablespoons unsalted butter or vegetable oil

2 large yellow onions, coarsely chopped

1 pound cremini or white mushrooms, stemmed, wiped clean, and thinly sliced (see headnote)

2 large garlic cloves, finely minced

2 tablespoons sweet paprika, or to taste

2½ pounds boneless pork shoulder (not too lean), cut in 1½-inch chunks

1 cup chicken broth

1 can (14½ ounces) diced tomatoes, with their liquid

1 tablespoon minced fresh savory, marjoram, or thyme, or 1 teaspoon dried herb, crumbled

1 teaspoon salt, or to taste

½ teaspoon freshly ground black pepper, or to taste

1 cup sour cream blended with 2 tablespoons all-purpose flour, at room temperature

1. Preheat oven to 325°F.

2. Melt butter in a large heavy nonreactive Dutch oven over moderately high heat for about a minute until bubbly. Add onions and sauté, stirring often, until limp and touched with brown—10 to 12 minutes. Add mushrooms and garlic and sauté, stirring now and then, until mushrooms have released their juices and these have evaporated—about 10 minutes.

3. Blend in paprika, then add pork and all remaining ingredients except sour cream mixture. Bring to a boil over moderately high heat, stirring often.

4. Cover Dutch oven, slide onto middle oven shelf, and braise until pork is fork-tender—about 1½ hours to 2 hours, stirring well at half-time.

5. Smooth in sour cream mixture, taste for paprika, salt, and pepper, and adjust as needed. Serve with buttered egg noodles or boiled redskin or fingerling potatoes.

MAKES 6 SERVINGS

pueblo posole with pork and green chilies

Posole (spelled *pozole* in Mexico) is nothing more than dried hominy, white kernels of field corn—or yellow—soaked in a lye bath until they puff and slip their skins. One of the most popular ways to use posole in New Mexico is in this peppery pork stew. Some cooks go all out using pig's trotters and other hard-to-find pork parts (the Mexican way) but for me this simple version, given to me years ago by a good cook at San Ildefonso Pueblo some 15 or 20 miles north of Santa Fe, is less daunting. You can buy dried posole in Latino groceries, but it takes time to soak and cook. Canned hominy, more readily available and a colossal time-saver, is what I use. Note: If you have no stomach for chili peppers, use one 7-ounce can chopped green chilies instead of two, or one 7-ouncer and one 4½-ouncer. The green chilies most often canned are jalapeños and poblanos, neither of which ranks very high on the Scoville scale used to measure chili heat. Tip: Mexican oregano is key here because of its distinctive flavor. Look for it in specialty food shops or Latino groceries.

3 tablespoons bacon drippings, lard, or vegetable oil

2 medium yellow onions, coarsely chopped

5 large garlic cloves, finely minced

1½ teaspoons Mexican oregano (see Tip above)

¾ teaspoon ground cumin

2 pounds boned pork shoulder (not too lean), cut in 1½-inch chunks

5¼ cups chicken broth

1 cup water

1 teaspoon salt, or to taste

2 cans (15 ounces each) white or yellow posole (whole hominy), well drained

2 cans (7 ounces each) chopped green chili peppers, well drained (see Note above)

OPTIONAL GARNISHES

12 large bright red radishes, stemmed, washed, and thinly sliced

2 large limes, cut in slim wedges

1. Heat drippings about 1 minute in a large heavy nonreactive Dutch oven over moderately high heat. Add onions, garlic, oregano, and cumin and cook, stirring occasionally, until limp and lightly browned—10 to 12 minutes.

2. Add pork, broth, water, and salt. Adjust heat so liquid barely ripples, cover, and simmer slowly, stirring from time to time, until pork is nearly tender—about 1½ hours.

3. Mix in posole and chilies and simmer uncovered until pork is fork-tender, flavors meld, and liquid reduces slightly—about 30 minutes more. Taste for salt and adjust as needed.

4. Spoon into heated large soup bowls and if you like, put out a platter of garnishes so everyone can add whatever they like to their posole. Accompany with tortillas or chunks of country bread. Good, too, with corn bread.

MAKES 6 SERVINGS

pork bowl of red

The original chili, a fiery cowboy concoction called "a bowl of red," did not contain hamburger, only diced leathery longhorn meat, water, plenty of chili powder, and plenty of heat. Pork, it seemed to me, would make an equally good chili. And so it does. Note: Masa harina, also called "tortilla flour," is made of pulverized dried field corn that's been given a lye bath, hence its unique flavor. You should find it in the baking or international section of your supermarket, and if not, head to the nearest Latino grocery. Tip: Bacon drippings give this chili especially good flavor, but cowboys, I suspect, would have used suet (beef fat).

¼ cup bacon drippings or vegetable oil

3 pounds boneless pork shoulder (not too lean),
cut in ¼- to-½-inch cubes

3 large garlic cloves, finely minced

¼ cup chili powder, or more,
depending on how "hot" you like things

1 tablespoon crumbled dried oregano
(preferably Mexican oregano)

1 teaspoon ground cumin

1½ teaspoons salt, or to taste

1 teaspoon ground hot red pepper (cayenne),
or to taste

1 quart (4 cups) water or, if you prefer, beef broth
(about)

2 tablespoons masa harina or stone-ground cornmeal
(see Note above)

1. Heat drippings in a large heavy nonreactive Dutch oven over moderately high heat until ripples appear on pan bottom—1½ to 2 minutes.

2. Brown pork in batches in drippings, allowing 8 to 10 minutes per batch and lifting each to a large bowl as it browns.

3. Add garlic to drippings and cook, stirring constantly until limp—2 to 3 minutes. Blend in chili powder, oregano, cumin, salt, and cayenne. Cook and stir over low heat to intensify flavors—3 to 5 minutes. Add water, and bring to a boil over high heat.

4. Return pork to pot along with accumulated juices. Adjust heat so liquid bubbles gently, cover, and simmer until pork is tender—1¼ to 1½ hours.

5. Blend in masa harina, cover, and cook over lowest heat just until chili has thickened slightly—about 30 minutes. Taste for salt and cayenne and adjust as needed. If chili seems thick, stir in about ½ cup hot water.

6. Ladle into heated soup bowls and serve with tortillas or corn bread.

MAKES 6 SERVINGS

gypsy goulash

Though this recipe comes out of Middle Europe, it's the sort of husky, economical stew that would have been bubbled up over campfires wherever gypsies roamed. I saw many gypsy encampments in my years of traveling about Portugal, particularly on the back roads of Alentejo, that vast land of cork, pork, and olives east of Lisbon. Note: This stew is equally good made with lamb shoulder.

3 pounds boneless pork shoulder (not too lean), cut in 1-inch cubes

1½ cups unsifted all-purpose flour combined with 2 teaspoons sweet paprika, 1½ teaspoons salt, and ¾ teaspoon freshly ground black pepper (seasoned flour)

6 tablespoons bacon drippings, lard, or vegetable oil

2 large yellow onions, halved lengthwise and each half thinly sliced

1 teaspoon caraway seeds

1¾ cups chicken broth plus enough cold water to total 4 cups

1 can (14½ ounces) diced tomatoes, drained well

TOPPING

1 large Spanish onion, halved lengthwise and each half thinly sliced

2 tablespoons lard or vegetable oil

1. Dredge pork, a few pieces at a time, by shaking with seasoned flour in a large plastic zipper bag and set aside.

2. Heat 4 tablespoons drippings in a large heavy nonreactive Dutch oven over moderately high heat until ripples appear on pan bottom—1½ to 2 minutes. Brown pork in three batches in drippings, allowing 8 to 10 minutes per batch and lifting each to a bowl as it browns.

3. Add remaining 2 tablespoons drippings to Dutch oven along with onions and caraway seeds and sauté, stirring often, until onions are limp and lightly browned—10 to 12 minutes.

4. Return pork to pot along with accumulated juices, add broth and tomatoes, and bring to a boil. Adjust heat so liquid bubbles gently, cover, and simmer until pork is fork-tender—1½ to 2 hours.

5. Meanwhile, prepare Topping: Stir-fry onion in lard in a large heavy skillet over moderately high heat until crisp and brown—about 10 to 12 minutes. Drain on paper toweling.

6. If stew gravy seems thin when pork is done, scoop pork from pot and boil gravy uncovered until slightly thinner than pasta sauce. Return pork to pot and heat 2 to 3 minutes. Taste for salt and pepper and adjust as needed.

7. To serve, ladle stew onto a heated large deep platter and sprinkle with reserved fried onions. Accompany with crusty chunks of country bread.

MAKES 6 SERVINGS

pork hot pot with parslied apple and carrot gravy

Simmering ever so gently and gathering flavor all the way, this stew needs nothing more to accompany than a green salad and a good country bread to catch any extra gravy. Like most stews, it's better if made one day and served the next.

3½ pounds boned pork shoulder (not too lean), cut in 1½-inch cubes

Cold water to cover pork by about 1 inch

4 medium carrots, peeled, and thickly sliced

2 medium tart green apples, peeled, cored, and thickly sliced

2 large yellow onions, halved lengthwise and each half thickly sliced

1 large garlic clove, coarsely chopped

2 large sprigs fresh thyme (preferably lemon thyme) or ½ teaspoon crumbled dried leaf thyme

1¾ cups chicken broth

1¼ cups apple juice blended with ¼ cup dry vermouth

½ cup heavy cream blended with 1 teaspoon Dijon mustard

¼ cup moderately finely chopped fresh Italian parsley

Salt to taste

Freshly ground black pepper to taste

1. Bring pork and water to a boil in a large heavy nonreactive Dutch oven over moderate heat, adjust heat so water barely bubbles, and cook uncovered until a scum rises to the top—about 10 minutes. Drain pork in a colander, then rinse both it and the pot to remove every trace of scum.

2. Return pork to pot, add next seven ingredients (carrots through apple juice mixture), and bring to a boil over moderate heat. Adjust heat so liquid barely ripples, cover, and simmer until pork is tender—about 1½ hours.

3. Using a slotted spoon, transfer pork to a heat-proof bowl. Also remove thyme sprigs, if used, and discard. Boil pot mixture uncovered 20 to 25 minutes until reduced by about one-third.

4. Set off heat, cool 20 minutes, then purée in three or four batches in a food processor or electric blender.

5. Return to Dutch oven along with pork, stir well, and bring to serving temperature over lowest heat (use a diffuser if gravy threatens to stick).

6. Blend in cream-mustard mixture, add parsley, then season to taste with salt and pepper. Heat 1 to 2 minutes longer, dish up, and serve.

MAKES 6 TO 8 SERVINGS

pork paprika

Paprikash, the Hungarian stew reddened with paprika and mellowed with sour cream, is usually made with veal. But why not pork? It's cheaper than veal and more readily available. Serve over rice or, to be more traditional, poppy-seed noodles. Delicious, too, over fresh sauerkraut. Note: To boost the nutritional value, I've added red bell peppers.

4 tablespoons vegetable oil or a 50/50 mix of bacon drippings and vegetable oil

3 pounds boneless pork shoulder (not too lean), cut in 1½-inch cubes

2 large yellow onions, halved lengthwise and each half thinly sliced

4 medium red bell peppers, cored, seeded, and slivered lengthwise

1 can (6-ounces) tomato paste

2 tablespoons sweet paprika, or to taste

1 tablespoon coarsely chopped fresh thyme or 1 teaspoon crumbled dried leaf thyme

1½ teaspoons salt, or to taste

½ teaspoon freshly ground black pepper, or to taste

Cold water to cover stew ingredients by about ½ inch

1 cup sour cream, at room temperature

1. Heat 2 tablespoons oil in a large heavy nonreactive Dutch oven over moderately high heat until ripples appear on pan bottom—1½ to 2 minutes.

2. Brown pork in batches in oil, allowing 8 to 10 minutes per batch and lifting each to a bowl as it browns.

3. Add remaining oil, or, for better flavor, bacon drippings, heat 1 to 2 minutes, add onions and bell peppers and cook, stirring often, until limp and lightly browned—about 10 minutes.

4. Return pork to pot along with accumulated juices, mix in all but last ingredient (sour cream), and bring to a boil over moderately high heat. Adjust heat so liquid barely ripples, cover, and simmer until pork is fork-tender—about 1½ hours.

5. Taste for paprika, salt, and pepper and adjust as needed. Smooth in sour cream, heat a minute or two longer, and serve.

MAKES 6 SERVINGS

pork à la normande

Traveling about Normandy on article assignment, I was struck by the number of pork and apple combinations, among them a stew very much like this one. Begin it on the top stove, finish it in the oven. I like to accompany it with little redskin potatoes, boiled whole and unpeeled. Note: Calvados, if you don't know it, is the smooth apple fire-water for which Normandy is famous.

2 tablespoons vegetable oil

2 tablespoons unsalted butter

2½ pounds boneless pork shoulder (not too lean),
cut in 1- to 1½-inch cubes

1 teaspoon salt, or to taste

½ teaspoon freshly ground black pepper,
or to taste

2 large yellow onions, coarsely chopped

4 medium tart green apples,
peeled, cored, and coarsely chopped

2 large garlic cloves, finely minced

2 tablespoons tomato paste

½ cup chicken broth

¼ cup Calvados or brandy (see Note above)

1 small sprig fresh rosemary
or 1 teaspoon crumbled dried leaf rosemary

1 cup heavy cream

1. Preheat oven to 350°F.

2. Heat oil and 1 tablespoon butter in a medium-size heavy nonreactive Dutch oven over moderately high heat until ripples appear on pan bottom—1½ to 2 minutes.

3. Sprinkle pork with salt and pepper and brown in two to three batches, allowing 8 to 10 minutes per batch and lifting each to a large bowl as it browns.

4. Add remaining butter to Dutch oven, heat 1 minute or so, then add onions, and sauté, stirring often, until limp and lightly browned—about 10 minutes.

5. Add apples and garlic and sauté, stirring occasionally, until limp—about 10 minutes. Add tomato paste and cook and stir 2 minutes. Mix in broth and Calvados, then drop in rosemary sprig. Return pork to pot along with accumulated juices and bring to a boil.

6. Cover, slide onto middle oven shelf, and braise pork for 1 hour. Smooth in cream, cover, and continue braising until pork is tender—½ to ¾ hour longer. Discard rosemary sprig, if used. Taste for salt and pepper and adjust as needed. Note: If mixture seems soupy, lift pork to a large bowl, set Dutch oven over moderate heat, and boil uncovered until the consistency of gravy. Spoon pork back into gravy and heat 1 or 2 minutes.

7. Dish up and serve with boiled redskin potatoes.

MAKES 4 TO 6 SERVINGS

smothered pork and caraway cabbage

Few recipes are easier or more economical than this one. And few more flavorful. Cabbage and caraway are one of those magical combos made even better when a few fennel seeds are added.

2 tablespoons bacon drippings or vegetable oil

2 pounds boneless pork shoulder (not too lean),
cut in 1-inch cubes

1 medium yellow onion, coarsely chopped

1½ teaspoons salt, or to taste

½ teaspoon freshly ground black pepper,
or to taste

3 cups chicken or vegetable broth

6 cups coarsely shredded or thinly sliced cabbage
or Savoy cabbage

¾ teaspoon caraway seeds, lightly crushed

¾ teaspoon fennel seeds, lightly crushed

2 tablespoons cider vinegar, or to taste

¼ cup water blended with
2 tablespoons all-purpose flour
(thickener)

1. Heat drippings in a medium-size heavy nonreactive Dutch oven over moderately high heat until ripples appear on pan bottom—1½ to 2 minutes.

2. Brown pork in two batches in drippings, allowing 8 to 10 minutes per batch and lifting each to a large bowl as it browns.

3. Return pork to pot along with accumulated juices, add onion, and sauté 5 to 8 minutes until golden. Add ½ teaspoon salt, the pepper, and broth, and bring to a boil over high heat. Adjust heat so liquid ripples gently, cover, and simmer, stirring occasionally, until pork is nearly tender—about 1 hour.

4. Add cabbage, caraway and fennel seeds, vinegar, and remaining 1 teaspoon salt, and mix well. Cover and simmer until cabbage is tender—about 30 minutes.

5. Blend in thickener, then cook and stir over moderate heat until liquid is lightly thickened and no raw floury taste lingers—about 5 minutes. Taste for vinegar, salt, and pepper and adjust as needed.

6. Serve with baked or mashed sweet potatoes or Irish potatoes.

MAKES 4 SERVINGS

sancocho

Before food processors made short shrift of long-winded recipes, this Puerto Rican pork stew was for intrepid cooks only. Who wanted to reduce onions and garlic and seven other seasonings to paste in a mortar and pestle? Today a quick whiz in the processor—or electric blender at high speed—and the pork's in the pot. No preliminary browning. How hard is that? Note: Once hard to find, plantains now routinely show up in supermarkets and are a Latino grocery staple.

1 large Spanish onion, cut in slim wedges

3 to 4 medium jalapeño peppers, stemmed, seeded, and chunked, depending on how "hot" you like things

3 large whole garlic cloves, peeled

½ cup fresh Italian parsley leaves (measure loosely packed)

½ cup fresh cilantro leaves (measure loosely packed)

¼ cup fresh lime juice

2 large bay leaves, crumbled

1½ teaspoons salt, or to taste

¼ teaspoon freshly ground black pepper, or to taste

3 pounds boneless pork shoulder (not too lean), cut in 1½-inch cubes

Cold water to cover pork by about ¼ inch

1 medium sweet potato, peeled and cut in 1-inch cubes

2 medium plantains, peeled and cut in 1-inch cubes (see headnote)

1½ cups frozen whole-kernel yellow corn, thawed

½ cup loosely packed fresh cilantro leaves puréed with 1 cup chicken broth

1. Purée first nine ingredients (onion through black pepper) in a food processor until smooth, then scoop into a large nonreactive Dutch oven.

2. Distribute pieces of pork evenly in mixture, add water, and bring to a boil over moderately high heat. Adjust heat so liquid bubbles gently, cover, and cook until pork is nearly fork-tender—about 1 hour.

3. Mix in sweet potato and plantains, cover, and simmer just until a fork pierces them easily—about 20 minutes. Mash sweet potato and plantains lightly to thicken sauce a bit.

4. Mix in corn, cover, and cook 15 minutes. Taste for salt and pepper and adjust as needed. Blend in cilantro purée.

5. Ladle into heated large soup plates and serve with corn tortillas, corn sticks, or other corn bread right out of the oven. Note: I sometimes top each portion with a few cubes of freshly diced firm-ripe Hass avocado—for this amount of stew, 2 medium avocados is about right. If you work fast, there's no need to dip the avocado cubes in lime juice because they'll be eaten before they darken.

MAKES 6 SERVINGS

polish pot roast of pork with red wine and tomatoes

What distinguishes this pot roast is the rich vegetable gravy spooned over it. Don't be daunted by the lengthy ingredient list—many are pantry staples, quickly measured. Note: If you should spot parsley root at your greengrocer's, buy one, trim, peel, dice until you have ½ cup, and substitute for the parsley sprigs. Adding a peeled and chunked parsnip to the pot wouldn't be amiss, either.

A 4- to 5-pound bone-in pork shoulder blade or picnic roast (not too lean)

1 teaspoon salt, or to taste

½ teaspoon freshly ground black pepper, or to taste

2 tablespoons unsalted butter

1 tablespoon vegetable oil

2 medium yellow onions, halved lengthwise and each half thinly sliced

2 medium carrots, peeled and cut in 1-inch chunks

1 large celery rib, cut in 1-inch chunks (include some leafy tops)

1 small celery root, peeled and diced (about 1 cup)

12 large fresh Italian parsley sprigs (see Note above)

1 can (14½ ounces) diced tomatoes, with their liquid

½ cup dry red wine

½ cup chicken broth

½ teaspoon crumbled dried leaf marjoram

½ teaspoon caraway seeds

⅛ to ¼ teaspoon ground allspice, depending on how spicy you like things

¼ cup unsifted all-purpose flour blended with ½ cup cold water (thickener)

1. Rub pork shoulder all over with salt and pepper and let stand at room temperature 1 hour.

2. Heat butter and oil in a large heavy nonreactive Dutch oven over moderately high heat until ripples appear on pan bottom—1½ to 2 minutes. Add pork shoulder and brown well on all sides—10 to 12 minutes.

3. Add all but final ingredient (thickener) and bring to a boil. Adjust heat so liquid bubbles gently, cover, and simmer until pork is fork-tender—about 1¾ to 2 hours.

4. Lift pot roast from Dutch oven, tent loosely with foil, and keep warm. Strain pan liquid through a fine sieve and blend ½ cup of it into thickener. Return remaining strained pan liquid to pot, add thickener mixture, and cook and stir over moderate heat until gravy is thickened, smooth, and no raw floury taste lingers—about 5 minutes. Taste for salt and pepper and adjust as needed.

5. Slice pot roast—not too thick—and ladle gravy over each portion as well as over any mashed potatoes served alongside (for me, the best possible accompaniment).

MAKES 6 SERVINGS

braised pork shoulder smitane

I've always been fond of the sour cream sauces so popular in eastern Europe. Called smitanes, they may be ladled over meat, fish, or fowl and their flavors vary according to what goes into them. The one constant? Sour cream. According to culinary historian Alan Davidson, smitane derives from *smetana* and *smietana,* the Russian and Polish words for sour cream. The smitanes I've enjoyed in restaurants are usually reserved for pricey pheasant or tenderloins of beef, veal, or pork. Much as I dote on 24-carat pork tenderloin, I decided to develop a cents-saving Pork Smitane using boned and rolled pork shoulder. I think you'll like the results.

A 3-pound boned and rolled pork shoulder roast (not too lean)

1 teaspoon salt, or to taste

½ teaspoon freshly ground black pepper, or to taste

¼ cup (½ stick) unsalted butter

¼ pound thickly sliced smoked bacon

1 large yellow onion, halved lengthwise and each half thinly sliced

2 small parsnips, peeled and diced

1 small celery root, peeled and diced (about 1 cup)

1¾ cups chicken broth plus enough cold water to total 4 cups

¼ cup unsifted all-purpose flour blended with ½ cup cold water or chicken broth (thickener)

1 cup sour cream, at room temperature

1. Rub pork all over with salt and pepper. Melt butter in a large heavy Dutch oven over moderately high heat and as soon as it froths and subsides, add pork and brown well on all sides—10 to 12 minutes. Lift to a large plate, drape with bacon, and set aside.

2. Add onion, parsnips, and celery root to pot and sauté, stirring now and then, until nicely browned—10 to 12 minutes.

3. Anchor bacon-draped pork in vegetables, add chicken broth mixture, and bring to a boil. Adjust heat so liquid bubbles gently, cover, and simmer until pork is fork-tender—1½ to 1¾ hours.

4. Lift pork to a heated platter, leaving bacon in place, tent loosely with foil, and keep warm. Ladle out and reserve 1 cup cooking liquid. Cool the rest along with all vegetables 15 to 20 minutes, then purée in 3 or 4 batches in the food processor and return to Dutch oven.

5. Blend reserved 1 cup cooking liquid into thickener, add to purée in pot, and cook and stir over moderate heat until thickened, smooth, and no raw flour taste lingers—about 5 minutes. Smooth in sour cream, taste for salt and pepper, and adjust as needed. Do not boil or sauce may curdle.

6. Slice pork—not too thick—and ladle sauce over each portion. Be generous! Serve with boiled redskin or fingerling potatoes.

MAKES 6 SERVINGS

alsatian fresh ham braised with sauerkraut and vermouth

A fresh ham is nothing more than the hind leg of a hog—unbrined, uncured, unsmoked. Unlike the tenderloin, which can be roasted, a fresh ham is best when braised—browned briefly, then cooked slowly with a little liquid and/or vegetables to keep it moist as it cooks. The choice here? Sauerkraut plus vermouth, chicken broth, thinly sliced onions and carrots. Note: Fresh sauerkraut may be sold by the quart or by the pound. For the record, 1 quart equals 2 pounds. Tip: If top halves of carrots are chunky, halve lengthwise before slicing.

**A 4-pound bone-in fresh ham,
skin or rind and excess fat removed**

1 teaspoon salt

½ teaspoon freshly ground black pepper

6 ounces smoked slab bacon, cut in ¼-inch dice

SAUERKRAUT

2 tablespoons bacon drippings (from bacon above)

1 tablespoon vegetable oil

**1 large yellow onion,
halved lengthwise and each half thinly sliced**

**2 small carrots, peeled and thinly sliced
(see Tip above)**

**1 quart (4 cups) firmly packed fresh sauerkraut,
rinsed and squeezed dry (see Note above)**

1½ teaspoons caraway seeds

**½ cup dry vermouth or dry white wine
such as Riesling or Gewürztraminer**

1¾ cups chicken broth

**6 small fresh parsley sprigs tied in cheesecloth
with 2 large whole bay leaves (preferably fresh),
10 lightly crushed black peppercorns, and
4 juniper berries (bouquet garni)**

1. Rub ham well with salt and pepper and set aside. Cook bacon over moderately low heat in a heavy nonreactive Dutch oven large enough to accommodate the ham until all drippings render out and only crisp brown bits remain—about 8 to 10 minutes. Scoop browned bits to paper toweling and reserve.

2. Heat drippings until ripples appear on pan bottom—1½ to 2 minutes. Add ham and brown well on all sides—about 15 minutes. Lift ham to a large bowl and reserve. Preheat oven to 325°F.

3. For Sauerkraut: Spoon all but 2 tablespoons drippings from Dutch oven, add oil, onion, and carrots and sauté, stirring occasionally, until limp and touched with brown—about 10 minutes. Mix in sauerkraut and caraway seeds and cook 10 minutes, stirring now and then. Add vermouth, broth, and bouquet garni and bring to a boil.

4. Set Dutch oven on open oven door, center ham in sauerkraut, and add accumulated ham juices. Cover Dutch oven tight, slide onto middle oven shelf, and braise until ham is tender—2 to 2½ hours. Discard bouquet garni.

5. Lift ham to a cutting board, let rest 15 minutes, then slice thin. Stir sauerkraut well so it mixes nicely with pan juices.

6. To serve, overlap slices of ham down middle of a heated large platter, wreathe sauerkraut around edge, and sprinkle with reserved bacon bits.

MAKES 6 SERVINGS

rhineland pork shoulder

Once everything's in the pot, no tending needed for this shoulder roast if you keep the heat low and check occasionally to see that the pot isn't boiling dry. If so, top off with a bit of additional broth. Along the Rhine boiled potatoes accompany this pot roast but in Bavaria, it's more likely to be potato dumplings. I prefer boiled potatoes—less muss, less fuss.

1 teaspoon Dijon mustard

1 teaspoon salt, or to taste

½ teaspoon freshly ground black pepper, or to taste

A 3-pound boneless pork shoulder (not too lean)

¼ cup (½ stick) unsalted butter

1 large yellow onion, coarsely chopped

2 medium carrots, peeled and thinly sliced

1 large ripe tomato, peeled, cored, seeded, and coarsely chopped, or 1 cup canned diced tomato

2 large whole bay leaves (preferably fresh)

4 large fresh Italian parsley sprigs

2 large fresh thyme sprigs or 1 teaspoon crumbled dried leaf thyme

3 whole cloves

1½ cups chicken broth (about)

½ cup good Rhine wine such as Riesling

3 tablespoons all-purpose flour blended with ½ cup cold water (thickener)

1. Combine mustard, salt, and pepper and rub all over pork. Melt butter in a large heavy nonreactive Dutch oven over moderately high heat and as soon as it froths and subsides, add pork and brown well on all sides—10 to 12 minutes. Lift to a large plate and set aside.

2. Add onion and carrots to drippings and sauté, stirring now and then, until nicely browned—10 to 12 minutes. Return pork to pot, add all but last ingredient (thickener), and bring to a boil. Adjust heat so liquid barely bubbles, cover, and cook until pork is fork-tender—1¾ to 2 hours.

3. Lift pork to a heated platter, tent loosely with foil, and keep warm. Ladle out and reserve ½ cup cooking liquid, and discard bay leaves, parsley and thyme sprigs, and cloves.

4. Cool remaining pan liquid 15 to 20 minutes, then purée along with all vegetables in 2 or 3 batches in a food processor and return to Dutch oven.

5. Blend reserved ½ cup cooking liquid into thickener, add to purée, and cook and stir over moderate heat until thickened, smooth, and no raw floury taste lingers—about 5 minutes. Taste gravy for salt and pepper and adjust as needed.

6. Slice pork—not too thick—and ladle gravy over each portion. Also over the boiled potatoes that accompany it.

MAKES 6 SERVINGS

braised shoulder of pork with herb stuffing and pan gravy

Fresh pork shoulder, boned, filled with sage-and-thyme-scented bread stuffing, and braised until tender is elegant but economical party food. Have the butcher bone the shoulder for you, making a neat cavity that's ready to stuff. Turn the pan drippings into a flavorful gravy and round out the main course with steamed broccoli or asparagus. Note: Use firm-textured or home-style white bread for the crumbs and make them good and coarse. One slice, buzzed to crumbs in a food processor, equals ½ cup, so for this stuffing you'll need six slices. Tip: Lemon thyme is lovely in this stuffing so if you grow your own or can find it, by all means use it.

PORK

A 4½- to 5-pound pork shoulder, boned and trimmed of excess fat (see headnote)

1 teaspoon salt

½ teaspoon freshly ground black pepper

2 cups chicken broth

STUFFING

¼ cup (½ stick) unsalted butter

1 large yellow onion, coarsely chopped

2 large garlic cloves, finely minced

1 tablespoon finely chopped fresh thyme or ¾ teaspoon crumbled dried leaf thyme (see Tip above)

1 tablespoon finely chopped fresh sage or 1 teaspoon rubbed sage

3 cups coarse white breadcrumbs (see Note above)

½ teaspoon finely grated lemon zest

½ teaspoon salt

¼ teaspoon freshly ground black pepper

¼ cup chicken broth (about)

GRAVY

½ cup pan drippings (the fatty ones on top make the best gravy)

⅓ cup unsifted all-purpose flour

1½ cups chicken broth

1½ cups milk

1 tablespoon minced fresh sage or ½ teaspoon rubbed sage

1½ teaspoons minced fresh thyme or ½ teaspoon crumbled dried leaf thyme

½ teaspoon salt, or to taste

¼ teaspoon freshly ground black pepper, or to taste

1. For Pork: Preheat oven to 325°F. Rub pork shoulder inside and out with salt and pepper and set aside.

2. For Stuffing: Melt butter in a large deep heavy skillet over moderately high heat, add onion, garlic, thyme, and sage and sauté, stirring often, until limp and golden—5 to 8 minutes. Mix in all remaining ingredients, adding only enough broth to moisten stuffing.

3. Spoon stuffing lightly into cavity in pork, tie into a compact shape, and place fat side up on a rack in a roasting pan. Pour the 2 cups broth over pork and cover pan with heavy-duty foil.

4. Braise on middle oven rack 1 hour. Remove foil and continue braising until pork is fork-tender and an instant-read thermometer thrust into meatiest part of shoulder, not touching stuffing, registers 160°F—1½ to 2 hours. Remove pork from oven, tent loosely with foil, and let rest while you prepare gravy.

5. For Gravy: Pour pan drippings into a small heavy saucepan and cool 5 minutes. Bend in flour, and cook and stir over moderate heat 1 minute. Add broth, milk, sage, and thyme and cook, stirring constantly, until thickened, smooth, and no raw flour taste remains—about 5 minutes. Season to taste with salt and pepper.

6. Remove strings from pork and transfer to a heated platter. Slice slightly on the bias so that more of the stuffing shows. Pass the gravy separately.

MAKES 8 TO 10 SERVINGS

pork swiss steak with root vegetables

Say "Swiss Steak" and beef springs to mind, a tough cut that requires low 'n' slow cooking in a small amount of liquid if it's to be juicy and tender. But why not pork? Blade and arm steaks—also called blade, round-bone, or shoulder chops—cut from the sinewy shoulder are just the thing for this recipe. Three steaks or chops—each weighing about 1½ pounds—will serve six nicely.

½ cup unsifted all-purpose flour mixed with
1 teaspoon salt and ½ teaspoon each freshly ground
black pepper and ground ginger (seasoned flour)

4 to 4½ pounds 1½- to 2-inch-thick bone-in pork arm
or blade steaks (see headnote)

3 tablespoons vegetable oil

1 tablespoon unsalted butter

2 large yellow onions, coarsely chopped

2 large garlic cloves, minced

1 cup chicken broth

½ cup apple cider

3 medium carrots, peeled and cut in 2-inch chunks

3 medium parsnips, peeled and cut in 2-inch chunks

3 medium turnips, peeled and cut in slim wedges
or 2 cups 1-inch rutabaga chunks

⅓ cup coarsely chopped fresh Italian parsley

1. Preheat oven to 325°F. Rub seasoned flour into both sides of each steak.

2. Heat 2 tablespoons oil and the butter in a large heavy nonreactive skillet over moderately high heat until ripples appear on skillet bottom—1½ to 2 minutes.

3. Add steaks and brown well on both sides—about 12 minutes in all. Transfer to a shallow nonreactive roasting pan and set aside.

4. Add remaining oil, onions, and garlic to skillet and sauté, stirring often, until lightly browned—about 10 minutes. Scoop on top of steaks.

5. Add broth and cider to skillet and cook, scraping up brown bits, 1 to 2 minutes. Pour over steaks, cover with foil, and bake 1½ hours on middle oven shelf.

6. Uncover, arrange carrots, parsnips, and turnips around steaks, cover, and bake 30 to 40 minutes longer or until steaks and vegetables are tender. Taste pan gravy for salt and pepper and adjust as needed.

7. To serve, halve each steak, transfer to a heated large platter, and wreathe with vegetables. Spoon pan gravy over all and sprinkle with parsley.

MAKES 6 SERVINGS

pork shoulder steaks creole

Everyone gets their own steak, superbly tender thanks to long and lazy cooking plus the softening effect of tomatoes. Plenty of flavor here. Accompany with boiled rice—a perfect sop for that spicy Creole tomato sauce.

⅓ cup unsifted all-purpose flour
mixed with 1 teaspoon salt and
½ teaspoon freshly ground black pepper
(seasoned flour)

6 boneless blade steaks (about 8 ounces each)

6 slices smoked bacon, stacked and thinly sliced

1 large yellow onion, coarsely chopped

1 small red bell pepper,
cored, seeded, and coarsely chopped

1 small green bell pepper,
cored, seeded, and coarsely chopped

2 large garlic cloves, finely chopped

2 cans (10 ounces each) diced tomatoes and
green chilies, with their liquid

½ teaspoon crumbled dried leaf thyme

½ teaspoon crumbled dried leaf oregano

¼ cup coarsely chopped fresh Italian parsley

1. Rub seasoned flour into both sides of each steak.

2. Sauté bacon in a large deep heavy nonreactive skillet over moderately high heat, stirring occasionally, until all drippings render out and only crisp brown bits remain—about 10 minutes. Using a slotted spoon, lift browned bits to paper toweling to drain and reserve.

3. Brown steaks well on both sides in skillet drippings over moderately high heat—about 12 minutes in all. Transfer to a large plate and set aside.

4. Add onion, bell peppers, and garlic to skillet and sauté, stirring occasionally, until limp and touched with brown—10 to 12 minutes. Mix in tomatoes, thyme, and oregano, then return steaks to skillet along with accumulated juices and scoop tomato mixture on top.

5. Adjust heat so mixture bubbles gently, cover, and simmer until steaks are fork-tender—1 to 1½ hours. Mix in parsley and reserved bacon, taste for salt and pepper, and adjust as needed.

6. To serve, plate each steak and top with a generous ladling of tomato-y sauce. Accompany with fluffy boiled rice.

MAKES 6 SERVINGS

pork shoulder steaks braised the brazilian way

The cooking of Brazil is a brilliant fusion of flavors—Portuguese, from the Europeans who colonized this vast South American country early in the 16th century, African, from those who were brought there to work the sugar plantations, and native Indians. Peppers sweet and hot play prominent roles as do tomatoes, onions, garlic, and pork. I like this stove-top way of braising gristly shoulder cuts—it's slightly faster than oven-braising. And I also like to serve these shoulder steaks as Brazilians might—over boiled rice or roasted sweet potatoes.

⅓ cup unsifted all-purpose flour mixed with
3 tablespoons cornmeal, 1 teaspoon salt,
and ½ teaspoon freshly ground black pepper
(seasoned flour)

4 to 4½ pounds 1½- to 2-inch-thick bone-in pork arm
or blade steaks (see headnote, Pork Swiss Steak
with Root Vegetables, page 223)

3 tablespoons extra-virgin olive oil or vegetable oil

1 large yellow onion, halved,
and each half thinly sliced

1 large red bell pepper, cored, seeded,
and cut lengthwise into slim wedges

4 large garlic cloves, thinly sliced

2 cans (10 ounces each) diced tomatoes
and green chilies, with their liquid

¼ cup seedless raisins, preferably golden sultanas

2 tablespoons cider or red wine vinegar

2 tablespoons raw sugar

1 teaspoon ground ginger

1 teaspoon crumbled dried leaf oregano

½ teaspoon hot red pepper sauce, or more,
depending on how "hot" you like things

⅓ cup coarsely chopped fresh cilantro

1. Rub seasoned flour into both sides of each steak.

2. Heat oil in a large heavy nonreactive Dutch oven over moderately high heat until ripples appear on pan bottom—1½ to 2 minutes.

3. Add steaks and brown well on both sides—about 12 minutes in all. Transfer to a large plate and set aside.

4. Add onion, bell pepper, and garlic to drippings, and sauté, stirring often, until lightly browned—8 to 10 minutes. Mix in all but the final ingredient (cilantro), return steaks to pot along with accumulated juices, pushing underneath vegetable mixture, and bring to a boil over high heat.

5. Adjust heat so liquid bubbles gently, cover, and simmer until steaks are fork-tender—1 to 1½ hours. Transfer steaks to a heated large platter and keep warm.

6. Stir cilantro into pan mixture (sauce), taste for salt and pepper, and adjust as needed.

7. To serve, ladle sauce over steaks and accompany with boiled rice (brown or white) or roasted sweet potatoes. Good, too, with black beans.

MAKES 6 SERVINGS

pork shoulder steaks braised with garlic and olives

Here's another "Swiss" steak made with arm or blade steaks cut from the pork shoulder, this one with a Spanish accent. Note: Olive salad (chopped pimiento-stuffed olives sold by the jar in many supermarkets) is a time-saving substitute for whole olives, which must be chopped.

⅓ cup unsifted all-purpose flour mixed with
1 tablespoon hot paprika, 1 teaspoon salt, and
½ teaspoon each freshly ground black pepper
and crumbled dried leaf thyme
(seasoned flour)

4 to 4½ pounds 1½- to 2-inch-thick bone-in pork arm
or blade steaks (see headnote, Pork Swiss Steak
with Root Vegetables, page 223)

3 tablespoons extra-virgin olive oil

1 large yellow onion, halved,
and each half thinly sliced

4 large garlic cloves, thinly sliced

1 cup chicken broth

½ cup dry sherry

⅔ cup coarsely chopped pimiento-stuffed olives
(see Note above)

2 tablespoons leftover seasoned flour (above)
blended with ½ cup chicken broth (thickener)

¼ cup coarsely chopped fresh Italian parsley

1. Preheat oven to 325°F. Rub seasoned flour into both sides of each steak. Reserve 2 tablespoons leftover seasoned flour to thicken gravy.

2. Heat oil in a large heavy nonreactive skillet over moderately high heat until ripples appear on skillet bottom—1½ to 2 minutes.

3. Add steaks and brown well on both sides—about 12 minutes in all. Transfer to a shallow nonreactive roasting pan and set aside.

4. Add onion and garlic to drippings, and sauté, stirring often, until lightly browned—8 to 10 minutes. Add broth, sherry, and olives, bring to a simmer, then pour over steaks.

5. Cover with foil, slide onto middle oven shelf, and bake until steaks are fork-tender—1½ to 2 hours.

6. Halve steaks, transfer to a heated large platter, tent loosely with foil, and keep warm while you make pan gravy.

7. Blend about ½ cup hot pan liquid into thickener and stir back into roasting pan. Set directly over moderate heat and cook, stirring constantly, until gravy thickens and no longer tastes of raw flour—about 5 minutes. Mix in parsley, taste for salt and pepper, and adjust as needed.

8. To serve, ladle gravy over steaks and accompany with fingerling or redskin potatoes boiled or roasted in their skins.

MAKES 6 SERVINGS

spicy braised pork belly with glazed carrots

Pork belly (bacon, not cured, not smoked) is the meat of the moment and it has chefs scrambling to one-up one another in their dash to create new and novel recipes. This one and the one that follows are my own. Unfortunately, few supermarkets sell pork belly, so head for your nearest boutique butcher or high-end grocery. The best way to describe pork belly? Rich, rich, rich—but the good news is that pork fat is less saturated than beef or lamb fat. Note: Begin this recipe a day before you serve it so that the spicy rub permeates the meat. Tip: The fastest way to grind spices for the dry rub is in a little electric coffee grinder. The texture should be about that of cracked pepper. Failing that, use a mortar and pestle, or simply whack the spices with a rolling pin or meat pounder.

2 star anise

2 whole cloves

1 teaspoon coriander seeds

1 teaspoon black peppercorns

½ teaspoon cardamom seeds (the little black seeds inside the pithy pods; you'll need 11 to 12 pods)

1½ teaspoons kosher or coarse salt

2½ pounds pork belly, skin removed

3 tablespoons peanut oil or vegetable oil

1 medium yellow onion, coarsely chopped

6 large garlic cloves, smashed and skins removed

2 medium carrots, peeled and coarsely chopped

2 medium celery ribs, trimmed and coarsely chopped (include a few leaves)

3 large whole bay leaves (preferably fresh)

¾ cup dry white wine such as a spicy Gewürztraminer or Riesling

1¾ cups chicken or vegetable broth

CARROTS

1 pound peeled baby carrots

½ cup strained braising liquid (from pork above)

2 tablespoons drippings (from pork above)

2 tablespoons raw sugar or maple sugar

Salt, if needed to taste

Freshly ground black pepper, if needed to taste

1. Grind or pound star anise, cloves, coriander seeds, peppercorns, and cardamom seeds until texture of cracked pepper, then combine with salt. Rub into pork belly—both sides—and place in a large nonreactive baking pan. Cover and marinate 24 to 30 hours in the refrigerator.

2. When ready to proceed, preheat oven to 325°F. Pat pork dry with paper toweling, reserving any bits of dry rub that fall off.

3. Heat oil in a large, heavy nonreactive Dutch oven over moderately high heat until ripples appear on pan bottom—1½ to 2 minutes. Add pork belly and brown well on both sides—about 15 minutes in all. Lift to a large plate. Pour drippings from Dutch oven and reserve, then spoon 3 tablespoons back into pot.

4. Add onion, garlic, carrots, celery, and bay leaves and sauté, stirring often, until lightly browned—about 5 minutes. Add wine, scraping up browned bits on pan bottom, and boil uncovered until reduced to a thick glaze—about 5 minutes.

5. Return pork to Dutch oven along with accumulated juices and add broth and reserved bits of dry rub. Cover, slide onto middle oven shelf, and braise, turning once, until richly flavorful—about 1½ hours, turning at half-time.

6. Remove pork from oven, lift to cutting board, cool until easy to handle, and cut into six pieces of equal size. Skim fat from braising liquid, strain liquid, and reserve; discard solids. Preheat broiler.

7. For Carrots: Bring all ingredients except salt and pepper to a boil in a medium-size heavy skillet over high heat. Adjust heat so liquid bubbles gently, cover, and simmer until carrots are tender—about 15 minutes, then boil uncovered over moderately high heat, shaking skillet often, until liquid evaporates and carrots are nicely glazed—about 15 minutes. Taste for salt and pepper and season as needed.

8. Arrange pork belly in single layer on broiler pan and broil 4 inches from heat until nicely browned—about 2 minutes.

9. To serve, mound pork belly in a heated large deep platter, spoon on remaining reserved braising liquid, and wreathe with carrots. Accompany with redskin or Yukon gold potatoes, boiled in their skins.

MAKES 6 SERVINGS

braised pork belly on collard greens

Strong-flavored greens and pork belly are one of those perfect duos, the greens tempering the oh-so-rich pork belly. Accompaniments? Roasted fingerling potatoes are delicious, ditto fresh-baked corn bread. Note: Because the collards are seasoned with pork drippings and broth, they're not likely to need salt, but taste before serving. Tip: To dress up the platter, brown about a fourth of the bacon until crisp in Step 2, crumble on paper toweling, and scatter over pork and collards just before serving.

2½ pounds pork belly, skin removed and meat cut in 6 pieces of equal size

¼ teaspoon freshly ground black pepper

3 ounces (2 to 3 slices) thick-cut bacon, cut in 1-inch pieces (see Tip above)

1 large yellow onion, coarsely chopped

6 large garlic cloves, finely chopped

1 teaspoon crumbled dried leaf thyme

1¾ cups chicken or vegetable broth

COLLARDS

3 pounds collards or turnip greens, stems and coarse ribs discarded, leaves cut crosswise in 2-inch ribbons

3 tablespoons pork and bacon drippings (from pork above)

2 cups water

¼ cup strained broth (from pork above)

Salt, if needed to taste (see Note above)

¼ teaspoon freshly ground black pepper, or to taste

2 teaspoons cider vinegar

1. Preheat oven to 325°F. Season pork belly with pepper and set aside.

2. Cook bacon in a large, heavy nonreactive Dutch oven over moderately high heat until beginning to brown—2 to 3 minutes. Using a slotted spoon, lift bacon to a small bowl and reserve (see Tip above).

3. Brown pork belly well on both sides in bacon drippings—about 15 minutes; lift to a large plate and reserve. Pour drippings from Dutch oven, then spoon 3 tablespoons back in. Save remaining drippings; you'll need 3 tablespoons for the collards; the balance can be refrigerated and used later to flavor vegetables, soups, and stews.

4. Add onion to Dutch oven and sauté, stirring often, until lightly browned—about 5 minutes. Add garlic and thyme and cook and stir until garlic begins to brown—1 to 2 minutes. Add broth and bring to a boil, scraping up browned bits on pan bottom.

5. Return pork to pot along with accumulated juices and reserved bacon. Cover, slide onto middle oven shelf, and braise, turning once, until richly flavorful—about 1½ hours.

6. Meanwhile, prepare Collards: Bring to a boil with drippings and water in a large heavy saucepan over high heat. Adjust heat so water bubbles gently, cover, and simmer collards until very tender—about 45 minutes. Remove lid and cook until all water evaporates.

7. Remove pork from oven and preheat broiler. Arrange pork belly in single layer on broiler pan and broil 4 inches from heat until nicely browned—about 2 minutes. Meanwhile, strain pork broth and reserve; discard solids.

8. Mix ¼ cup strained broth into collards, season to taste with salt and pepper, and bring to a boil. Note: Save remaining broth for soup or stew another day.

9. To serve, mound collards on a heated large deep platter, drizzle with vinegar, top with pork belly, and if you browned and crumbled some of the bacon, scatter decoratively on top.

MAKES 6 SERVINGS

pickled pig's feet

Throughout the South, pickled pig's feet are beloved snackin' food. "My uncles used to nibble on them when they were drinking moonshine," says my North Carolina friend Bob Holmes. "It would have never occurred to any of those fellas to use anything other than their fingers. It was customary in country stores and many service stations to have a big jar of pickled pig's feet on the counter along with jars of purple boiled eggs and smoked sausage." Bob goes on to say that his grandmother canned pig's feet "just like pickles." But most southerners simply keep pickled pig's feet in the refrigerator (as they do pickled shrimp) and eat them within a few days. The recipe that follows is an old North Carolina one and it's pretty typical. Note: Many butchers, even supermarkets, sell split or quartered pig's feet. For pickled pig's feet, they should be split. If only the whole are available, have your butcher split them.

6 to 8 pig's feet (6 pounds), well scrubbed, hairs singed off, and feet split lengthwise (see Note above)

Cold water to cover pig's feet by about 1 inch

1½ quarts (6 cups) cider vinegar

2 small white onions, thinly sliced

⅓ cup firmly packed light brown sugar

¼ cup pickling salt or kosher salt

6 large whole bay leaves, preferably fresh

4 teaspoons whole cloves

1½ cinnamon sticks

1 teaspoon black peppercorns

8 cups cooking liquid (from pig's feet above; if insufficient, round out measure with water)

1. Bring pig's feet and water to a boil in a covered large Dutch oven over high heat—this may take 15 to 20 minutes. Adjust so water bubbles gently, cover, and simmer 1 hour. Skim froth from surface and discard, re-cover, and continue simmering until meat nearly falls from bones—1½ to 2 hours.

2. One hour before pig's feet are done, combine all but last ingredient (cooking liquid) in a large nonreactive saucepan and bring to a boil over high heat. Adjust heat so mixture barely bubbles and simmer uncovered 1 hour.

3. Lift pig's feet to a large nonreactive bowl or crock and measure out 8 cups cooking liquid. Stir cooking liquid into vinegar mixture, strain, then pour over pig's feet; they should be completely submerged so add a little more water, if necessary.

4. Cool to room temperature, cover, and refrigerate for two days before serving. Note: The pickling liquid will gel as the pig's feet chill, so bring them to room temperature before serving.

MAKES 4 TO 6 SERVINGS

crispy fried trotters with milk and cornmeal gravy

Pickled pig's feet may be the southern favorite but running a close second in the Blue Ridge and Smokies are these crispy fried "trotters." They're best, I think, browned in bacon drippings or butter, but use vegetable oil if you must. Note: Frugal cooks save bacon drippings for frying and flavoring. If you don't, you should know that you'll get about ½ cup drippings from a pound of bacon, a bit more if bacon is fatter. I pour any excess drippings into a small preserving jar, screw the lid down tight, and store in the refrigerator.

6 to 8 pig's feet (6 pounds), well scrubbed, hairs singed off, and feet split or quartered lengthwise (see Pickled Pig's Feet headnote, page 232)

Cold water to cover pig's feet by about 1 inch

3 large yellow onions, quartered

4 large celery ribs, sliced ½ inch thick (include some leaves)

1½ teaspoons salt

12 black peppercorns

3 large eggs beaten until frothy with ½ cup cold water

3 cups stone-ground yellow or white cornmeal mixed with ½ teaspoon each salt and freshly ground black pepper (seasoned cornmeal)

⅔ cup bacon drippings, unsalted butter, or vegetable oil (see Note above)

GRAVY

4 tablespoons bacon drippings or unsalted butter

⅓ cup stone-ground yellow or white cornmeal mixed with 2 tablespoons flour

1 quart (4 cups) milk

Salt to taste

Freshly ground black pepper to taste

1. Bring pig's feet, water, onions, celery, salt, and peppercorns to a boil in a covered large Dutch oven over high heat—this may take 15 to 20 minutes. Adjust so water bubbles gently, cover, and simmer 1 hour. Skim froth from the surface and discard, re-cover, and continue simmering until meat nearly falls from bones—1½ to 2 hours.

2. Lift pig's feet to paper toweling and pat dry; strain cooking liquid, if you like, and freeze to use another day for soup or stew.

3. Place beaten eggs in a pie plate and seasoned cornmeal in a second pie plate. Dip pig's feet, piece by piece, in beaten eggs, then roll in seasoned cornmeal until evenly coated and set aside.

4. Heat drippings in a large heavy non-stick skillet over moderately high heat until ripples appear on pan bottom—1 to 1½ minutes.

5. Brown pig's feet in two batches in drippings, allowing 10 to 12 minutes per batch and turning so they brown evenly. Work carefully—pig's feet splatter in hot fat. As pig's feet brown, lift to paper toweling, cover loosely with foil, and keep warm while you make the gravy.

6. For Gravy: Melt drippings in a medium-size saucepan, blend in cornmeal mixture, and cook and stir a second or two over moderate heat. Add milk and cook, stirring constantly, until thickened, smooth, and no raw starchy taste remains—about 5 to 7 minutes. Season to taste with salt and pepper.

7. To serve, arrange browned pig's feet on six heated dinner plates, ladle a little gravy over each portion, and pass the rest.

MAKES 6 SERVINGS

pig's feet the alentejo way with garlic and cilantro

The only Portuguese province flat enough for big-scale farming, Alentejo is a vast sweep of plains east of Lisbon. It's the least spoiled part of this colorful little country and for that reason, my favorite. It is also where Maria de Lourdes Modesto (Portugal's Julia Child) grew up and an area, she says, "where the grand destiny of the pig" is to be turned into all things delicious. I remember, in particular, eating *Pezinhos de Porco de Coentrada* (pig's feet with fresh cilantro [*coentros,* in Portuguese]) at Fialho, a popular family restaurant on a quiet alley in the provincial capital of Évora, and to be honest, was surprised that I liked a dish with what was described as "enough garlic to blow a safe." Here's my stab at this Portuguese classic.

6 to 8 pig's feet (6 pounds), well scrubbed, hairs singed off, and feet split or quartered lengthwise (see Pickled Pig's Feet headnote, page 232)

Cold water to cover pig's feet by about 1 inch

3 large whole yellow onions, each peeled and stuck with 2 large cloves

1 large bulb of garlic, separated into cloves and each clove peeled (about 12 garlic cloves)

¼ cup extra-virgin olive oil

1 teaspoon kosher or coarse salt, or to taste

¼ teaspoon freshly ground black pepper, or to taste

½ cup loosely packed moderately finely chopped fresh cilantro

2 tablespoons white wine vinegar blended with 2 tablespoons all-purpose flour (thickener)

3 cups strained cooking liquid (from pig's feet above)

1. Bring pig's feet, water, and onions to a boil in a covered large Dutch oven over high heat—this may take 15 to 20 minutes. Adjust heat so water bubbles gently, cover, and simmer 1 hour. Skim froth from surface and discard, re-cover, and continue simmering until meat nearly falls from bones—1½ to 2 hours.

2. Toward end of cooking, purée garlic with oil, salt, and pepper in a food processor or electric blender, then spread over bottom of a medium-size, broad-bottomed, nonreactive saucepan or sauté pan.

3. When pig's feet are tender, lift to a cutting board, strip meat from bones. Discard bones, then coarsely chop or cut meat in thin strips and set aside. Also, strain 3 cups cooking liquid and reserve.

4. Set saucepan of puréed garlic over moderate heat and cook, stirring constantly, just until garlic begins to color—about 5 minutes. Mix in cilantro, thickener, and strained cooking liquid, and cook, stirring constantly, until thickened and smooth—3 to 5 minutes.

5. Add reserved meat, reduce heat to low, and cook uncovered, stirring now and then, until sauce is a good gravy consistency—about 20 minutes. If sauce seems thick, thin with a little chicken broth or water. Note: The broth has considerable body thanks to long, slow simmering, which converts pig's feet sinew to gelatin.

6. Taste for salt and pepper, adjust as needed, ladle into heated soup plates, and serve with chunks of rustic country bread—French, Italian, or if you can find it, Portuguese.

MAKES 6 SERVINGS

slow cooker pork ossobuco

Veal ossobuco has always been a favorite of mine, but pork ossobuco? Never heard of it until it appeared on the menu at Ben and Karen Barker's award-winning Magnolia Grill in Durham, NC. At the restaurant, pork ossobuco is often plated with Creole baked beans but at home, I settle for pasta or rice. The recipe here, inspired by one that appears in *Not Afraid of Flavor* (University of North Carolina Press, 2000), a collection of Ben and Karen's signature recipes, is adapted for the slow cooker. Note: Pork shanks are hardly a supermarket staple, but any good butcher will order and cut them for you. Also ask him to tie each shank around the middle so it holds its shape as it slow-cooks. For this recipe, the shanks should marinate overnight in a sweet-sour marinade, so begin this recipe the day before you serve it.

1 cup Pinot Grigio or other dry white wine

3 tablespoons cider vinegar

3 tablespoons molasses

6 large garlic cloves, smashed and skins removed

6 small sprigs fresh rosemary

6 small sprigs fresh thyme (preferably lemon thyme)

4 large whole bay leaves (preferably fresh)

½ teaspoon chili flakes (crushed dried hot red chili peppers), or to taste

6 center-cut meaty pork shanks 2½ inches in diameter and 2 inches thick, tied (about 3¼ pounds; see Note above)

1 teaspoon salt, or to taste

½ teaspoon freshly ground black pepper, or to taste

½ cup unsifted all-purpose flour

¼ cup extra-virgin olive oil

2 cups chicken broth

Cold water, if needed

GREMOLATA
¼ cup finely chopped fresh Italian parsley mixed with 2 finely minced garlic cloves and 1 teaspoon each finely grated lemon and orange zest

1. Combine first eight ingredients (wine through chili flakes) in a very large nonreactive bowl, add shanks, and turn well to coat. Cover and refrigerate overnight, turning shanks several times.

2. When ready to proceed, lift shanks from marinade, reserving marinade. Wipe shanks dry and season on both sides with salt and pepper. Dredge well in flour, shaking off excess.

3. Heat oil in a large heavy skillet over high heat until ripples appear on pan bottom—about 1½ minutes. Add shanks and brown well—5 to 7 minutes per side.

4. Arrange browned shanks in a single layer around walls of a large (4- to 6-quart) slow cooker, then add broth and reserved marinade.

5. Cover and cook on HIGH 1 hour. Reduce to LOW and continue cooking until meat nearly falls from bones—3½ to 4 hours. Note: Check cooker at half-time and if liquid seems skimpy, add a little water. Liquid should not quite half cover shanks. Discard bay leaves, rosemary and thyme sprigs. Taste for salt, black pepper, and chili flakes and adjust as needed.

6. Arrange shanks on a heated large platter, spoon some of the pan juices on top, then scatter gremolata evenly over all. Serve with a pasta like pappardelle or with hot boiled rice. Pass remaining pan juices separately.

MAKES 6 SERVINGS

fricadellen

The ways of tenderizing tough (read "economical") cuts are mechanical as well as culinary—pounding sinew into submission, for example, scoring or slicing meat across the grain to sever the gristle, but best of all, grinding. So is it any wonder that meatloaves and meatballs are staples nearly everywhere? Among my own favorites is this Belgian meatball recipe—pork, veal, and beef balls simmered in cream sauce lightly blushed with tomato. I picked the recipe up years ago in Brussels and find it an ideal dinner party make-ahead. Prepare one day, refrigerate overnight, and reheat just before serving. The best accompaniment? Mashed potatoes are traditional but I often serve boiled brown or white rice instead. And sometimes wild rice for special occasions. Note: You'll find meatballs easier to shape if the meat is good and cold. Tip: Use your food processor to crumb the bread; simply tear the slices directly into the work bowl, then alternately churn and pulse to fairly fine crumbs.

2 pounds refrigerator-cold ground pork shoulder (not too lean; see Note above)

½ pound refrigerator-cold ground veal shoulder

½ pound refrigerator-cold ground beef chuck

2 cups soft white breadcrumbs (4 slices firm-textured white bread; see Tip above)

⅓ cup milk or evaporated skim milk

2 large eggs, lightly beaten

1 teaspoon salt, or to taste

¼ teaspoon freshly ground black pepper, or to taste

¼ teaspoon freshly grated nutmeg

¼ cup (½ stick) unsalted butter

1 cup beef broth

2 tablespoons tomato paste

1 cup heavy cream

1 tablespoon fresh lemon juice, or to taste

2 tablespoons finely snipped fresh dill or chives

1. Mix first nine ingredients thoroughly (pork through nutmeg) and shape into Ping-Pong-size balls.

2. Melt 2 tablespoons butter in a large heavy nonstick skillet over moderately high heat and as soon as it froths and subsides, add half the meatballs and brown well on all sides—about 12 minutes. Using a slotted spoon, lift to a large plate. Melt remaining butter in skillet, brown remaining meatballs the same way, and lift to plate.

3. Add broth to skillet and cook 1 to 2 minutes, scraping up browned bits. Smooth in tomato paste and return meatballs to skillet along with accumulated juices. Adjust heat so mixture bubbles gently, cover, and simmer 10 minutes.

4. Add cream and simmer uncovered until meatballs are cooked through and sauce is lightly thickened—about 10 minutes. Mix in lemon juice, taste for salt and pepper, and adjust as needed.

5. To serve, stir in dill and accompany with boiled rice. I like to ladle the meatballs and sauce directly over the rice on heated large dinner plates and add a few spears of steamed or roasted asparagus—the perfect partner.

MAKES 6 SERVINGS

danish fricadeller in onion sauce

Like Belgians and other northern Europeans, Danes make a specialty of pork meatballs, most of which also contain lesser amounts of ground beef or veal. I find these particularly good because they simmer lazily in onion sauce. Note: The point of having the ground pork and beef cold is that the meatballs are easier to shape. Tip: By substituting evaporated skim milk for half-and-half, you trim fat and calories. It's deceptively rich and creamy.

2 pounds refrigerator-cold ground pork shoulder
(not too lean; see Note above)

1 pound refrigerator-cold ground lean beef chuck

1 cup soft white breadcrumbs
(2 slices firm-textured white bread)

1 medium-size yellow onion, finely chopped

1/3 cup milk

1/3 cup half-and-half or evaporated skim milk
(see Tip above)

1 large egg, lightly beaten

1 tablespoon Dijon mustard

1 teaspoon salt

1/4 teaspoon freshly ground black pepper

1/4 cup (1/2 stick) unsalted butter

SAUCE

1/4 cup (1/2 stick) unsalted butter

3 large yellow onions, coarsely chopped

1/4 cup unsifted all-purpose flour

1/2 teaspoon salt, or to taste

1/4 teaspoon freshly ground black pepper,
or to taste

1/4 teaspoon freshly grated nutmeg

2 cups milk

1 cup half-and-half

1. Mix first ten ingredients thoroughly (ground pork through black pepper) and shape into Ping-Pong-size balls.

2. Melt 2 tablespoons butter in a large heavy non-stick skillet over moderately high heat and as soon as it froths and subsides, add half the meatballs and brown well on all sides—about 12 minutes. Using a slotted spoon, lift to a large plate. Melt remaining butter in skillet, brown remaining meatballs the same way, and lift to plate.

3. For Sauce: Melt butter in same skillet over moderate heat, add onions, and sauté, stirring often, until limp and golden—6 to 8 minutes. Blend in flour, salt, pepper, and nutmeg and cook and stir a few seconds. Add milk and half-and-half and cook, stirring constantly, until lightly thickened and smooth—3 to 5 minutes.

4. Return meatballs to skillet along with accumulated juices. Adjust heat so mixture barely bubbles, cover, and simmer slowly until meatballs are cooked through—about 20 minutes. Don't allow mixture to boil, for if it does, sauce will curdle. Watch carefully, and if sauce threatens to scorch, slide a diffuser underneath skillet. Taste for salt and pepper and adjust as needed.

5. Serve with buttered noodles or boiled potatoes—either alongside or on top. I also like these meatballs ladled over hot cooked rice—white or brown.

MAKES 6 SERVINGS

german pork-and-veal balls in sour cream sauce

Called *Königsberger Klopse* in German, these meatballs are "fluffed" with club soda and their flavor sharpened with anchovy paste. Like other meatballs, they're easier to shape if the meat mixture is well chilled. Note: Because of the saltiness of the anchovy paste and capers, this recipe is not likely to need salt. But taste the sauce before serving and adjust as needed. Tip: To crumb bread, tear slices directly into a food processor, then alternately pulse and churn till uniformly fine.

1 pound refrigerator-cold ground pork shoulder
(not too lean)

½ pound refrigerator-cold ground veal shoulder

4 slices firm-textured white bread,
buzzed to fine crumbs (see Tip above)

3 tablespoons finely chopped fresh Italian parsley

Finely grated zest of 1 medium lemon

1 large egg, lightly beaten

1 tablespoon anchovy paste

¼ teaspoon freshly grated nutmeg

¼ teaspoon freshly ground black pepper

⅔ cup club soda (its fizz fluffs the meatballs)

1¾ cups chicken or beef broth

1 quart (4 cups) water

SAUCE

3 tablespoons unsalted butter

6 medium scallions, trimmed and finely chopped
(white part only)

4 tablespoons all-purpose flour

2 cups reduced poaching liquid
(from meatballs above)

¾ cup firmly packed sour cream or crème fraîche,
at room temperature

¼ cup small capers (the tiniest you can find),
well drained

1. Mix all but last two meatball ingredients (broth and water) thoroughly, cover, and chill several hours or until firm enough to shape.

2. When ready to proceed, shape into 1-inch balls, arrange in single layer on a foil-lined baking sheet, cover loosely, and refrigerate 2 to 3 hours. Note: This additional chilling is necessary because the meatball mixture is softer than most. Moreover, the meatballs are poached, not sautéed.

3. To cook, bring broth and water to a boil in a medium-size Dutch oven over moderately high heat, adjust heat so liquid barely bubbles, then ease in half the meatballs and poach uncovered 20 minutes. With a mesh skimmer or slotted spoon, gently transfer meatballs to a large shallow bowl, cover loosely, and keep warm. Poach remaining meatballs the same way, add to bowl, cover, and keep warm.

4. Strain poaching liquid through a cheesecloth-lined sieve, return to Dutch oven (now wiped clean), and boil uncovered over high heat until reduced to 2 cups—15 to 20 minutes.

5. For Sauce: Melt butter in a small heavy saucepan over moderate heat, add scallions, and sauté, stirring often, until limp—about 5 minutes; do not brown. Blend in flour and cook and stir 2 minutes. Add 1 cup reduced poaching liquid, whisking hard, stir back into reduced liquid in Dutch oven, and cook, whisking constantly, until smooth—3 to 5 minutes.

6. Mix in sour cream and capers, then ease in meatballs, set lid on askew, and bring just to serving temperature over lowest heat—about 15 minutes. Do not boil or the sauce will curdle. Also, resist temptation to stir because meatballs are fragile and may break apart. Taste for salt and pepper and adjust as needed.

7. Serve hot with boiled redskin potatoes (I leave the skins on) and steamed broccoli or asparagus.

MAKES 6 SERVINGS

pork loaf with capers and dill

Our grandmothers knew the easiest way to tenderize a tough cut of meat: feed it through a meat grinder. As a little girl, I got this job in both my mother's and grandmother's kitchens. Today supermarkets sell portioned, packaged, and ready-to-use ground pork. And as for those old clamp-to-the-counter meat grinders, I'll bet these relics still show up at tag sales. Note: Use firm-textured white bread (also called "home-style bread") for the crumbs. One slice, buzzed to crumbs in a food processor, equals ½ cup crumbs, so for this recipe you'll need four slices, crusts and all.

1½ pounds ground pork shoulder (not too lean)

1 pound ground smoked ham

2 cups moderately coarse soft white breadcrumbs (see Note above)

2 medium yellow onions, moderately finely chopped

1 large garlic clove, finely minced

1 cup buttermilk or evaporated skim milk

2 large eggs

⅓ cup coarsely chopped fresh dill (measure loosely packed) or 1½ teaspoons dill weed

⅓ cup well drained small capers

¼ cup moderately finely chopped fresh Italian parsley

2 tablespoons well drained dill pickle relish or finely chopped dill pickle

½ teaspoon salt

½ teaspoon freshly ground black pepper

1. Preheat oven to 350°F. Lightly coat a 9 x 5 x 3-inch loaf pan with nonstick cooking spray and set aside.

2. Using your hands, combine all ingredients thoroughly and pack in pan, mounding slightly in center. Set pan on a rimmed baking sheet (to catch drips), then slide onto middle oven shelf and bake uncovered until nicely browned and an instant-read meat thermometer, thrust into center of loaf, registers 160°F—1¾ to 2 hours.

3. Cool loaf in the upright pan on a wire rack 15 minutes, then with a thin-blade spatula loosen around the edge. Before turning loaf out, cool to room temperature.

4. To serve, pour any juices that may have accumulated into a small bowl, then turn loaf out on a platter, arranging right side up. Slice about ½-inch thick, then spoon a little of the pan juices, if any, over each slice.

MAKES A 9 X 5 X 3-INCH LOAF

party pork ring with spicy sauce

Why do we consider prime ribs and crown roasts, loin chops and T-bones—and only them—fittin' party food? I frankly find meatloaves made from tougher cuts equally appropriate and ever so much more imaginative. This one, for example, has won plenty of kudos over the years.

2½ pounds ground pork shoulder (not too lean)

¾ pound veal shoulder or ground turkey

1½ cups coarse soda cracker crumbs soaked in ¾ cup milk or evaporated skim milk

½ cup finely chopped yellow onion

⅓ cup finely chopped red or green bell pepper

¼ cup finely chopped fresh Italian parsley

2 large eggs

2 tablespoons steak sauce

2 teaspoons salt

½ teaspoon freshly ground black pepper

SAUCE

¼ cup (½ stick) unsalted butter

1 small yellow onion, finely chopped

1 small garlic clove, finely chopped

⅓ cup unsifted all-purpose flour

2 teaspoons curry powder

½ teaspoon salt, or to taste

¼ teaspoon freshly ground black pepper, or to taste

⅛ teaspoon freshly grated nutmeg

3 cups chicken broth

1. Preheat oven to 325°F. Line bottom of an 8-cup ring mold with foil (dull side up), baking parchment, or wax paper, then spritz well with nonstick cooking spray, making sure sides and central tube are also well coated.

2. Using your hands, mix all meatloaf ingredients thoroughly and pack firmly in mold. Set mold on a rimmed baking sheet (to catch drips), slide onto middle oven shelf, and bake uncovered until nicely browned, firm to the touch and an instant-read meat thermometer, thrust into loaf midway between central tube and edge registers 160°F—about 1½ hours.

3. Remove meatloaf from oven and cool upright in pan on a wire rack 20 minutes, then loosen around edge and central tube with a thin-blade spatula and invert on heated large round platter. Tip: If you lightly spritz platter, it will be easier to center meatloaf.

4. For Sauce: Melt butter in a medium-size saucepan over moderate heat, add onion and garlic, and sauté, stirring occasionally, until limp—2 to 3 minutes. Blend in all but final ingredient (broth), cook and stir a few seconds. Add broth and cook, stirring constantly, until thickened, smooth, and no floury taste remains—about 5 minutes. Taste for salt and pepper and adjust as needed.

5. To serve, ladle some of the sauce decoratively over the meatloaf and pass the rest. Accompany with boiled rice, brown rice, wild rice, or a favorite pilaf or risotto.

MAKES 8 TO 10 SERVINGS

finnish layered pork and apple loaf

With its echoes of Russian occupation during the 18th and 19th centuries, Finland is for me one of the most interesting Scandinavian countries. I'm smitten with its innovative designs (furniture, tableware) and soaring futuristic architecture, the splashy Marimekko fabrics and haunting music of Sibelius, but most of all with the food—different in many ways from that of Denmark, Norway, and even Sweden to which it also once belonged. This meatloaf, for example, is unlike anything I've enjoyed elsewhere in Scandinavia. It's layered and baked in a casserole—apples, meat, apples, meat, and so forth. It's quick, it's economical, it's delicious, it's nutritious. A hard combo to beat.

1½ pounds ground pork shoulder (not too lean)

1 pound ground lean beef chuck

1 medium-size yellow onion, finely chopped

2 medium-size carrots, peeled and finely grated

¼ cup finely chopped fresh Italian parsley

⅓ cup milk or evaporated skim milk

1 large egg, lightly beaten with
2 tablespoons cornstarch, 2 teaspoons salt,
and ½ teaspoon each ground ginger and
freshly ground black pepper

3 small Granny Smith or other tart apples,
peeled, cored, and thinly sliced

2 tablespoons unsalted butter

1. Preheat oven to 375°F. Spritz a shallow 6-cup casserole with nonstick cooking spray and set aside.

2. Using your hands, mix first seven ingredients well (ground pork through egg mixture), then layer into casserole this way: ⅓ apples, ½ pork mixture, ⅓ apples, remaining pork mixture, remaining apples. Spread each layer as evenly as possible, pressing lightly into one below. Dot with butter.

3. Set on a rimmed baking sheet (to catch drips), slide onto middle oven shelf, and bake uncovered until brown—about 30 minutes. Cover loosely with foil and continue baking until firm to the touch and an instant-read meat thermometer, thrust into middle of a meat layer, registers 160°F—about 1½ hours.

4. Serve at table directly from the casserole and accompany with redskin potatoes or fingerlings boiled in their jackets.

MAKES 6 SERVINGS

SOURCES

WHERE TO FIND ADDITIONAL INFORMATION

www.americanveal.com
American Veal Association
Website tells story of veal in America, offers industry information and updates, veal recipes, and related links.

www.atlanticveal.com/plume_de_veau.php
All about Plume de Veau, a brand of choice milk-fed veal.

www.beef.org
National Cattlemen's Beef Association
Organization information plus links to other websites devoted to beef.

www.delftblueveal.com
Another quality brand of milk-fed veal, what it is, where to buy it.

www.freeraised.com
All about fine pasture-raised veal from a French heritage breed as well as a directory of stores that now sell it.

www.nppc.org
National Pork Producers Council
Basic information plus other website links.

www.ag.purdue.edu/ansc
Purdue University Animal Sciences
Useful information about beef, lamb, pork, and veal (click animal icons at bottom of home page). Also offers links to pertinent websites.

www.slowfoodusa.org
Not specifically about meat, but a website I find indispensable for food news, facts, and features.

www.theotherwhitemeat.com
Recipes plus tips on buying, handling, and storing pork. This site is devoted specifically to America's "new lean pork" introduced some 25 years ago in an effort to attract the calorie-and-cholesterol-conscious who had begun to substitute chicken for pork.

www.usda.gov
U.S. Department of Agriculture
Click on Food and Nutrition, then enter search for detailed fact sheets on beef, veal, lamb, and pork.

www.veal.ca
Veal Information Gateway
Veal defined, veal recipes, related links.

WHERE TO BUY WHAT YOUR SUPERMARKET DOESN'T CARRY

ONLINE (RETAIL)

www.allenbrothers.com
Supplying prime beef since 1893, this Chicago firm now ships quality lamb, pork, and veal as well—mostly pricey roasts and chops but also a few tougher cuts like shanks, spareribs, and back ribs.

www.dartagnan.com
Founded some 25 years ago by Ariane Daguin, daughter of Michelin-starred Gascon chef André Daguin, this purveyor of fine meats is headquarters for the very best. Despite its emphasis on tender steaks, chops, and roasts, d'Artagnan also sells tough cuts like beef flank, veal shanks, and lamb shoulder. Expensive but worth it.

www.foxfirefarms.com
Organic grass-fed beef (chuck, brisket, stew meat, oxtail) and lamb (shoulder roasts and chops, shanks, stew meat, ground lamb), also organic apple-fed pork (spareribs, Boston butt), all from a family that's been ranching in Colorado for nearly 100 years.

www.heritagefoodsusa.com
Among the offerings of this valuable website, a directory of where to buy heritage breeds of meat online.

www.lobels.com
This fancy Upper East Side New York butcher now ships cuts of beef, veal, lamb, and pork—the tough as well as the tender.

www.nimanranch.com
For more than 40 years, Niman Ranch has supported farmers and ranchers who humanely raise meat animals. No hormones, no antibiotics. Niman Ranch meats are sold at high-end groceries but can also be ordered directly through this website.

www.pastacheese.com
This Long Island importer of Italian foods also fills online orders for tougher cuts of beef (brisket, stew meat, round), lamb (shoulder blade chops), pork (back ribs), and veal (shanks, shoulder, stew meat).

www.penzeys.com
The place to order herbs, spices, exotic seasonings.

LOCAL FARMS AND MARKETS

www.buyappalachian.org
This website lists scores of family farms across Appalachia; some sell beef, lamb, pork, and/or veal; a few pack and ship.

www.buylocalvirginia.org
Its directory will lead you to the Virginia farms and farmer's markets selling home-grown meats.

www.canecreekfarm.us
Headquarters for the famously succulent Ossabaw pork, this central North Carolina farm sells at local farmer's markets and a few groceries (check website for market schedule). No shipping.

www.csumeats.com
To learn which farms and markets sell locally grown beef, lamb, pork, and veal, click on this Community Supported Agriculture website.

www.freshdirect.com
More and more of my New York colleagues now order groceries from FreshDirect, which delivers throughout the greater metropolitan area. Its inventory includes a variety of meats, even Plume de Veau milk-fed veal.

www.localharvest.org
Among the information on this website, a directory of farms, farmer's markets, and online sources where locally grown organic meats can be bought. A few pack and ship.

www.naturesharmonyfarm.com
Another farm that sells Ossabaw pork, this one near Elberton, Georgia, east of Atlanta. The website tells how and where to buy.

INDEX

Page numbers in *italics* refer to photographs or illustrations.

Istanbul, of Lamb and Vegetables, 160
    of Ribs and White Beans, 199
    See also pie (meat)
cattle, 2, 84
Cauliflower, Veal Stew with Mushrooms and, 88
Celery, Veal Rump Pot-Roasted with Carrots, Potatoes, and, 99
Celery Root, Veal Braised with Carrots, Port-Plumped Prunes, and, 106–7, *107*
cheese, xiv, 148
chicken, Puchero, 70
chilies, 32, 207
    Green Chile with Pinto Beans, 32, *33*
    Pork Bowl of Red, 208
    Texas Beef 'n' Beans, 35
    That Fiery Beef Bowl of Red, 29
chili peppers, xii, 207
    Pueblo Posole with Pork and Green Chiles, *206, 207*
    Sancocho, 215
Chinese cuisine
    Far East Spareribs on Sesame Sauerkraut, 198
    Gingery Lacquered Spareribs, 196
Cho Cho, 62
chopping techniques for meat, 8, 20, 29, 32, 35, 58
Chunks of Beef Fricaseed with Fresh Basil and Wine, 26
Cider, Sauce, Welsh Honied Lamb with, 178
cilantro
    Persian Green Stew, 161
    Pig's Feet the Alentejo Way with Garlic and, 234
citrus, xii. *See also* lemon; orange
Coffee, and Cream Gravy, Braised Blade Chops of Lamb with, 172
Cold Sliced Veal with Tuna Mayonnaise (Vitello Tonnato), *110,* 111
collagen, ix
collard(s; greens), 188
    Black-Eyed Pea Soup with Ham Hocks and, 188, *189*
    Braised Pork Belly on, 230–31
connective tissue, ix, xi
cooling or chilling tips, xvi
corn, 19, 69
    Beef Stew with Carrots, Potatoes, and, *18,* 19
    Cozido, *68,* 69
    Sancocho, 215
    Slow Cooker Brunswick Stew with Pork, 200, *201*
    See also cornmeal; masa harina; posole
Corned Beef and Cabbage, 71
cornmeal
    and Milk Gravy, Crispy Fried Trotters with, 233
    See also polenta *entry*
Country-Fried Steak, 49
Country-Fried Steak with Mushrooms and Madeira, *50,* 51
Cozido, *68,* 69
Cranberries, Ragout of Beef with Wild Mushrooms and, 24, *25*

cream
    and Coffee Gravy, Braised Blade Chops of Lamb with, 172
    Swiss Skillet Veal in, 114
    Vegetable Gravy, Swiss-Style Rump of Veal with, 104
Creole cuisine, Pork Shoulder Steaks, 224, *225*
Crispy Fried Trotters with Milk and Cornmeal Gravy, 233
Crofter's Lamb and Potato Pie, 144, *145*
Cucumbers, Turkish Lamb with Yogurt and, on Pita Bread, 158–59

D
Danish Fricadeller in Onion Sauce, 237
Deviled Short Ribs, 76
dill
    and Lemon Sauce, Lamb Neck Slices in, 169
    Pork Loaf with Capers and, 240
dry rub, 170, 194, 228
dumpling(s), 8
    -Balls, Jade Soup with Pork-and-Veal, *190,* 191

E
Easy Oven Dinner, 27
Eggplant and Roasted Garlic Tahini, Braised Blade Chops with, 173
eggs, hard-cooked, xiii
English cuisine
    Lancashire Hot Pot, 168
    Old English Steak and Kidney Pie, 57

F
Far East Spareribs on Sesame Sauerkraut, 198
fat
    bacon drippings, xi, 233
    butter, xii, 136
    de-fatting techniques, 136, 142, 178
    lard, xiii
    and pork, 184–85, 228
    suet, 58
Fennel Stew, Aegean Lamb and, 156, *157*
Filipino cuisine, Morcon, 60–61
Finnish Layered Pork and Apple Loaf, 242
fish. *See* tuna *entry*
Flavors-of-the-East Sicilian Lamb Bake, 152
Flemish cuisine, Braised Veal Rump with Broccoli and Lemon Sauce, 102
flour, xiii, 40, 208
Forfar Bridies, 58
freezer tips, xvi, 3, 77, 85, 123, 185
French cuisine
    Alsatian Fresh Ham Braised with Sauerkraut and Vermouth, *218,* 219
    Beef Bourguignon, 36
    Navarin of Lamb, 143
    Pork à la Normande, 213